how firm a FOUNDATION

365 DEVOTIONS FROM GENESIS TO REVELATION FOR

HELP, HOPE, AND STRENGTH

Our Daily Bread

Our Daily Bread
Publishing.

Bible book introductions are taken from *Our Daily Bread Bible Sourcebook: The Who, What, Where, Wow Guide to the Bible* by Dave Branon (Grand Rapids, MI: Our Daily Bread Publishing, 2019). Used by permission.

The devotional readings collected in this book were first published over a span of years in the *Our Daily Bread* devotional booklets that are distributed around the world in more than fifty languages.

Scripture quotations, unless otherwise indicated, are taken from the Holy Bible, New International Version®, NIV®. Copyright © 1973, 1978, 1984, 2011 by Biblica, Inc.™ Used by permission of Zondervan. All rights reserved worldwide. www.zondervan.com.
    Scripture quotations marked ESV are taken from the ESV® Bible (The Holy Bible, English Standard Version®), copyright © 2001 by Crossway, a publishing ministry of Good News Publishers. Used by permission. All rights reserved.
    Scripture quotations marked GNT are from the Good News Translation in Today's English Version—Second Edition Copyright © 1992 by American Bible Society. Used by permission.
    Scripture quotations marked KJV are taken from the Authorized Version, or King James Version, of the Bible.
    Scripture quotations marked NKJV are taken from the New King James Version®. Copyright © 1982 by Thomas Nelson. Used by permission. All rights reserved.
    Scripture quotations marked NLT are taken from the Holy Bible, New Living Translation, copyright © 1996, 2004, 2015 by Tyndale House Foundation. Used by permission of Tyndale House Publishers, Inc., Carol Stream, Illinois 60188. All rights reserved.
    Scripture quotations marked PHILLIPS are from The New Testament in Modern English, copyright © 1958, 1959, 1960 J.B. Phillips and 1947, 1952, 1955, 1957 The Macmillian Company, New York. Used by permission. All rights reserved.

ISBN: 978-1-64070-181-6

Printed in China
23 24 25 26 27 28 29 30 / 9 8 7 6 5 4 3 2

CONTENTS

◆

INTRODUCTION

◆

It's surprising how much you can learn about God and His love for us in a year. Many followers of Jesus use a read-through-the-Bible plan to guide them on a day-by-day quest to learn more about what God wants us to know as revealed in what we often call God's Word.

Since 1956, another way millions of believers in Jesus have gained a growing knowledge of God's truth has been through reading *Our Daily Bread*. Each day, readers have been exposed to a nugget of truth from the Bible's pages—a sure way to strengthen fellowship with God, discover God's teaching, and be encouraged by the breadth and depth of God's inspired Book.

In a sense, this book offers you a combination of those two methods. It carries you on a daily journey straight through the Bible, allowing you to read much of what it says and giving you stopping points along the way to dwell on specific passages. Using the time-tested method of *Our Daily Bread's* encouraging and challenging teaching, *How Firm a Foundation* walks you through the Word and guides you to take daily action on your faith. You will find help in both familiar and unfamiliar passages—helping you to dig into portions of the Bible that most of us routinely ignore.

In addition, we've provided some teaching about each section of the Bible and each book of the Bible—helping you to round out your knowledge of the greatest Book ever written.

We hope you enjoy the journey, and we desire that it will enhance your relationship with God and nudge you closer to Him than you've ever been before.

It's our prayer that as you spend a year in this approach to the devotional articles and Scripture readings, you'll build on what you already know and construct a firmer base on which to build your life in Christ. We trust that when you're done, you can sing with increasing confidence, "How firm a foundation . . . is laid for your faith in His excellent Word."

Dave Branon
Compiler and Editor

PART 1

◆

The Pentateuch

Genesis, Exodus, Leviticus, Numbers, Deuteronomy

The Pentateuch, which literally means "five scrolls," is a series of books that gives us a clear look at beginnings. God's inspired record of the creation of the world, the creation of mankind, and the creation of God's chosen people, the Jews, is found in these five books. We see mankind's fall from his original sinless state, and we see the beginnings of God's eternal plan to redeem mankind from the sin that infected all people after Adam's sin in the garden of Eden. The Pentateuch gives us the stories of some of the Bible's most interesting and remarkable characters: Noah, Abraham, Joseph, and Moses.

GENESIS

◆

Contained in the pages of Genesis are some of the seminal events in mankind's history. Without a record of creation, we would not know how we got here. Without the story of the fall, we would not understand why we need a Savior. Without the retelling of the flood story, we would not grasp God's hatred for sin and His grace to provide salvation. Without the details about Abraham and his family, we would not be able to fully understand the sacrificial system that pointed to the true Lamb of God. Genesis provides us all of that background—establishing our need for a Savior, the promise of a Savior, and the beginnings of the story of the people through whom the Savior would come to earth to save us.

OUTLINE

Creation Genesis 1:1–2:25

Fall of Man Genesis 3:1–24

The Great Flood Genesis 6:1–10:32

The Tower of Babel Genesis 11:1–32

The Call and Answer of Abraham Genesis 12:1–20:18

The Life of Isaac Genesis 21:1–26:25

The Life of Jacob Genesis 27:1–36:43

The Life of Joseph Genesis 37:1–50:26

Whodunit?

Read Genesis 1

Then God said, "Let us make mankind in our image, in our likeness, so that they may rule over the fish in the sea and the birds in the sky, over the livestock and all the wild animals, and over all the creatures that move along the ground."

GENESIS 1:26

The word *whodunit* is actually in the dictionary. It means "detective story." The most important whodunit of all time is the question of creation.

Some people wish the Bible said, "In the beginning, God wasn't needed." To them, it's unacceptable to say, "In the beginning God created the heavens and the earth" (Genesis 1:1), or "Let us make mankind in our image" (v. 26).

Instead, they believe that after an explosion of unsourced energy and uncreated matter, somehow an atmosphere conducive to life was formed. Then single-celled organisms morphed on their own into the exceedingly complex life forms we have today.

No need for God, they say, for it all happened naturally. On an earth and in an atmosphere not of anyone's making, forces with a blueprint designed by no one joined together to place the earth in the perfect location for life to thrive.

What we do with "In the beginning God" is at the center of it all. We must either believe His Word—and everything His Word claims—or we must believe that our meaningless lives resulted from an accidental, mindless chain reaction. What a stark contrast to "Let us make mankind in our image"!

In the beginning. Was it God? Or was it chance? Our answer to this whodunit reveals whether or not we truly worship the awesome God of creation.

Dave Branon

JANUARY 2

Made for Each Other

Read Genesis 2

*The LORD God said, "It is not good for the man
to be alone. I will make a helper suitable for him."*

GENESIS 2:18

"I take care of him. When he's happy, I'm happy," says Stella. Merle replies, "I'm happy when she's around." Merle and Stella had been married for seventy-nine years when they said that. When Merle was admitted to a nursing home, he was miserable—so Stella gladly brought him home. He was one hundred and one, and she was ninety-five. Though she needed a walker to get around, she lovingly did what she could for her husband, such as preparing the food he liked. But she couldn't do it on her own. Grandchildren and neighbors helped with the things Stella couldn't manage. When Merle died in 2019 at the age of one hundred and two, they had been married for eighty years.

Stella and Merle's life together is an example of Genesis 2, where God said, "It is not good for the man to be alone. I will make a helper suitable for him" (v. 18). None of the creatures God brought before Adam fit that description. Only in Eve, made from the rib of Adam, did Adam find a suitable helper and companion (vv. 19–24).

Eve was the perfect companion for Adam, and through them God instituted marriage. This wasn't only for the mutual aid of individuals but also to begin a family and to care for creation, which includes other people (1:28). From that first family came a community so that, whether married or single, old or young, none of us would be alone. As a community, God has given us the privilege of sharing "each other's burdens" (Galatians 6:2).   *Alyson Kieda*

Buyer's Remorse

Read Genesis 3:1–8

*I delight greatly in the LORD; my soul rejoices in my God. For
he has clothed me with garments of salvation and arrayed me
in a robe of his righteousness, as a bridegroom adorns his head
like a priest, and as a bride adorns herself with her jewels.*

ISAIAH 61:10

Have you ever experienced buyer's remorse? I have. Just prior to making
a purchase, I feel the surge of excitement that comes with getting something new. After buying the item, however, a wave of remorse sometimes
crashes over me. Did I really need this? Should I have spent the money?

In Genesis 3, we find the first record of a buyer's remorse. The whole
thing began with the crafty serpent and his sales pitch. He persuaded Eve
to doubt God's Word (v. 1). He then capitalized on her uncertainty by
casting doubt on God's character (vv. 4–5). He promised that her eyes
would "be opened" and she would become "like God" (v. 5).

So Eve ate. Adam ate. And sin entered the world. But the first man
and woman got more than they bargained for. Their eyes were opened
all right, but they didn't become like God. In fact, their first act was to
hide from God (vv. 7–8).

Sin has dire consequences. It always keeps us from God's best. But
God in His mercy and grace clothed Adam and Eve in garments made
from animal skins (v. 21)—foreshadowing what Jesus Christ would do
for us by dying on the cross for our sins. His blood was shed so that we
might be clothed with His righteousness—with no remorse!

Poh Fang Chia

Shopping with Liam

Read Genesis 3:14-19

And I will put enmity between you and the woman,
and between your offspring and hers; he will crush
your head, and you will strike his heel.

GENESIS 3:15

My son Liam loves to pick dandelions for his mother. To date, she hasn't wearied of receiving them. One man's weed is a little boy's flower.

One day I took Liam shopping with me. As we hurried past the floral section, he pointed excitedly to an arrangement of yellow tulips. "Daddy," he exclaimed, "you should get those dandelions for Mommy!" His advice made me laugh. It made a pretty good Facebook post on his mother's page too. (By the way, I bought the tulips.)

Some see in weeds a reminder of Adam's sin. By eating the forbidden fruit, Adam and Eve brought on themselves the curse of a fallen world—relentless work, agonizing birth, and eventual death (Genesis 3:16–19).

But Liam's youthful eyes remind me of something else. There is beauty even in weeds. The anguish of childbirth holds hope for us all. Death is ultimately defeated. The "Seed" God spoke of in Genesis 3:15 would wage war with the serpent's offspring. That Seed is Jesus himself, who rescued us from the curse of death (Galatians 3:16).

The world may be broken, but wonder awaits us at every turn. Even weeds remind us of the promise of redemption and a Creator who loves us.

Tim Gustafson

One Window

Read Genesis 6:9–16

*Make a roof for it, leaving below the roof an opening
one cubit high all around. Put a door in the side of
the ark and make lower, middle and upper decks.*

GENESIS 6:16

Windows have two primary functions: one is to let people look out, the other is to let the light shine in.

When God gave Noah the instructions for an ark to save his family, He designed it with only one window in the entire huge structure. It was to be near the top of the boat, perhaps encircling the entire vessel. Noah could look out upon the waters and up toward heaven.

We have here many spiritual lessons. The ark is a picture of Christ (1 Peter 3:20–22), who bears His own through the waters of judgment to the heavenly places of security and divine fellowship (Ephesians 2:6). Even as Noah and his family were not to be touched by the waters of God's wrath, so also we will be delivered.

Darkness may surround the believer, but the clear blue of God's love and the warmth and light of His smile await the ransomed soul who will simply look to God in His Word. If the Lord Jesus does not return soon and physical death comes to us, we need not fear the passage through the deep valley of death or the lashing waves of judgment.

Through the window of the Bible we may look up with hope into the shining realities of eternity! *Henry Bosch*

On a Hill Far Away

Read Genesis 22:1–12

Then God said, "Take your son, your only son, whom you love—Isaac—and go to the region of Moriah. Sacrifice him there as a burnt offering on a mountain I will show you."

GENESIS 22:2

I often find myself thinking back to the years when my children were young. One particular fond memory is our morning wake-up routine. Every morning I'd go into their bedrooms, tenderly call them by name, and tell them that it was time to get up and get ready for the day.

When I read that Abraham got up early in the morning to obey God's command, I think of those times when I woke up my children and wonder if part of Abraham's daily routine was going to Isaac's bed to waken him—and how different it would have been on that particular morning when he was planning to take him to a hill far away as a sacrifice. How heart-rending for Abraham to waken his son that morning!

Abraham bound his son and laid him on an altar, but then God provided an alternate sacrifice. Hundreds of years later, God would supply another sacrifice—the final sacrifice—His own Son. Think of how agonizing it must have been for God to sacrifice His Son, His only Son whom He loved! And He went through all of that because He loves you.

If you wonder whether you are loved by God, wonder no more.

Joe Stowell

14

Whose Will?

Read Genesis 39:1–6, 20–23

Going a little farther, he fell with his face to the ground and prayed, "My Father, if it is possible, may this cup be taken from me. Yet not as I will, but as you will."

MATTHEW 26:39

"May all things happen according to your will," is a greeting frequently exchanged during Chinese New Year. As wonderful as that may sound, events turn out best when God's will plays out and not mine.

Given a choice, Joseph would not have wished to be a slave in Egypt (Genesis 39:1). But despite his captivity, he "prospered" because "the LORD was with [him]" (v. 2). The Lord even blessed his master's home "because of Joseph" (v. 5).

Joseph would never have chosen to go to prison in Egypt. But he did when falsely accused of sexual assault. However, for the second time we read: "the LORD was with [Joseph]" (v. 21). There, he gained the trust of the warden (v. 22) so that he had "success in whatever he did" (v. 23). His downward spiral into prison turned out to be the start of his rise to the top position in Egypt. Few people would choose to be promoted the way God promoted Joseph. But Joseph's God blesses, despite, and even through, adverse circumstances.

God had a purpose for bringing Joseph to Egypt, and He has a purpose for placing us where we are. Instead of wishing that all things happened according to our will, we could say, as our Savior did before going to the cross, "Not as I will, but as you will" (Matthew 26:39).

C. P. Hia

EXODUS

◆

In the book of Exodus, God leaves no doubt about who He is and what He can do. For the rest of the Old Testament and into the New, the things God accomplishes in these forty chapters set the tone for belief and faith of all who need a solid foundation of truth and greatness. First, by wresting the Hebrews from the hands of the Pharaoh and rescuing them from the frightening armies of Egypt—and then leading the people back to the Promised Land—God shows that He is the King of redemption. Each of His miracles along the wilderness way and even into the Promised Land as Israel reestablished herself in the land demonstrated the trustworthiness of His power. In addition, God reveals His presence with His covenant people—both in the wilderness and in the homeland. The tabernacle allowed the people to experience firsthand His presence with them.

OUTLINE

✦

Who Am I?

Read Exodus 3:10–17

*God said to Moses, "I AM WHO I AM. This is what you
are to say to the Israelites: 'I AM has sent me to you.'"*

EXODUS 3:14

Dave enjoyed his job, but for a long time he had sensed a pull toward
something else. Now he was about to fulfill his dream and step into
mission work. But strangely, he began to have serious doubts.

"I don't deserve this," he told a friend. "The mission board doesn't
know the real me. I'm not good enough."

Dave has some pretty good company. Mention the name of Moses,
and we think of leadership, strength, and the Ten Commandments. We
tend to forget that Moses fled to the desert after murdering a man. We
lose sight of his forty years as a fugitive. We overlook his anger problem
and his intense reluctance to say yes to God.

When God showed up with marching orders (Exodus 3:1–10),
Moses played the I'm-not-good-enough card. He even got into a lengthy
argument with God, asking Him: "Who am I?" (v. 11). Then God
told Moses who He was: "I AM WHO I AM" (v. 14). It's impossible for
us to explain that mysterious name because our indescribable God is
describing His eternal presence to Moses.

A sense of our own weaknesses is healthy. But if we use them as an
excuse to keep God from using us, we insult Him. What we're really
saying is that God isn't good enough.

The question isn't Who am I? The question is Who is the I AM?

Tim Gustafson

The Passover Picture

Read Exodus 12:1–20

Christ, our Passover lamb, has been sacrificed.
1 Corinthians 5:7

The day of Israel's first Passover was full of excitement and mystery for the Hebrew boys and girls. They saw their fathers roast lambs over an open fire. They watched them sprinkle blood from the lambs on the sides and tops of the doorframes of their houses. They listened with wide-eyed wonder as their fathers told them that an angel of death would kill the firstborn in every house that was not marked by the blood.

In the evening, wearing their sandals and dressed for immediate departure, family members gathered in groups just large enough to consume a whole lamb. They ate the Passover meal, which included bitter herbs and bread made without yeast. After midnight they gathered up their possessions and left Egypt to begin a new way of life as a free people.

Israel's slavery in Egypt pictures for us as believers in Christ the bondage to sin from which we have been delivered. The slaughtered lamb points to Jesus Christ, "our Passover Lamb, [who] has been sacrificed for us" (1 Corinthians 5:7 NLT). The sprinkling of the blood speaks of the act of faith by which we receive salvation.

Have you experienced the joy of salvation that comes to those who put their trust in the Lamb of God? *Herb Vander Lugt*

The Law Side of Love

Read Exodus 20:1–17

*It is easier for heaven and earth to disappear than for
the least stroke of a pen to drop out of the Law.*

LUKE 16:17

A cartoon in *Christianity Today* portrayed Moses atop Mount Sinai
holding the stone tablets containing the Ten Commandments. Looking
heavenward, he says to God, "They tend to lose interest rather quickly.
Could I have a one-liner instead?"

In a sense, God did give "one-liners." His ten laws are clear and pointed.

1. Love the only true God.
2. Don't make an image of God.
3. Hallow His name.
4. Keep His day holy.
5. Honor your parents.
6. Don't murder.
7. Don't commit adultery.
8. Don't steal.
9. Don't lie.
10. Don't covet.

These laws express God's holy nature, and we function best as His
image-bearers when we obey them.

Sinners don't lose interest in God's laws because they are complex,
but because they have an aversion to obeying them. The Hebrew word
for *law* is *torah*, which refers to the kind of instruction loving parents
give their children so they will be happy. And when we trust Jesus as
Savior, His Spirit gives us the desire to obey.

God's commandments work for our good. They are the law side of
love.   *Dennis DeHaan*

The Craftsman's Touch

Read Exodus 31:1–5

*For we are God's handiwork, created in
Christ Jesus to do good works, which God
prepared in advance for us to do.*

EPHESIANS 2:10

I recently saw a documentary about the making of a Steinway piano. It traced the meticulous care that goes into crafting this fine instrument. From the cutting of trees until the piano appears on a showroom floor, it goes through countless delicate adjustments by skilled craftsmen. When the year-long process is complete, accomplished musicians play the piano and often comment on how the same rich sounds could never be produced by a computerized assembly line. The secret to the final product is the craftsman's touch.

When the tabernacle was built, we see that God also valued the craftsman's touch. He chose the craftsman Bezalel and said of him: "I have filled him with the Spirit of God, with wisdom, with understanding, with knowledge, and with all kinds of skills—to make artistic designs for work in gold, silver and bronze, to cut and set stones, to work in wood, and to engage in all kinds crafts" (Exodus 31:3–5).

Today God dwells in the hearts of believers. Yet the call to craftsmanship has not ended. Now each individual believer is God's "handiwork" (Ephesians 2:10). The Master Craftsman is the Holy Spirit, who chips away at flaws in our character to make each of us like Jesus (Romans 8:28–29). And as we yield to His workmanship, we will find that the secret to the final product is the Craftsman's touch.   *Dennis Fisher*

LEVITICUS

If you were to sign up to be an Old Testament priest, this would be a great book to be handed. It spells out the tasks the priests will perform and the sacrifices that must be made. Since you are not an Old Testament priest, what is the book's value to you? Both Paul and Peter, writing in the New Testament, suggested that we can learn from such Old Testament teachings (See Romans 15:4, 1 Corinthians 10:11). Despite the fact that the specific sacrifices and ceremonies of the book of Leviticus don't apply to us today, we can learn from them about God's holiness and His high regard for strong biblical standards.

OUTLINE

Laws Regarding Offerings to God Leviticus 1:1–7:38

Laws Regarding the Priesthood Leviticus 8:1–10:20

Laws Regarding Purity Leviticus 11:1–15:33

Laws Regarding Atonement and Sacrifices Leviticus 16:1–17:16

How to Live: Sanctification and Holiness Leviticus 18:1–27:34

Unintentional

Read Leviticus 4:1–3; Romans 3:21–26

*Say to the Israelites: "When anyone sins unintentionally and
does what is forbidden in any of the LORD's commands—
If the anointed priest sins, bringing guilt on the people,
he must bring to the LORD a young bull without defect
as a sin offering for the sin he has committed."*

LEVITICUS 4:2–3

When I was returning our grandson Alex to his family after a visit, the traffic seemed especially challenging. Fast-maneuvering cars blocked me from the correct toll lane, forcing me to go through a lane where only cars with a prepaid pass are permitted, which I didn't have. Alex told me that my license plate would be photographed and a ticket might be mailed to me. I was frustrated because a penalty would have to be paid even though my infraction was unintentional.

For the ancient Jews, a violation of God's laws committed even in ignorance was taken very seriously. The Old Testament recognized and provided for unintentional sins through appropriate sacrifices: "When anyone sins unintentionally and does what is forbidden in any of the LORD's commands . . . he must bring to the LORD a young bull without defect as a sin offering" (Leviticus 4:2–3).

Old Testament sacrifices were more than a reminder that accidental wrongs have consequences. They were given in anticipation that God in His grace would provide atonement even for wrongs we didn't realize we were doing. He did this through the death of Jesus in our place. God's grace is far greater than we could ever imagine! *Dennis Fisher*

Whose Property?

Read Leviticus 6:1–7

If anyone sins and is unfaithful to the LORD by deceiving a
neighbor about something entrusted to them or left in their care
or about something stolen, or if they cheat their neighbor, . . .
when they sin in any of these ways and realize their guilt, they
must return what they have stolen or taken by extortion, or
what was entrusted to them, or the lost property they found.

LEVITICUS 6:2, 4

A thief in New Jersey stole $7,000 in jewelry, old coins, and cash from a widow. The items taken were all she had left from her husband's estate.

In sorting through his loot, the thief came across several church offering envelopes containing money the woman intended to give to the Lord. Leaving their contents inside, he put them in another envelope, addressed it to the woman's church, and then dropped it in the mail.

When the pastor found out what had happened, he commented, "It is a characteristic of the moral confusion of our times that someone would consider stealing from a widow and her children, yet think it reprehensible to steal from the church."

That thief overlooked an important truth: A sin against our neighbor is a sin against God (Leviticus 6:2). All of us, I'm afraid, are prone to think that God's property line ends somewhere near the back of the church. But it doesn't. Everything and everyone belongs to God. To reverence Him is to respect the property that He has entrusted to His children.

Wise is the person who fears God and recognizes that to sin against others is to sin against Him. *Mart DeHaan*

The Leviticus Reminder

Read Leviticus 11:41–45

I am the LORD your God; consecrate yourselves and be holy, because I am holy. Do not make yourselves unclean by any creature that moves along the ground.

LEVITICUS 11:44

Leviticus may be one of the least-read books in the Bible, and you might be wondering what its purpose really is. Why all those laws and rules about clean and unclean animals? (chapter 11). What message was God giving to the Israelites—and to us?

Bible commentator Gordon Wenham says, "As the laws distinguished clean from unclean animals, so the people were reminded that God had distinguished them from all the other nations on earth to be His own possession. . . . Man's highest duty is to imitate his creator."

Five times in Leviticus God says, "Be holy, because I am holy" (11:44–45; 19:2; 20:7, 26). And forty-five times He says, "I am the LORD" or "I am the LORD your God." One of the most important themes in the book is God's call for His people to be holy. Jesus echoed that theme when He said, "Be perfect, therefore, as your heavenly Father is perfect" (Matthew 5:48).

As you read Leviticus 11, remember that you are special to God and are to "declare the praises of him who called you out of darkness into his wonderful light" (1 Peter 2:9).

We need the Leviticus reminder every day. *Anne Cetas*

Fixing Elevators

Read Leviticus 19:9–18

Love your neighbor as yourself. I am the LORD.
LEVITICUS 19:18

Sarah has a rare condition that causes her joints to dislocate, making her reliant on an electric wheelchair to get around. On her way to a meeting recently, Sarah rode her wheelchair to the train station but found the elevator broken. Again. With no way of getting to the platform, she was told to take a taxi to another station forty minutes away. The taxi was called but never arrived. Sarah gave up and went home.

Unfortunately, this is a regular occurrence for Sarah. Broken elevators stop her from boarding trains, forgotten ramps leave her unable to get off them. Sometimes Sarah is treated as a nuisance by railway staff for needing assistance. She's often close to tears.

Out of the many biblical laws governing human relationships, "love your neighbor as yourself" is key (Leviticus 19:18; Romans 13:8–10). And while this love stops us from lying, stealing, and abusing others (Leviticus 19:11, 14), it also changes how we work. Employees must be treated fairly (v. 13), and we should all be generous to the poor (vv. 9–10). In Sarah's case, those who fix elevators and drag out ramps aren't doing inconsequential tasks but offering important service to others.

If we treat work as just a means to a wage or other personal benefit, we will soon treat others as annoyances. But if we treat our jobs as opportunities to love, then the most everyday task becomes a holy enterprise.

Sheridan Voysey

Sacred Gathering

Read Leviticus 23:33–36, 39–44

Rejoice before the LORD your God for seven days.
LEVITICUS 23:40

Our group of friends reunited for a long weekend together on the shores of a beautiful lake. The days were spent playing in the water and sharing meals, but it was the evening conversations I treasured the most. As darkness fell, our hearts opened to one another with uncommon depth and vulnerability, sharing the pains of faltering marriages and the aftermath of trauma some of our children were enduring. Without glossing over the brokenness of our realities, we pointed one another to God and His faithfulness throughout such extreme difficulties. Those evenings are among the most sacred in my life.

I imagine those nights are similar to what God intended when He instructed His people to gather each year for the Festival of Tabernacles. This feast, like many others, required the Israelites to travel to Jerusalem. Once they arrived, God instructed His people to gather together in worship and to "do no regular work" for the duration of the feast— about a week! (Leviticus 23:35). The Festival of Tabernacles celebrated God's provision and commemorated their time in the wilderness after leaving Egypt (vv. 42–43).

This gathering cemented the Israelites' sense of identity as God's people and proclaimed His goodness despite their collective and individual hardships. When we gather with those we love to recall God's provision and presence in our lives, we too are strengthened in faith.

Kirsten Holmberg

NUMBERS

◆

This book begins with a census of "the whole Israelite community" (1:2). It details the journey of the people of Israel beginning in Year Two of their escape from Egypt. The narrative covers the next thirty-eight years and takes the people to the east side of the Jordan as they prepare to enter the Promised Land.

OUTLINE

Ancient Promises

Read Numbers 6:22–27

The LORD bless you and keep you.

NUMBERS 6:24

In 1979, Dr. Gabriel Barkay and his team discovered two silver scrolls in a burial ground outside the Old City of Jerusalem. In 2004, after twenty-five years of careful research, scholars confirmed that the scrolls were the oldest biblical text in existence, having been buried in 600 BC. What I find particularly moving is what the scrolls contain—the priestly blessing that God wanted spoken over His people: "The LORD bless you and keep you; the LORD make his face shine on you" (Numbers 6:24–25).

In giving this benediction, God showed Aaron and his sons (through Moses) how to bless the people on His behalf. The leaders were to memorize the words in the form God gave so they would speak to them just as God desired. Note how these words emphasize that God is the one who blesses, for three times they say, "the LORD." And six times He says, "you," reflecting just how much God wants His people to receive His love and favor.

Ponder for a moment that the oldest existing fragments of the Bible tell of God's desire to bless. What a reminder of God's boundless love and how He wants to be in a relationship with us. If you feel far from God today, hold tightly to the promise in these ancient words. May the Lord bless you; may the Lord keep you.   *Amy Boucher Pye*

Sound the Trumpets

Read Numbers 10:8–10

At your times of rejoicing—your appointed festivals and
New Moon feasts—you are to sound the trumpets.

NUMBERS 10:10

"Taps" is a trumpet call played by the US military at the end of the day as well as at funerals. I was amazed when I read the unofficial lyrics and discovered that many of the verses end with the phrase "God is nigh" (God is near). Whether before the dark of each night settles in or while mourning the loss of a loved one, the lyrics offer soldiers the beautiful assurance that God is near.

In the Old Testament, trumpets were also a reminder to the Israelites that God was near. In the middle of celebrating the feasts and festivals that were part of the covenant agreement between God and the nation of Israel, the Jews were to "sound the trumpets" (Numbers 10:10). Blowing a trumpet was a reminder not only of God's presence but also that He was available when they needed Him most—and He longed to help them.

Today, we still need reminders that God is near. And in our own style of worship, we too can call out to God in prayer and song. Perhaps our prayers can be thought of as trumpets asking God to help us. And the beautiful encouragement is that God always hears those calls (1 Peter 3:12). To each of our pleas, He responds with the assurance of His presence that strengthens and comforts us in the difficulties and sorrows of life.   *Lisa Samra*

Getting a Grip on Gratitude

Read Numbers 11:1–11

*Would they have enough if all the fish in
the sea were caught for them?*

Numbers 11:22

The years of weariness caused by chronic pain and frustrations with my limited mobility had finally caught up with me. In my discontent, I became demanding and ungrateful. I began complaining about my husband's caregiving skills. I griped about the way he cleaned the house. Even though he's the best cook I know, I fussed about the lack of variety in our meals. When he finally shared that my grumbling hurt his feelings, I was resentful. He had no idea what I was going through. Eventually, God helped me see my wrongs, and I asked my husband and the Lord for forgiveness.

Longing for different circumstances can lead to complaining, and even a form of relationship damaging self-centeredness. The Israelites were familiar with this dilemma. It seems they were never satisfied and always griping about God's provision (Exodus 17:1–3). Even though the Lord cared for His people in the wilderness by sending them "bread from heaven" (16:4), they began craving other food (Numbers 11:4). Instead of rejoicing over the daily miracles of God's faithful and loving care, the Israelites wanted something more, something better, something different, or even something they used to have (vv. 4–6). They took out their frustrations on Moses (vv. 10–14).

Trusting God's goodness and faithfulness can help us get a good grip on gratitude. Today we can thank Him for the countless ways He cares for us. *Xochitl Dixon*

Don't Just Retire

Read Numbers 8:23–26

They may minister with their brethren . . . to attend to needs.

NUMBERS 8:26 NKJV

The first people to climb Mount Everest, the world's highest mountain, were Edmund Hillary and Tenzing Norgay in 1953. Hillary was just thirty-three years old. His feat afforded him fame, wealth, and the realization that he had already lived a remarkable life.

So, what did Hillary do for the next fifty-five years? Did he retire and rest on his laurels? Absolutely not.

Although Hillary had no higher mountains to climb, that didn't stop him. He achieved other notable goals, including a concerted effort to improve the welfare of the Nepalese people living near Mount Everest—a task he carried on until his death in 2008.

Did you know that God told the Levites to retire from their regular duties at age fifty? (Numbers 8:24–25). But He did not want them to stop helping others. He said that they should "minister with their brethren . . . to attend to needs" (v. 26 NKJV). We cannot take this incident as a complete teaching on retirement, but we can see a godly implication that continuing to serve others after our working days are over is a good idea.

Many people find that when they retire they have nothing meaningful to do with their time. But as the Levites and Sir Edmund Hillary did, we can refocus when we retire—giving of our time to help others.

C. P. Hia

Chimp Eden

Read Numbers 14:1–10

*If the LORD is pleased with us, he will lead us
into that land . . . and will give it to us.*

NUMBERS 14:8

Eugene Cussons rescues chimpanzees. Orphaned by those in the business of bush-meat trade and taken from the jungle as infants, many have lived their entire lives confined in a space smaller than a prison cell. When Cussons arrives to take them to the game reserve he calls "Chimp Eden," he often finds them hostile and untrusting.

"These chimps don't realize that I am one of the good guys," Cussons says. When he tries to put them into a smaller crate for the trip to their new home, they put up quite a fight. "They don't know that I'm going to take them back to Chimp Eden and give them a life so much better."

On a much grander scale, God's offer to liberate us from the slavery of sin is often met with resistance. When He rescued the children of Israel from Egypt, God took them through difficult places that caused them to doubt His good intentions. "Would it not be better for us to go back to Egypt?" they cried (Numbers 14:3 ESV).

On our journey of faith, there are times when the "freedom" of sin that we left behind is more appealing than the restrictions of faith that lie ahead. We must trust the protective boundaries found in God's Word as the only way to get to the place of ultimate freedom.

Julie Ackerman Link

Look at the Tassels

Read Numbers 15:37–41

*Remember all the commands of the
LORD, that you may obey them.*

NUMBERS 15:39

Best-selling author Chaim Potok began his novel *The Chosen* by describing a baseball game between two Jewish teams in New York City. Reuven Malter, the book's main character, notices that the opposing players' uniforms have a unique accessory—four long ropelike tassels that extend below each teammate's shirt. Reuven recognizes the tassels as a sign of strict obedience to God's Old Testament laws.

The history of these fringes—known as *tzitzit*—began with a message from God. Through Moses, God told His people to create tassels containing some strands of blue thread and attach them to the four corners of their top garments (Numbers 15:38). God said, "When you see the tassels, you will remember and obey all the commands of the LORD" (v. 39 NLT).

God's memory device for the ancient Israelites has a parallel for us today. We can look at Christ who consistently kept the whole law in our place and obeyed His heavenly Father (John 8:29). Having received His work on our behalf, we now "put on the Lord Jesus Christ, and make no provision for the flesh, to fulfill its lusts" (Romans 13:14 NKJV). Keeping our eyes on God's Son helps us to honor our heavenly Father.

Jennifer Benson Schuldt

Are You Listening?

Read Numbers 20:1–13

*Speak to that rock before their eyes
and it will pour out its water.*

NUMBERS 20:8

He was frustrated. He was angry. He was tired of being blamed for everything that went wrong. Year after year, he had gotten them through one disaster after another. He was continually interceding on their behalf to keep them out of trouble. But all he got for his efforts was more grief. Finally, in exasperation, he said, "Listen, you rebels, must we bring you water out of this rock?" (Numbers 20:10).

That suggestion might sound preposterous, but it wasn't. Forty years earlier, the previous generation had the same complaint: no water. God told Moses to strike a rock with his staff (Exodus 17:6). When he obeyed, water gushed out—plenty of water. When the grumbling started again so many years later, Moses did the thing that worked before. But this time it was the wrong thing to do. What Moses told the Israelites to do—to listen—he himself had not done. God had told him to speak to the rock this time, not strike it.

Sometimes in exhaustion or exasperation, we don't pay close attention to God. We assume He will always work the same way. But He doesn't. Sometimes He tells us to act; sometimes He tells us to speak; sometimes He tells us to wait. That is why we must always be careful to listen before we take action. *Julie Ackerman Link*

The One Who Sees

Read Numbers 32:16–24

You may be sure that your sin will find you out.

NUMBERS 32:23

"Oh no!" My wife's voice rang out when she stepped into the kitchen. The moment she did, our ninety-pound Labrador retriever, Max, bolted from the room.

Gone was the leg of lamb that had been sitting too close to the edge of the counter. Max had consumed it, leaving only an empty pan. He tried to hide under a bed. But only his head and shoulders fit. His uncovered rump and tail betrayed his whereabouts when I went to track him down.

"Oh, Max," I murmured, "Your sin will find you out." The phrase was borrowed from Moses, when he admonished two tribes of Israel to be obedient to God and keep their promises. He told them: "But if you fail to do this, you will be sinning against the LORD; and you may be sure that your sin will find you out" (Numbers 32:23).

Sin may feel good for a moment, but it causes the ultimate pain of separation from God. Moses was reminding his people that God misses nothing. As one biblical writer put it, "Everything is uncovered and laid bare before the eyes of him to whom we must give account" (Hebrews 4:13).

Though seeing all, our holy God lovingly draws us to confess our sin, repent of it (turn from it), and walk rightly with Him (1 John 1:9). May we follow Him in love today.   *James Banks*

DEUTERONOMY

◆

The book of Deuteronomy contains three messages delivered by Moses to his people as a farewell to them. One message centers on the history of the people (1:1–4:43). The second message reviews the law of God (4–26). And the third message (27–30) is a review of the covenant God made with His chosen people. After Moses completed his sermons to the people, we read about the transition of leadership from Moses to Joshua (chapters 31–34). The book ends with a record of the death of Moses.

OUTLINE

Moses reviews God's Dealings Deuteronomy 1:1–4:49

Moses reviews God's Law Deuteronomy 5:1–6:25

Securing the Land Deuteronomy 7:1–26

Calls for Obedience Deuteronomy 8:1–13:18

Laws of Separation Deuteronomy 14:1–29

Calendar Events, Feasts Deuteronomy 15:1–16:22

Governance, Prophecies, and Laws Deuteronomy17:1–30:20

Moses's Final Acts Deuteronomy 31:1–33:29

Moses Dies Deuteronomy 34:1–12

JANUARY 25

Trust Tally

Read Deuteronomy 1:21-33

See, the LORD your God has given you the land.
. . . Do not be afraid; do not be discouraged.

DEUTERONOMY 1:21

Before my husband and I surrendered our lives to Christ, we seriously considered divorce. But after committing to love and obey God, we recommitted to each other. We sought wise counsel and invited the Holy Spirit to transform us individually and as a couple. Our heavenly Father continues to help us develop healthy communication skills. He's teaching us how to love and trust Him—and one another—no matter what happens.

Yet, even as we head toward celebrating our twenty-fifth anniversary, I occasionally forget everything God has done in and through our trials. Sometimes, I struggle with a deep-seated fear of the unknown— experiencing unnecessary anxiety instead of relying on God's track record.

In Deuteronomy 1, Moses affirmed the Lord's reliability. He encouraged the Israelites to move forward in faith so they could enjoy their inheritance (v. 21). But God's people demanded details about what they'd be up against and what they'd receive before committing to trust Him with their future (vv. 22–33).

Followers of Christ are not immune to succumbing to fear or anxiety. Worrying about what difficulties we may or may not encounter can keep us from depending on faith and may even damage our relationships with God and others. But the Holy Spirit can help us create a trust tally of the Lord's past faithfulness. He can empower us with courageous confidence in God's trustworthiness yesterday, today, and forever.

Xochitl Dixon

JANUARY 26

Doing What He Says

Read Deuteronomy 5:28–33

Walk in obedience to all that the LORD
your God has commanded you.
DEUTERONOMY 5:33

I needed an underground water tank and knew precisely how I wanted it constructed, so I gave clear instructions to the builder. The next day when I inspected the project, I was annoyed when I realized that he had failed to carry out my instructions. He had changed the plan and therefore the effect. The excuse he gave was as irritating as his failure to follow my directives.

As I watched him redo the concrete work, and as my frustration diminished, a guilty conviction swept over me: How many times have I needed to redo things in my life in obedience to the Lord?

Like the ancient Israelites who frequently failed to do what God asked them to do, we too often go our own way. Yet obedience is a desired result of our deepening relationship with God. Moses told the people, "Be careful to do what the LORD your God has commanded you. . . . Walk in obedience to all that [he] has commanded you" (Deuteronomy 5:32–33). Long after Moses, Jesus urged His disciples to trust Him and to love one another.

This is still the kind of surrender of our hearts that leads to our well-being. As the Spirit helps us to obey, it is good to remember that He "works in [us] to will and to act in order to fulfill his good purpose" (Philippians 2:13). *Lawrence Darmani*

Keeping Close

Read Deuteronomy 6:1–9

*Tie them as symbols on your hands and
bind them on your foreheads.*

DEUTERONOMY 6:8

My mile-long walk home from dropping off my daughter at her school gives me the opportunity to memorize some verses from the Bible—if I'm intentional about doing so. When I take those minutes to turn over God's Word in my mind, I often find them coming back to me later in the day, bringing me comfort and wisdom.

When Moses prepared the Israelites to enter the promised land, he urged them to hold close to God's commands and decrees (Deuteronomy 6:1–2). Wanting them to flourish, he said they should turn these instructions over in their minds and discuss them with their children (vv. 6–7). He even said to tie them to their wrists and bind them to their foreheads (v. 8). He didn't want them to forget God's instructions to live as people who honored the Lord and enjoyed His blessings.

How might you consider God's words today? One idea is to write out a verse from Scripture, and every time you wash your hands or take a drink, read the words and turn them over in your mind. Or before you go to sleep, consider a short passage from the Bible as the last act of the day. Many are the ways of keeping God's Word close to our hearts!

Amy Boucher Pye

Grateful for Everything

Read Deuteronomy 8:6–18

*When you have eaten and are satisfied, praise the LORD
your God for the good land he has given you.*

DEUTERONOMY 8:10

In Australia, it can take hours to drive between towns and fatigue can lead to accidents. So at busy holiday times rest stops are set up on major highways with volunteers offering free coffee. My wife, Merryn, and I grew to enjoy these stops during our long drives there.

On one trip, we pulled in and walked over to order our coffee. An attendant handed the two cups over, and then asked me for two dollars. I asked why. She pointed to the small print on the sign. At this stop, only the driver got free coffee; you had to pay for passengers. Annoyed, I told her this was false advertising, paid the two dollars, and walked off. Back at the car, Merryn pointed out my error: I had turned a gift into an entitlement and become ungrateful for what I received. She was right.

When the Israelites were about to enter the Promised Land, Moses urged them to be a grateful people (Deuteronomy 8:10). Thanks to the blessings of God, the land was abundant, but they could easily treat this prosperity as something they deserved (vv. 17–18). From this, the Jews developed a practice of giving thanks for every meal, no matter how small. For them, it was all a gift.

I went back to the woman and apologized. A free cup of coffee was a gift I didn't deserve—and something for which to be thankful.

Sheridan Voysey

The Bill Is Paid

Read Deuteronomy 26:12–15

You shall give it to the Levite, the foreigner,
the fatherless and the widow.

DEUTERONOMY 26:12

"What happened to you?" asked Zeal, a Nigerian businessman, as he bent over a hospital bed in Lagos. "Someone shot me," replied the young man, his thigh bandaged. Although the injured man was well enough to return home, he wouldn't be released until he settled his bill—a policy that many government hospitals in the region follow. After consulting with a social worker, Zeal anonymously covered the bill through the charitable fund he'd earlier set up as a way to express his Christian faith. In return, he hopes that those receiving the gift of release will one day give to others too.

The theme of giving from God's bounty pulses throughout the Bible. For instance, when Moses instructed the Israelites on how to live in the Promised Land, he told them to give back to God first (see Deuteronomy 26:1–3) and to care for those in need—the foreigners, orphans, and widows (v. 12). Because they dwelled in a "land flowing with milk and honey" (v. 15), they were to express God's love to the needy.

We too can spread God's love through sharing our material goods, whether big or small. We might not have the opportunity to personally give exactly like Zeal did, but we can ask God to show us how to give or who needs our help.   *Amy Boucher Pye*

Choose Life

Read Deuteronomy 30:11–20

*Choose life, so that both you and your children may
live and that you may love the LORD your God,
listen to his voice, and hold fast to him.*

DEUTERONOMY 30:19–20

What is God's will for my life? The question haunted me when I was growing up. What if I couldn't find it? What if I didn't recognize it? God's will seemed like a needle in a haystack. Hidden. Obscured by lookalikes. Outnumbered by counterfeits.

But my view of God's will was wrong because my view of God was wrong. God takes no pleasure in seeing us lost, wandering, searching. He wants us to know His will. He makes it clear, and He makes it simple. He doesn't even make it multiple-choice. He gives just two choices: "life and prosperity" or "death and destruction" (Deuteronomy 30:15). In case the best choice isn't obvious, He even says which one to choose: "Choose life" (v. 19). To choose life is to choose God himself and obey His Word.

When Moses addressed the Israelites for the last time, he pleaded with them to make the right choice by observing "all the words of this law. . . . they are your life" (32:46–47). God's will for us is life. His Word is life. And Jesus is the Word. God may not give a prescription for every decision, but He gave us a perfect example to follow—Jesus. The right choice may not be easy, but when the Word is our guide and worship is our goal, God will grant us the wisdom to make life-affirming choices. *Julie Ackerman Link*

What's Your Song?

Read Deuteronomy 31:15–22

*So Moses wrote down this song that day
and taught it to the Israelites.*

DEUTERONOMY 31:22

Most Americans knew little about Alexander Hamilton—until 2015, when Lin-Manuel Miranda wrote his hit musical *Hamilton*. Now schoolchildren know Hamilton's story by heart. They sing it to each other on the bus and at recess. He's their favorite founding father.

God knows the power of music, and He told Moses to "write down this song and teach it to the Israelites and have them sing it" (Deuteronomy 31:19). God knew that long after Moses was gone, when He had brought Israel into the Promised Land, they would rebel and worship other gods. So He told Moses, "This song will testify against them, because it will not be forgotten by their descendants" (v. 21).

Songs are nearly impossible to forget, so it's wise to be selective about what we sing. Some songs are just for fun, and that's fine, but we benefit from songs that boast in Jesus and encourage our faith. One of the ways we "[make] the most of every opportunity" is when we speak "to one another with psalms, hymns, and songs from the Spirit." So "sing and make music from your heart to the Lord" (Ephesians 5:15–19).

Songs can be an indicator of the direction of our heart. Do the words make much of Jesus? Do we sing them wholeheartedly? What we sing will influence what we believe, so choose wisely and sing loudly.

Mike Wittmer

PART 2

◆

The Histories

Joshua, Judges, Ruth, 1 & 2 Samuel,
1 & 2 Kings, 1 & 2 Chronicles,
Ezra, Nehemiah, Esther

While the first five books (Genesis through Deuteronomy) are historical in nature, they also have become a separate entity by virtue of their uniqueness. Written by Moses and labeled the Pentateuch, or five scrolls, they deserve to be set apart. Our Jewish friends call those books the Torah. But the history of God's redemption story continues in the next twelve books, which are referred to as the histories. They follow the story of the Jewish people from their entrance into the promised land, through the two periods of judges and kings, and on into the time of exile and return. Once we get to the end of Joshua through Esther, we have a complete picture of the Hebrew nation from Abraham through the last time we hear about them four hundred years before the Messiah Jesus is born.

JOSHUA

◆

Finally, after forty years, the Israelites are allowed to enter the land promised to Abraham and his offspring so long ago. A miraculous crossing of the flooded Jordan River gives them access to the land, but it is going to take much effort to settle it, call it their own, and distribute the population throughout the country. As the people take on this task, they must have the courage God spoke to Joshua about (1:6–9), and they must learn that obedience to God's directions is still the secret to accomplishing what He wants them to do. It is a happy prospect for these hundreds of thousands of people that it is now possible for them to stop traveling, settle down, and establish themselves in towns and villages throughout the land.

OUTLINE

Strong and Courageous

Read Joshua 1:1–9

As I was with Moses, so I will be with you;
I will never leave you nor forsake you.

JOSHUA 1:5

Each night, as young Caleb closed his eyes, he felt the darkness envelop him. The silence of his room was regularly suspended by the creaking of the wooden house in Costa Rica. Then the bats in the attic became more active. His mother had put a nightlight in his room, but the young boy still feared the dark. One night Caleb's dad posted a Bible verse on the footboard of his bed. It read: "Be strong and courageous. Do not be afraid; . . . for the LORD your God will be with you" (Joshua 1:9). Caleb began to read those words each night—and he left that promise from God on his footboard until he went away to college.

In Joshua 1, we read of the transition of leadership to Joshua after Moses died. The command to "be strong and courageous" was repeated several times to Joshua and the Israelites to emphasize its importance (vv. 6–7, 9). Surely, they felt trepidation as they faced an uncertain future, but God reassuringly said, "As I was with Moses, so I will be with you; I will never leave you nor forsake you" (v. 5).

It's natural to have fears, but it's detrimental to our physical and spiritual health to live in a state of constant fear. Just as God encouraged His servants of old, we too can be strong and courageous because of the One who promises to always be with us. *Cindy Hess Kasper*

Even Her?

Read Joshua 2:1–14

Was not Rahab the harlot also justified?

JAMES 2:25 NKJV

Imagine looking through your family tree and finding this description of your ancestor: "A prostitute, she harbored enemies of the government in her house. When she was confronted by the authorities, she lied about it."

What would you do about her? Hide her story from anyone inquiring about your family? Or spotlight and praise her in the legends of your family's story?

Meet Rahab. If what we read about her in Joshua 2 were all we knew, we might lump her in with all of the other renegades and bad examples in the Bible. But her story doesn't stop there. Matthew 1:5–6 reveals that she was King David's great-great grandmother—and that she was in the lineage of our Savior, Jesus. And there's more. Hebrews 11:31 names Rahab as a woman of faith who was saved from the fall of Jericho (see Joshua 6:17). And in James 2:25, her works of rescue were given as evidence of her righteous faith.

God's love is amazing that way. He can take people with a bad reputation, transform their lives, and turn them into examples of His love and forgiveness. If you think you're too bad to be forgiven or if you know someone else who feels that way, read about Rahab and rejoice. If God can turn her into a beacon of righteousness, there's hope for all of us.   *Dave Branon*

Standing on the Edge

Read Joshua 3:9–17

[The Israelites] broke camp to cross the JORDAN, the priests carrying the ark of the covenant went ahead of them.

JOSHUA 3:14

My little girl stood apprehensively at the pool's edge. As a nonswimmer, she was just learning to become comfortable in the water. Her instructor waited in the pool with outstretched arms. As my daughter hesitated, I saw the questions in her eyes: Will you catch me? What will happen if my head goes under?

The Israelites may have wondered what would happen when they crossed the Jordan River. Could they trust God to make dry ground appear in the riverbed? Was God guiding their new leader, Joshua, as He had led Moses? Would God help His people defeat the threatening Canaanites who lived just across the river?

To learn the answers to these questions, the Israelites had to engage in a test of faith—they had to act. So they "broke camp to cross the Jordan, the priests carrying the ark of the covenant went ahead of them" (v. 14). Exercising their faith allowed them to see that God was with them. He was still directing Joshua, and He would help them settle in Canaan (vv. 7, 10, 17).

If you are facing a test of faith, you too can move forward based on God's character and His unfailing promises. Relying on Him will help you move from where you are to where He wants you to be.

Jennifer Benson Schuldt

A Winning Strategy

Read Joshua 7:1–13

Israel has sinned; they have violated my covenant.

JOSHUA 7:11

During my days as a high school basketball coach, I made a huge mistake. I sent some of my players to scout an opponent. They returned with this report: We can take those guys easily. Overconfident, we lost to that team. Does that sound familiar? To me, it sounds like the situation at Ai when Joshua sent out his scouts, who misjudged their opponent's strength.

But there was more to the defeat at Ai than bad scouting. Israel lost the battle and thirty-six soldiers for several reasons that I think we can learn from.

Shortly before the loss at Ai, Joshua led his army successfully against Jericho because he knew God's plan of attack. But there is no mention of Joshua consulting God before Ai. Prior to the battle of Jericho, the men had consecrated themselves to God (Joshua 5:2–8). Before Ai—nothing is said about Joshua's men preparing themselves spiritually. The reason the Bible gives for the Israelites' loss is sin in the camp. Achan had stolen from the spoils of Jericho (7:1). They could not defeat Ai until the sin was confessed and the people had consecrated themselves (7:16–26). Then God gave them a plan for victory (8:1–7).

A winning strategy for our daily battles: confessing our sin and living in the power that God provides. *Dave Branon*

Help from Heaven

Read Joshua 10:6–15

Surely the LORD was fighting for Israel!
JOSHUA 10:14

SOS, the Morse code signal, was created in 1905 because sailors needed a way to indicate extreme distress. The signal gained renown in 1910 when used by the sinking steamer Kentucky, saving all forty-six people aboard.

While SOS may be a more recent invention, the urgent cry for help is as old as humanity. We hear it often in the Old Testament story of Joshua, who faced opposition from fellow Israelites (Joshua 9:18) and challenging terrain (3:15–17) for more than fourteen years as the Israelites slowly conquered and settled the land God had promised them. During this struggle "the LORD was with Joshua" (6:27).

In Joshua 10, the Israelites go to the aid of the Gibeonites, allies of Israel who were being attacked by five kings. Joshua knew that he needed the Lord's help to defeat so many powerful enemies (v. 12). God responded with a hailstorm, even stopping the sun in the middle of the sky to give Israel more time to defeat the enemy. Joshua 10:14 recounts, "Surely the LORD was fighting for Israel!"

If you are in the midst of a challenging situation, you can send out an SOS to God. Although help will look different than the assistance Joshua received, perhaps help comes through an unexpected job, an understanding doctor, or peace in the midst of grief. Be encouraged that these are ways He is responding to your call for help and fighting for you. *Lisa Samra*

With God's Help

Read Joshua 14:7–15

*So here I am today, eighty-five years old! . . . I'm just
as vigorous to go out to battle now as I was then.*

JOSHUA 14:10–11

As I've grown older, I've noticed more joint pain, especially when cold weather hits. Some days, I feel less like a conqueror and more like someone conquered by the challenges of becoming a senior citizen.

That's why my hero is an older man named Caleb—the former spy sent by Moses to scout out Canaan, the Promised Land (Numbers 13–14). After the other spies gave an unfavorable report, Caleb and Joshua were the only spies out of the twelve whom God favored to enter Canaan. Now, in Joshua 14, the time for Caleb to receive his portion of land had come. But there were enemies still to drive out. Not content to retire and leave the battle to the younger generation, Caleb declared, "You yourself heard then that the Anakites were there and their cities were large and fortified, but, the LORD helping me, I will drive them out just as he said" (Joshua 14:12).

"The LORD helping me." That's the kind of mindset that kept Caleb battle-ready. He focused on God's power, not his own, nor on his advanced age. God would help him do whatever needed to be done.

Most of us don't think of taking on anything monumental when we reach a certain age. But we can still do great things for God, no matter how old we are. When Caleb-sized opportunities come our way, we don't have to shy away from them. With the Lord helping us, we can conquer!   *Linda Washington*

We Have Fruit!

Read Joshua 24:2, 8–14

*I gave you a land on which you did not
toil and cities you did not build.*

JOSHUA 24:13

The young mother sighed as she scraped together lunch for her three-year-old daughter. Spying the empty fruit basket on the table in their tiny kitchen, she sighed and said aloud, "If we just had a basket of fruit, I would feel rich!" Her little girl overheard her.

Weeks passed. God sustained the small family. Still, the struggling mom worried. Then one day her little girl bounded into the kitchen. "Look, Mommy, we're rich!" she exclaimed, pointing at the full fruit basket on the table. Nothing had changed except that the family had purchased a bag of apples.

When Joshua, the leader of the Israelites, was about to die, he shared a message from the Lord that recounted all God had done for them. And he noted, "You lived in the wilderness for a long time" (Joshua 24:7). Then he said, "[God] gave you a land on which you did not toil and cities you did not build; and you live in them and eat from vineyards and olive groves that you did not plant" (v. 13). Joshua set up a large stone to remind Israel of God's provision (v. 26).

Like the Israelites, after a time of challenge and scarcity, that family now lives in a different place and enjoys fruit trees in a spacious yard, planted years earlier by a previous owner. If you visit them, you'll find a bowl of fruit in their kitchen. It reminds them of God's goodness and how a three-year-old infused her family with faith, joy, and perspective.

Tim Gustafson

Choose Your God

Read Joshua 24:14–18

Choose for yourselves this day whom you will serve. . . .
But as for me and my household, we will serve the LORD.

JOSHUA 24:15

I recently saw a commercial for an online game based on Greek mythology. It spoke about armies, mythological gods, heroes, and quests. What got my attention was the description of how to get the game started. You go online to register, choose your god, then build your empire.

Wow! "Choose your god." Those words, though presented casually in the ad, struck me as being characteristic of one of the most dangerous things about our world. In a game, it may be insignificant what "god" you choose; but in the real world that choice has eternal consequences.

To a generation of Israelites surrounded by the gods of their day, Joshua declared that they must choose their god—but it must not be done in a cavalier way. He set the example as he said, "Choose for yourselves this day whom you will serve, whether the gods your ancestors served beyond the Euphrates, or the gods of the Amorites, in whose land you are living. But as for me and my house, we will serve the LORD" (Joshua 24:15).

Today, as in the days of Joshua, there are many options. But there is only one wise choice—the true God. Joshua made the right choice. "We will serve the Lord."   *Bill Crowder*

JUDGES

Under the leadership of Joshua, the Israelites had conquered the Promised Land and established themselves according to their ancestral tribes into their own territories. An entire generation grew old in this new land under the leadership of Joshua and the direction of God himself. After Joshua died, however, things changed in the land. After a preliminary victory led by Caleb, the Israelites began to lose their edge, beginning in Judges 1:19, which says, "they were unable to drive the people from the plains." Over and over, they fail to do as they were commanded, and that was to rid the region of pagan people. ("The Benjamites, however, did not drive out the Jebusites," v. 21; "Manasseh did not drive out the people of Beth Shan," v. 27.) Little by little, the people began to accept the ways of the Canaanites in their pagan religious practices. Judges 3:5–6 explains, "The Israelites lived among the Canaanites, Hittites, Amorites, Perizzites, Hivites and Jebusites. They took their daughters in marriage and gave their own daughters to their sons, and served their gods." A pattern of action for the people developed through this era. The people would disobey God's standards and adopt the idolatrous practice of surrounding people groups. God would bring judgment on the people through enemy nations, and then He would give them a judge to deliver them and lead them to repentance. Then the cycle would start all over.

OUTLINE

Secondhand Faith

Read Judges 2:6–12

*Another generation grew up who knew neither
the LORD nor what he had done for Israel.*

JUDGES 2:10

When I was growing up in Singapore, I remember that some of my school friends were kicked out of their homes by their non-Christian parents for daring to believe in Jesus Christ. They suffered for their beliefs and emerged with stronger convictions. By contrast, I was born and raised in a Christian family. Though I didn't suffer persecution, I too had to make my convictions my own.

The Israelites who first entered the promised land with Joshua saw the mighty acts of God and believed (Judges 2:7). But sadly, the very next generation "knew neither the LORD nor what he had done for Israel" (v. 10). So it was not long before they turned aside to worship other gods (v. 12). They didn't make their parents' faith their own.

No generation can live off the faith of the previous generation. Every generation needs a firsthand faith. When faced with trouble of any kind, the faith that is not personalized is likely to drift and falter.

Those who are second, third, or even fourth generation Christians have a wonderful legacy, to be sure. However, there's no secondhand faith! Find out what God says in His Word and personalize it so that yours is a fresh, firsthand faith (Joshua 1:8). *C. P. Hia*

Who's That Hero?

Read Judges 3:7-11

Let your light so shine before others, that they may see your good deeds and glorify your Father in heaven.

MATTHEW 5:16

Reading the book of Judges, with its battles and mighty warriors, can sometimes feel like reading about comic book superheroes. We have Deborah, Barak, Gideon, and Samson. However, in the line of judges (or deliverers), we also find Othniel.

The account of his life is brief and straightforward (Judges 3:7–11). No drama. No display of prowess. But what we do see is what God did through Othniel: "The LORD . . . raised up for them a deliverer" (v. 9), "the Spirit of the LORD came upon him" (v. 10), and "the LORD gave Cushan-Rishathaim king of Aram into the hands of Othniel" (v. 10).

The Othniel account helps us focus on what is most important—the activity of God. Interesting stories and fascinating people can obscure that. We end up concentrating on those and fail to see what the Lord is doing.

When I was young, I wished I could be more talented so that I could point more people to Christ. But I was looking at the wrong thing. God often uses ordinary people for His extraordinary work. It is His light shining through our lives that glorifies God and draws others to Him (Matthew 5:16).

When others look at our life, it is more important that they see God—not us. *Poh Fang Chia*

Beat Again

Read Judges 5:19–21

March on, my soul; be strong!

Judges 5:21

In 2012, Phillips, Craig and Dean released their song "Tell Your Heart to Beat Again." It was inspired by the true story of a heart surgeon. After removing a patient's heart to repair it, the surgeon returned it to the chest and began gently massaging it back to life. But the heart wouldn't restart. More intense measures followed, but the heart still wouldn't beat. Finally, the surgeon knelt next to the unconscious patient and spoke to her: "Miss Johnson," he said, "this is your surgeon. The operation went perfectly. Your heart has been repaired. Now tell your heart to beat again." Her heart began to beat.

The idea that we could tell our physical heart to do something might seem strange, but it has spiritual parallels. "Why, my soul, are you downcast?" the psalmist says to himself. "Put your hope in God" (Psalm 42:5). "Return to your rest, my soul," says another, "for the Lord has been good to you" (116:7). After beating Israel's enemies in war, Deborah, a judge, revealed that she too had spoken to her heart during battle. "March on, my soul," she told it, "be strong!" (Judges 5:21), because the Lord had promised victory (4:6–7).

Our capable Surgeon has mended our heart (Psalm 103:3). So when fear, depression, or condemnation come, perhaps we too should address our souls and say: March on! Be strong! Feeble heart, beat again.

Sheridan Voysey

Plod On

Read Judges 6:7–16

Am I not sending you?
JUDGES 6:14

What's God calling you to do that you can't do in your own strength? How can you rely on His power today?

God loves to use people the world might overlook. William Carey was raised in a tiny village in the 1700s and had little formal education. He had limited success in his chosen trade and lived in poverty. But God gave him a passion for sharing the good news and called him to be a missionary. Carey learned Greek, Hebrew, and Latin and eventually translated the first New Testament into the Bengali language. Today he is regarded as a "father of modern missions," but in a letter to his nephew he offered this humble assessment of his abilities: "I can plod. I can persevere."

When God calls us to a task, He also gives us strength to accomplish it regardless of our limitations. In Judges 6:12 the angel of the Lord appeared to Gideon and said, "The LORD is with you, mighty warrior." The angel then told him to rescue Israel from the Midianites who were raiding their towns and crops. But Gideon, who hadn't earned the title of "mighty warrior," humbly responded, "How can I save Israel? . . . I am the least in my family" (v. 15). Still, God used Gideon to set His people free.

The key to Gideon's success was in the words, "the LORD is with you" (v. 12). As we humbly walk with our Savior and rely on His strength, He will empower us to accomplish what's only possible through Him.

James Banks

God of My Strength

Read Judges 7:1–8

I will strengthen you and help you.

Isaiah 41:10

No one could have mistaken the ancient Babylonian soldiers for gentlemen. They were ruthless, resilient, and vicious, and they attacked other nations the way an eagle overtakes its prey. Not only were they powerful, they were prideful as well. They practically worshiped their own combat abilities. In fact, the Bible says that their "strength [was] their god" (Habakkuk 1:11).

God did not want this kind of self-reliance to infect Israel's forces as they prepared to battle the Midianites. So He told Gideon, Israel's army commander, "You have too many men. I cannot deliver Midian into their hands, or Israel would boast against me, 'My own strength has saved me'" (Judges 7:2). As a result, Gideon discharged anyone who was fearful. Twenty-two thousand men hightailed it home, while ten thousand fighters stayed. God continued to downsize the army until only three hundred men remained (vv. 3–7).

Having fewer troops meant that Israel was dramatically outnumbered—their enemies, who populated a nearby valley, were as "thick as locusts" (v. 12). Despite this, God gave Gideon's forces victory.

At times, God may allow our resources to dwindle so that we rely on His strength to keep going. Our needs showcase His power, but He is the One who says, "I will strengthen you and help you; I will uphold you with my righteous right hand" (Isaiah 41:10).

Jennifer Benson Schuldt

Good Intentions

Read Judges 8:22–27

[The ephod] became a snare to Gideon and his family.

Judges 8:27

Have you ever had one of those "I was just trying to help" moments? Maybe you offered to carry the cake to the table and you dropped it. Or perhaps you offered to dog-sit your neighbor's pooch and the little guy ran away.

In Judges 8, it appears that Gideon tried to do a good thing. But the result was tragic. Impressed by his military exploits, the men of Israel asked Gideon to be their king. To his credit, he refused (Judges 8:22–23). But then he asked them to donate gold earrings, which he made into an "ephod" (v. 27). This was either a sacred garment worn by the high priest or some type of image. Why did he do this? We don't know for sure, but Gideon may have been trying to provide spiritual leadership. Whatever his motive was, God hadn't told him to do this.

When Gideon set up the ephod in Ophrah, it drew the people's attention away from worship of the Lord and led them into idolatry (v. 27). And as soon as Gideon died, the people found it easy to go back to worshiping the Baals (v. 33).

Gideon may have had good intentions, but he made the mistake of acting without consulting the Lord. Let's be careful not to allow anything to take our eyes off our loving, holy God—or it will lead us and others astray.   *Dave Branon*

A Lock of Hair

Read Judges 16:4–17

*The LORD . . . [shows] Himself strong on behalf
of those whose heart is loyal to Him.*

2 CHRONICLES 16:9 NKJV

After his return from the moon, Neil Armstrong was often plagued by the media. Seeking greater privacy, he moved his family into a small town. But notoriety was a nuisance even there. Armstrong's barber found out that people would pay good money to get a lock of his hair. So after giving the space hero several haircuts, he sold the clippings to a buyer for $3,000! Armstrong was shocked at the barber's disloyalty.

The Scriptures tell of another story of disloyalty and a haircut. As a symbol of God's calling of Samson as a Nazirite, he was never to cut his hair (Judges 13:5). When the Spirit of God came upon him, he was given super-human strength over his enemies (15:14). Wanting to overpower him, the Philistines hired Delilah, a woman who had a relationship with him, to find out the secret of that strength. He foolishly told her that his power would be gone if his hair were cut. She lulled him to sleep and had him shorn (16:5, 19).

Greed can drive us to be disloyal to others and to God, causing us to make sinful choices. Our desire should be to exhibit a heart that is fully committed to love the Lord and others. He shows "Himself strong on behalf of those whose heart is loyal to Him" (2 Chronicles 16:9 NKJV).

Dennis Fisher

RUTH

◆

Who does not like this story! It has drama (family has to move across the river in order to get food). It has tragedy (when Naomi loses her husband and her sons to death). We don't know the details about these three deaths—perhaps in a battle, perhaps to a disease, perhaps an accident. But we can imagine the heartbreak and sadness that must have accompanied these three women. They have no means of support as they arrive in Bethlehem, and they must depend on the kindness of others. But God has gone before to set things up for them, and by the surprising outcome will become a flashpoint of joy in the midst of a dark time in Israel's history.

OUTLINE

Dig It Up

Read Ruth 1:3–5, 20–21

Get rid of all bitterness.

EPHESIANS 4:31

When Rebecca's brother and sister-in-law started having marriage problems, Rebecca prayed earnestly for their reconciliation. But they divorced. Then her sister-in-law took the children out of state and their dad didn't protest. Rebecca never again saw the nieces she dearly loved. Years later she said, "Because of trying to handle this sadness on my own, I let a root of bitterness start in my heart, and it began to spread to my family and friends."

The book of Ruth tells about a woman named Naomi who struggled with a heart of grief that grew into bitterness. Her husband died in a foreign land, and ten years later both her sons died. She was left destitute with her daughters-in-law, Ruth and Orpah (1:3–5). When Naomi and Ruth returned to Naomi's home country, the whole town was excited to see them. But Naomi told her friends: "The Almighty has made my life very bitter. . . . The LORD has afflicted me" (vv. 20–21). She even asked them to call her "Mara," meaning "bitter."

Who hasn't faced disappointment and been tempted toward bitterness? Someone says something hurtful, an expectation isn't met, or demands from others make us resentful. When we acknowledge to ourselves and God what's happening deep in our hearts, our tender Gardener can help us dig up any roots of bitterness—whether they're still small or have been growing for years—and can replace them with a sweet, joyful spirit. *Anne Cetas*

Renamed

Read Ruth 1:19–22

*"Don't call me Naomi," she told them. "Call me Mara,
because the almighty has made my life bitter."*

RUTH 1:20

Riptide. Batgirl. Jumpstart. These are a few names given to counselors at
the summer camp our family attends every year. Created by their peers,
the camp nicknames usually derive from an embarrassing incident, a
funny habit, or a favorite hobby.

Nicknames aren't limited to camp—we even find them used in the
Bible. For example, Jesus dubs the apostles James and John the "Sons
of Thunder" (Mark 3:17). It is rare in Scripture for someone to give
themselves a nickname, yet it happens when a woman named Naomi
asks people to call her "Mara," which means "bitterness" (Ruth 1:20),
because both her husband and two sons had died. She felt that God
had made her life bitter (v. 21).

The new name Naomi gave herself didn't stick, however, because
those devastating losses were not the end of her story. In the midst of her
sorrow, God had blessed her with a loving daughter-in-law, Ruth, who
eventually remarried and had a son, creating a family for Naomi again.

Although we might sometimes be tempted to give ourselves bitter
nicknames, like "failure" or "unloved," based on difficulties we've experienced or mistakes we've made, those names are not the end of our
stories. We can replace those labels with the name God has given each
of us, "loved one" (Romans 9:25), and look for the ways He's providing
for us in even the most challenging of times.   *Lisa Samra*

Managing the Mess

Read Ruth 1:15–22

Why call me Naomi? The LORD has afflicted me;
the Almighty has brought misfortune upon me.

RUTH 1:21

When we meet Naomi in the Scriptures, her life is a mess. She and her husband had gone to Moab searching for food during a famine. While in that land, their two sons married Moabite women, and life was good—until her husband and sons died and she was stuck, widowed in a foreign land.

Though honest about her pain, Naomi obviously had a sense of who was in control: "The LORD has afflicted me; the Almighty has brought misfortune upon me" (Ruth 1:21).

The Hebrew word for *Almighty* (*Shaddai*) indicates God's sufficiency for any situation. The word *Lord* (*Yahweh*) refers to His faithfulness as the loving covenant-keeping God. I love how Naomi put these two names together. In the midst of her complaint, she never lost sight of the fact that her God was a capable and faithful God. And, sure enough, He proved His capability to deliver her and His faithfulness to care for her to the very end.

If there seems to be no way out of your despair, remember that Naomi's God is your God as well. And He specializes in managing our messes to good and glorious outcomes. Thankfully, He is both capable and faithful. So, when your life is a mess, remember who your God is!

Joe Stowell

Gleaning the Fields

Read Ruth 2:1–12

*Ruth the Moabite said to Naomi, "Let me go to
the fields and pick up the leftover grain behind
anyone in whose eyes I find favor."*

Ruth 2:2

A Tanzanian friend has a vision for redeeming a piece of desolate land in the capital city of Dodoma. Recognizing the needs of some local widows, Ruth wants to transform these dusty acres into a place to keep chickens and grow crops. Her vision to provide for those in need is rooted in her love for God, and was inspired by her biblical namesake, Ruth.

God's laws allowed the poor or the foreigner to glean (harvest) from the edges of the fields (Leviticus 19:9–10). Ruth (in the Bible) was a foreigner, and was therefore allowed to work in the fields, gathering food for her and her mother-in-law. Gleaning in Boaz's field, a close relative, led to Ruth and Naomi ultimately finding a home and protection. Ruth used her ingenuity and effort in the work of the day—gathering food from the edges of the field—and God blessed her.

The passion of my friend Ruth and the dedication of the biblical Ruth stir me to give thanks to God for how He cares for the poor and downtrodden. They inspire me to seek ways to help others in my community and more broadly as a means of expressing my thanks to our giving God. How might you worship God through extending His mercy to others?   *Amy Boucher Pye*

Unexpected Encounter

Read Ruth 2:11–20

The LORD repay you for what you have done. May you be richly rewarded by the LORD, the God of Israel.

RUTH 2:12

Drew, young and enthusiastic, was leading the singing for the first time in a large church. Lois, a long-time attender, wanted to encourage him, but she thought it would be too difficult to get to the front of the church before he left. But then she saw a way to snake through the crowd. Lois told Drew, "I appreciate your enthusiasm in worship. Keep serving Him!"

As Lois walked away, she ran into Sharon, who she hadn't seen in months. After a short conversation, Sharon said, "Thank you for what you do for the Lord. Keep serving Him!" Because Lois had gone out of her way to give encouragement, she was now in the right place to receive unexpected encouragement.

After Ruth and her mother-in-law, Naomi, left Moab and returned to Israel, they received an unexpected blessing. They were both widows with no one to provide for them, so Ruth went to glean grain from a field (Ruth 2:2–3). The field happened to be owned by Boaz, a distant relative of Naomi's. He noticed Ruth, provided for her needs, and later became her husband (2:20; 4:13). Ruth received a blessing because she was in the right place at the right time (2:11–23).

Sometimes God uses unexpected encounters to bring unexpected blessings.   *Anne Cetas*

The Romance

Read Ruth 3:1–11

"Naomi has a [grand]son!" And they named him Obed.
He was the father of Jesse, the father of David.

RUTH 4:17

Widows in biblical times often faced a life of poverty. That's the situation Ruth and her mother-in-law, Naomi, were in after each woman lost her husband. But God had a plan to provide security for them while involving Ruth as an integral part of a much bigger plan.

Boaz, a wealthy landowner, knew of and admired Ruth (Ruth 2:5–12), but he was surprised when he awoke one night to see her lying at his feet (3:8). She asked him to "spread the corner" of his garment over her to indicate that as a close relative he was willing to be her "guardian-redeemer" (v. 9). This was more than a request for protection; she was requesting marriage. Boaz agreed to marry her (vv. 11–13; 4:13).

Not exactly your typical romantic tale. But Ruth's choice to follow Naomi's instructions (3:3–6) set up a series of events that placed her in God's plan of redemption! From Ruth's marriage to Boaz came a son (Obed), the eventual grandfather of King David (4:17). Generations later, Joseph was born to the family, and he became the "legal father" of Mary's child (Matthew 1:16–17; Luke 2:4–5)—our Guardian-Redeemer, Jesus.

Ruth trusted God and followed Naomi's instructions even though the ending was uncertain. We too can count on God to provide for us when life is unsure. *Cindy Hess Kasper*

1 SAMUEL

---◆---

This book marked the end of the theocracy—in which God was the head of the land—and the beginning of the monarchy, where a human king would be the leader of the country. Samuel became the last of the judges of Israel, but the people wanted a king, so Samuel anointed tall, good-looking Saul for that position. Saul and the next anointed king, David, had a rocky relationship because of Saul's jealousy of the young king in waiting. Eventually, Saul's monarchy went from good to bad to worse—and he eventually killed himself instead of face defeat on the battlefield.

OUTLINE

FEBRUARY 22

Words That Wound

Read 1 Samuel 1:1–8

The words *of the reckless pierce like* swords, *but the tongue of the wise brings healing.*
PROVERBS 12:18

"Skinny bones, skinny bones," the boy taunted. "Stick," another chimed. In return, I could have chanted "sticks and stones may break my bones, but words will never hurt me." But even as a little girl, I knew the popular rhyme wasn't true. Unkind, thoughtless words did hurt—sometimes badly, leaving wounds that went deeper and lasted much longer than a welt from a stone or stick.

Hannah certainly knew the sting of thoughtless words. Her husband, Elkanah, loved her, but she had no children, while his second wife, Peninnah, had many. In a culture where a woman's worth was often based on having children, Peninnah made Hannah's pain worse by continually "provoking her" for being childless. She kept it up until Hannah wept and couldn't eat (1 Samuel 1:6–7).

And Elkanah probably meant well, but his thoughtless response, "Hannah, why are you weeping? . . . Don't I mean more to you than ten sons?" (v. 8) was still hurtful.

Like Hannah, many of us have been left reeling in the wake of hurtful words. And some of us have likely reacted to our own wounds by lashing out and hurting others with our words. But all of us can run to our loving and compassionate God for strength and healing (Psalm 27:5, 12–14). He lovingly rejoices over us—speaking words of love and grace.   *Alyson Kieda*

The Servant Hears

Read 1 Samuel 3:1–10

*The LORD came and stood there, calling as at the
other times, "Samuel! Samuel!" Then Samuel
said, "Speak, for your servant is listening."*

1 SAMUEL 3:10

Had the wireless radio been on, they would have known the *Titanic*
was sinking. Cyril Evans, the radio operator of another ship, had tried
to relay a message to Jack Phillips, the radio operator on the *Titanic*—
letting him know they had encountered an ice field. But Phillips was
busy relaying passengers' messages and rudely told Evans to be quiet.
So Evans reluctantly turned off his radio and went to bed. Ten minutes
later, the *Titanic* struck an iceberg. Their distress signals went unanswered because no one was listening.

In 1 Samuel we read that the priests of Israel were corrupt and had
lost their spiritual sight and hearing as the nation drifted into danger.
"The word of the LORD was rare; there were not many visions" (1 Samuel 3:1). Yet God wouldn't give up on His people. He began to speak
to a young boy named Samuel who was being raised in the priest's
household. Samuel's name means "the Lord hears"—a memorial to
God's answering his mother's prayer. But Samuel would need to learn
how to hear God.

"Speak, for your servant is listening" (v. 10). It's the servant who
hears. May we also choose to listen to and obey what God has revealed
in the Scriptures. Let's submit our lives to Him and take the posture of
humble servants—those who have their "radios" turned on.

Glenn Packiam

Hidden Beauty

Read 1 Samuel 16:1–7

People look at the outward appearance,
but the LORD looks at the heart.

1 SAMUEL 16:7

Our children needed a little coaxing to believe that it was worth putting on snorkeling gear to peer beneath the surface of the Caribbean Sea off the shore of the island of Tobago. But after they dove in, they resurfaced ecstatic, "There are thousands of fish of all different kinds! It's so beautiful! I've never seen such colorful fish!"

Because the surface of the water looked similar to freshwater lakes near our home, our children could have missed the beauty hidden just below the surface.

When the prophet Samuel went to Bethlehem to anoint one of Jesse's sons to be the next king, Samuel saw the oldest son, Eliab, and was impressed by his appearance. The prophet thought he had found the right man, but the Lord rejected Eliab. God reminded Samuel that He "does not look at the things people look at. People look at the outward appearance, but the LORD looks at the heart" (1 Samuel 16:7).

So Samuel asked if there were more sons. The youngest boy wasn't present but caring for the family's sheep. This son, David, was summoned and the Lord directed Samuel to anoint him.

Often we look at people only on a surface level and don't always take the time to see their inner, sometimes hidden, beauty. We don't always value what God values. But if we take the time to peer beneath the surface, we may find great treasure. 　　　　*Lisa Samra*

Amani

Read 1 Samuel 16:14–23

The Spirit God gave us does not make us timid,
but gives us power, love and self-discipline.

2 TIMOTHY 1:7

Amani, which means "peace" in Swahili, is the name of a Labrador retriever pup that has some special friends. Amani lives with two young cheetahs at the Dallas Zoo. Zoologists placed the animals together so the cheetahs could learn Amani's relaxed ways. Since dogs are generally at ease in public settings, the experts predict that Amani will be a "calming influence" in the cheetahs' lives as they grow up together.

David was a soothing influence in King Saul's life when an "evil spirit" troubled him (1 Samuel 16:14). When Saul's servants learned of his problem, they thought music might ease his affliction. One servant summoned David, who was a skilled harpist. Whenever the king became troubled, David would play the harp. "Then relief would come to Saul; he would feel better" (v. 23).

We crave refreshment and well-being when we are plagued by anger, fear, or sadness. The God of the Bible is a "God of peace" (Hebrews 13:20–21), One who gives His Holy Spirit to everyone who believes in Him. When we're agitated or anxious, we can remember that God's Spirit produces power, love, and self-control (2 Timothy 1:7). God's influence in our lives can create a calming effect—one that leads to comfort and wholeness. *Jennifer Benson Schuldt*

Mighty

Read 1 Samuel 17:32, 41–47

[Goliath] looked David over and saw that
he was little more than a boy.

1 Samuel 17:42

Baby Saybie, born as a "micro-preemie" at twenty-three weeks, weighed eight and a half ounces. Doctors doubted Saybie would live and told her parents they'd likely have only an hour with their daughter. However, Saybie kept fighting. A pink card near her crib declared "Tiny but Mighty." After five months in the hospital, Saybie miraculously went home as a healthy five-pound baby. And she took a world record with her: the world's tiniest surviving baby.

It's powerful to hear stories of those who beat the odds. The Bible tells one of these stories. David, a shepherd boy, volunteered to fight Goliath—a mammoth warrior who defamed God and threatened Israel. King Saul thought David was ridiculous: "You are not able to go out against this Philistine and fight him; you are only a young man, and he has been a warrior from his youth" (1 Samuel 17:33). And when the boy David stepped onto the battlefield, Goliath "looked David over and saw that he was little more than a boy" (v. 42). However, David didn't step into battle alone. He came "in the name of the Lord Almighty, the God of the armies of Israel" (v. 45). And when the day was done, a victorious David stood above a dead Goliath.

No matter how enormous the problem, when God is with us there's nothing that we need to fear. With His strength, we're also mighty.

Winn Collier

God's Mercy at Work

Read 1 Samuel 24:1–10

May the LORD judge between you and me.

1 SAMUEL 24:12

My anger percolated when a woman mistreated me, blamed me, and gossiped about me. I wanted everyone to know what she'd done—wanted her to suffer as I'd suffered because of her behavior. I steamed with resentment until a headache pierced my temples. But as I began praying for my pain to go away, the Holy Spirit convicted me. How could I plot revenge while begging God for relief? If I believed He would care for me, why wouldn't I trust Him to handle this situation? Knowing that people who are hurting often hurt other people, I asked God to help me forgive the woman and work toward reconciliation.

The psalmist David understood the difficulty of trusting God while enduring unfair treatment. Though David did his best to be a loving servant, King Saul succumbed to jealousy and wanted to murder him (1 Samuel 24:1–2). David suffered while God worked things out and prepared him to take the throne, but still he chose to honor God instead of seeking revenge (vv. 3–7). He did his part to reconcile with Saul and left the results in God's hands (vv. 8–22).

When it seems others are getting away with wrongdoing, we struggle with the injustice. But with God's mercy at work in our hearts and the hearts of others, we can forgive as He's forgiven us and receive the blessings He's prepared for us.   *Xochitl Dixon*

◆

FEBRUARY 28

Hard Conversations

Read 1 Samuel 25:21–35

*If it is possible, as far as it depends on
you, live at peace with everyone.*

Romans 12:18

I once drove fifty miles to have a hard conversation with a remote staff person. I had received a report from another employee that suggested he was misrepresenting our company, and I was concerned for our reputation. I felt nudged to offer an opinion that might change his choices.

In 1 Samuel 25, an unlikely person took great personal risk to confront a future king of Israel who was about to make a disastrous choice. Abigail was married to Nabal, whose character matched the meaning of his name ("fool") (vv. 3, 25). Nabal had refused to pay David and his troops the customary wage for protecting his livestock (vv. 10–11). Hearing that David planned a murderous revenge on her household, and knowing her foolish husband wouldn't listen to reason, Abigail prepared a peace offering, rode to meet David, and persuaded him to reconsider (vv. 18–31).

How did Abigail accomplish this? After sending ahead donkeys loaded with food to satisfy David and his men and settle the debt, she spoke truth to David. She wisely reminded David of God's call on his life. If he resisted his desire for revenge, when God made him king, he wouldn't "have on his conscience the staggering burden of needless bloodshed" (v. 31).

You might also know someone dangerously close to a mistake that could harm others and compromise their own future effectiveness for God. Like Abigail, might God be calling you to a hard conversation?

Elisa Morgan

Recovering What's Lost

Read 1 Samuel 30:1–6, 18–19

But David found strength in the LORD his God.

1 SAMUEL 30:6

At the phone store, the young pastor steeled himself for bad news. His smart phone, accidentally dropped during our Bible class, was a total loss, right? Actually, no. The store clerk recovered all of the pastor's data, including his Bible videos and photos. She also recovered "every photo I'd ever deleted," he said. The store also "replaced my broken phone with a brand-new phone." As he said, "I recovered all I had lost and more."

David once led his own recovery mission after an attack by the vicious Amalekites. Spurned by Philistine rulers, David and his army discovered the Amalekites had raided and burned down their town of Ziklag—taking captive "the women and everyone else in it," including all their wives and children (1 Samuel 30:2–3). "So David and his men wept aloud until they had no strength left to weep" (v. 4). The soldiers were so bitter with their leader David that they talked of "stoning him" (v. 6).

"But David found strength in the LORD his God" (v. 6). As God promised, David pursued the Amalekites and "recovered everything the Amalekites had taken. . . . Nothing was missing: young or old, boy or girl, plunder or anything else they had taken. David brought everything back" (vv. 18–19). As we face spiritual attacks that "rob" us even of hope, may we find renewed strength in God. He will be with us in every challenge of life.   *Patricia Raybon*

2 SAMUEL

Because 1 and 2 Samuel were originally recorded as one scroll, it is logical that the story that ends with the conclusion of 1 Samuel continues into 2 Samuel. Second Samuel records the pertinent events of David's forty-year reign over Israel. Also supremely important to the overall story of the Bible is the Davidic Covenant, which we read about in 2 Samuel. We see David both as a benevolent and wise leader—completing the takeover of the Promised Land by the Jews. And we see him as a major sinner in the episode with Bathsheba and Uriah. Before the Bathsheba incident, David's reign was mostly smooth sailing; afterward, his kingdom was fraught with difficulties.

OUTLINE

An Emergency of the Spirit

Read 2 Samuel 1:17–27

David took up his lament concerning
Saul and his son Jonathan.

2 SAMUEL 1:17

In March 2011, a devastating tsunami struck Japan, taking nearly sixteen thousand lives as it obliterated towns and villages along the coast. Writer and poet Gretel Ehrlich visited Japan to witness and document the destruction. When she felt inadequate to report what she was seeing, she wrote a poem about it. In a *PBS NewsHour* interview she said, "My old friend William Stafford, a poet now gone, said, 'A poem is an emergency of the spirit.'"

We find poetry used throughout the Bible to express deep emotion, ranging from joyful praise to anguished loss. When King Saul and his son Jonathan were killed in battle, David was overwhelmed with grief (2 Samuel 1:1–12). He poured out his soul in a poem he called "the Song of the Bow": "Saul and Jonathan—in life they were loved and admired, and in their death they were not parted. . . . How the mighty have fallen in battle! . . . I grieve for you, Jonathan my brother; you were very dear to me" (vv. 23–26).

When we face "an emergency of the spirit"—whether glad or sad—our prayers can be a poem to the Lord. While we may stumble to articulate what we feel, our heavenly Father hears our words as a true expression of our hearts.   *David McCasland*

As Light as a Feather

Read 2 Samuel 6:12–23

A cheerful heart is good medicine.

PROVERBS 17:22

We Christians can sometimes be a joyless lot, preoccupied with maintaining our dignity. That's an odd attitude, though, since we're joined to a God who has given us His wonderful gift of joy and laughter.

It's okay to have fun! Each family expresses it in different ways, of course. I'm thankful that our house has been a house of laughter. Water fights, good-natured (albeit stiff) competition, gentle ribbing, and hilarity came easily to us. Laughter has been a gift of God's goodness that carried us through some of life's darkest days. The joy of the Lord has often been our refuge (Nehemiah 8:10).

When King David brought the ark of the covenant to Jerusalem from the house of Obed-Edom, he danced "with all his might" before the Lord (2 Samuel 6:14). The Hebrew word has the idea of joyful exuberance and is akin to our expression "kick up your heels." In fact, in verse 16 it says that David was "leaping and dancing." Michal, David's wife, felt that his antics were unbecoming to the dignity of a king and reacted with stern severity. David's response was to announce that he would "become even more undignified" (v. 22). His spirit was buoyant and he felt "as light as a feather."   *David Roper*

Intentional Kindness

Read 2 Samuel 9:3–11

I want to show God's kindness to them.

2 SAMUEL 9:3 NLT

Boarding a plane alone with her children, a young mom tried desperately to calm her three-year-old daughter who began kicking and crying. Then her hungry four-month-old son also began to wail.

A traveler seated next to her quickly offered to hold the baby while Jessica got her daughter buckled in. Then the traveler—recalling his own days as a young dad—began coloring with the toddler while Jessica fed her infant. And on the next connecting flight, the same man offered to assist again if needed.

Jessica recalled, "I [was] blown away by God's hand in this. [We] could have been placed next to anyone, but we were seated next to one of the nicest men I have ever met."

In 2 Samuel 9, we read of another example of what I call intentional kindness. After King Saul and his son Jonathan had been killed, some expected David to kill off any competition to his claim for the throne. Instead, he asked, "Is there no one still alive from the house of Saul to whom I can show God's kindness?" (v. 3). Mephibosheth, Jonathan's son, was then brought to David who restored his inheritance and warmly invited him to share his table from then on—just as if he were his own son (v. 11).

As beneficiaries of the immense kindness of God, may we look for opportunities to show intentional kindness toward others (Galatians 6:10).   *Cindy Hess Kasper*

MARCH 4

Where Are You Headed?

Read 2 Samuel 11:1–4

Then Nathan said to David, "You are the man!"

2 SAMUEL 12:7

In northern Thailand, the Wild Boars youth soccer team decided to explore a cave together. After an hour they turned to go back and found that the entrance to the cave was flooded. Rising water pushed them deeper into the cave, day after day, until they were finally trapped more than two miles (four kilometers) inside. When they were heroically rescued two weeks later, many wondered how they had become so hopelessly trapped. Answer: one step at a time.

In Israel, Nathan confronted David for killing his loyal soldier, Uriah. How did the man "after [God's] own heart" (1 Samuel 13:14) become guilty of murder? One step at a time. David didn't go from zero to murder in one afternoon. He warmed up to it, over time, as one bad decision bled into others. It started with a second glance that turned into a lustful stare. He abused his kingly power by sending for Bathsheba, then tried to cover up her pregnancy by calling her husband home from the front. When Uriah refused to visit his wife while his comrades were at war, David decided he would have to die.

We may not be guilty of murder or trapped in a cave of our own making, but we're either moving toward Jesus or toward trouble. Big problems don't develop overnight. They break upon us gradually, one step at a time. *Mike Wittmer*

Displaced

Read 2 Samuel 15:13–26

My flesh and my heart fail; but God is the strength
of my heart and my portion forever.

Psalm 73:26

David fled Jerusalem, driven from his home by his son Absalom, who had gathered an army of supporters. As he escaped, he instructed Zadok, his priest, to take the ark of God back to Jerusalem and to lead his people in worship there. "If I find favor in the Lord's eyes," he mused, "he will bring me back and let me see it and his dwelling place. But if he says, 'I am not pleased with you,' then I am ready; let him do to me whatever seems good to him" (2 Samuel 15:25–26).

Perhaps, like David, you've lost the power of self-determination. Someone has seized control of your life, or so it seems.

You may fear that circumstance and human caprice have overturned your plans. But nothing can frustrate God's loving intention. Tertullian (AD 150–220) wrote, "[Do not regret] a thing which has been taken away . . . by the Lord God, without whose will neither does a leaf glide down from a tree, nor a sparrow of one farthing's worth fall to the earth."

Our heavenly Father knows how to care for His children and will allow only what He deems best. We can rest in His infinite wisdom and goodness.

Thus we can echo David's words: "I am ready; let him do to me whatever seems good to him." *David Roper*

Preventing Regret

Read 2 Samuel 18:31–19:4

The king was shaken. He went up to the
room over the gateway and wept.

2 Samuel 18:33

In the 1980s, the British band Mike and the Mechanics recorded a powerful song titled, "The Living Years." The songwriter mourns his father's death, because their relationship had been strained and marked by silence rather than sharing. The singer remorsefully says, "I didn't get to tell him all the things I had to say." Struggling with regret over words unsaid and love unexpressed, he laments, "I just wish I could have told him in the living years."

King David similarly regretted his broken relationship with his son Absalom. Angered over David's refusal to punish Amnon for raping his sister Tamar, Absalom killed Amnon and fled (2 Samuel 13:21–34). David's servant Joab knew that he longed to go to his fugitive son, so he arranged for Absalom to be brought to him. But their relationship was never the same again. Absalom's bitterness sparked a conflict that ended with his death (18:14). It was a bitter victory for King David, causing him to lament his lost son and their failed relationship (18:33). No amount of grieving, however, could undo David's heartache.

We can learn from David's regret when dealing with broken relationships. The pain of trying to make things right can be hard. But it's much better to do what we can to make things right "in the living years."

Bill Crowder

Open Arms

Read 2 Samuel 22:1–7, 17–20

In my distress I called to the LORD. . . .
My cry came to his ears.

2 SAMUEL 22:7

Saydee and his family have an "open arms and open home" philosophy. People are always welcome in their home, "especially those who are in distress," he says. That's the kind of household he had growing up in Liberia with his nine siblings. Their parents always welcomed others into their family. He says, "We grew up as a community. We loved one another. Everybody was responsible for everybody. My dad taught us to love each other, care for each other, protect each other."

When King David was in need, he found this type of loving care in God. Second Samuel 22 (and Psalm 18) records his song of praise to God for the ways He had been a refuge for him throughout his life. He recalled, "In my distress I called to the LORD; I called out to my God. From his temple he heard my voice; my cry came to his ears" (2 Samuel 22:7). God had delivered him from his enemies, including King Saul, many times. He praised God for being his fortress and deliverer in whom he took refuge (vv. 2–3).

While our distresses may be small in comparison to David's, God welcomes us to run to Him to find the shelter we long for. His arms are always open. Therefore we "sing the praises of [His] name" (v. 50).

Anne Cetas

Who's It For?

Read 2 Samuel 23:13–17

He poured [the water] out before the LORD.

2 SAMUEL 23:16

The picture made me laugh out loud. Crowds had lined a Mexican avenue, waving flags and throwing confetti as they waited for the pope. Down the middle of the street strolled a stray puppy, appearing to grin as if the cheering was entirely for him. Yes! Every dog should have its day, and it should look like this.

It's cute when a puppy "steals the show," but hijacking another's praise can destroy us. David knew this, and he refused to drink the water his mighty warriors had risked their lives to get. He had wistfully said it would be great if someone would fetch a drink from the well in Bethlehem. Three of his soldiers took him literally. They broke through enemy lines, drew the water, and carried it back. David was overwhelmed by their devotion, and he had to pass it on. He refused to drink the water, but "poured it out before the LORD" as a drink offering (2 Samuel 23:16).

How we respond to praise and honor says a lot about us. When praise is directed toward others, especially God, stay out of the way. The parade isn't for us. When the honor is directed toward us, thank the person and then amplify that praise by giving all the glory to Jesus. The "water" isn't for us either. Give thanks, then pour it out before God.

Mike Wittmer

1 KINGS

---◆---

When 1 Kings begins, Israel's second king, David, is elderly and bed-ridden. The third king was almost Adonijah, but fortunately for Solomon, Nathan and Solomon's mother Bathsheba got wind of Adonijah's attempt to nab the crown. They marched in to David's bedroom and made sure Solomon became the ruling monarch—Israel's third king. The book then follows Solomon's reign, his construction projects, his wisdom, his administrative prowess, and finally, his death. The rest of the book details how the kingdom of Israel split into two lands: Israel and Judah; then it details the lives of the kings who followed Solomon. It is a fascinating look at this key portion of Israel's history.

OUTLINE

Missing: Wisdom

Read 1 Kings 3:5-12

Give your servant a discerning heart . . . to distinguish between right and wrong.

1 Kings 3:9

Two-year-old Kenneth went missing. Yet within three minutes of his mom's 9-1-1 call, an emergency worker found him just two blocks from home at the county fair. His mom had promised he could go later that day with his grandpa. But he'd driven his toy tractor there and parked it at his favorite ride. When the boy was safely home, his dad wisely removed the toy's battery.

Kenneth was actually rather smart to get where he wanted to go, but two-year-olds are missing another key quality: wisdom. And as adults we sometimes lack it too. Solomon, who'd been appointed king by his father David (1 Kings 2), admitted he felt like a child. God appeared to him in a dream and said, "Ask for whatever you want me to give you" (3:5). He replied, "I am only a little child and do not know how to carry out my duties. . . . So give your servant a discerning heart to govern your people and to distinguish between right and wrong" (vv. 7–9). God gave Solomon "a breadth of understanding as measureless as the sand on the seashore" (4:29).

Where can we get the wisdom we need? Solomon said the beginning of wisdom is a "fear" or awe of God (Proverbs 9:10). So we can start by asking Him to teach us about himself and to give us wisdom beyond our own.   *Anne Cetas*

Her Father's Zoo

Read 1 Kings 4:29–34

The righteous care for the needs of their animals,
but the kindest acts of the wicked are cruel.

PROVERBS 12:10

June Williams was only four when her father bought seven acres of land to build a zoo without bars or cages. Growing up she remembers how creative her father was in trying to help wild animals feel free in confinement. Today Chester Zoo is one of England's most popular wildlife attractions. Home to eleven thousand animals on one hundred ten acres of land, the zoo reflects her father's concern for animal welfare, education, and conservation.

Solomon had a similar interest in all creatures great and small. In addition to studying the wildlife of the Middle East, he imported exotic animals like apes and monkeys from far-off lands (1 Kings 10:22). But one of his proverbs shows us that Solomon's knowledge of nature went beyond intellectual curiosity. When he expressed the spiritual implications of how we treat our animals, he mirrored something of the heart of our Creator: "The righteous care for the needs of their animals, but the kindest acts of the wicked are cruel" (Proverbs 12:10).

With God-given wisdom, Solomon saw that our relationship to our Creator affects not only how we treat people but also how much thoughtful consideration we give to the creatures in our care.

Marvin Williams

Age-Old Wisdom

Read 1 Kings 12:1–7, 12–17

Is not wisdom found among the aged?
Does not long life bring understanding?
JOB 12:12

A few years ago, a newspaper in Singapore published a special report that contained life lessons gleaned from eight senior citizens. It opened with these words: "While aging brings challenges to mind and body, it can also lead to an expansion in other realms. There is an abundance of emotional and social knowledge; qualities which scientists are beginning to define as wisdom . . . the wisdom of elders."

Indeed, wise older people have much to teach us about life. But in the Bible, we meet a newly crowned king who failed to recognize this.

King Solomon had just died, and in 1 Kings 12:3, we read that "the whole assembly of Israel went to Rehoboam" with a petition. They asked the new king to lighten the harsh labor and heavy taxes his father Solomon had demanded of them. In return, they would loyally serve Rehoboam.

At first the young king consulted the elders (v. 6). But he rejected their advice and accepted the foolish counsel of the young men who had grown up with him (v. 8). He made the burden on the people even greater! His rashness cost him most of his kingdom.

All of us need the counsel that comes with years of experience, especially from those who have walked with God and listened well to His counsel. Think of the accumulated wisdom God has given them! They have much to share with us about the Lord. Let's seek them out and give a listening ear to their wisdom. *Poh Fang Chia*

Direct Instruction

Read 1 Kings 13:11–22

I have been told by the WORD of the LORD.
1 KINGS 13:17

My second child was eager to sleep in a "big-girl bed" in her sister's room. Each night I tucked Britta under the covers, issuing strict instructions to stay in bed, warning her I'd return her to the crib if she didn't. Night after night, I found her in the hallway and had to escort my discouraged darling back to her crib. Years later I learned her customarily-sweet older sister wasn't excited about having a roommate and repeatedly told Britta that she'd heard me calling for her. Britta heeded her sister's words, went to look for me, and thus landed herself back in the crib.

Listening to the wrong voice can have consequences for us all. When God sent a man to Bethel to speak on His behalf, He gave explicit instructions for him to not eat or drink while there, nor return home by the same route (1 Kings 13:9). When King Jeroboam invited him to share a meal, the prophet declined, following God's command. When an older prophet extended an invitation to dine, the man initially declined, but relented and ate when his elder deceived him, saying an angel told him it was okay. Just as I wanted Britta to enjoy her "big-girl bed," I imagine God was saddened the man didn't heed His instructions.

We can trust God completely. His words are our path to life; we are wise to listen and obey.   *Kirsten Holmberg*

MARCH 13

Only Trust

Read 1 Kings 17:8–16

*So there was food every day for Elijah and
for the woman and her family.*

1 KINGS 17:15

Three hundred children were dressed and seated for breakfast, and a prayer of thanks was offered for the food. But there was no food! Situations like this were not unusual for orphanage director and missionary George Mueller (1805–1898). Here was yet another opportunity to see how God would provide. Within minutes of Mueller's prayer, a baker who couldn't sleep the night before showed up at the door. Sensing that the orphanage could use the bread, he had made three batches. Not long afterward, the town milkman appeared. His cart had broken down in front of the orphanage. Not wanting the milk to spoil, he offered it to Mueller.

It's normal to experience bouts of worry, anxiety, and self-pity when we lack resources essential to our well-being—food, shelter, health, finances, friendships. First Kings 17:8–16 reminds us that God's help can come through unexpected sources like a needy widow. "I don't have any bread—only a handful of flour in a jar and a little olive oil in a jug" (v. 12). Earlier it was a raven that provided for Elijah (vv. 4–6). Concerns for our needs to be met can send us searching in many directions. A clear vision of God as the Provider who has promised to supply our needs can be liberating. Before we seek solutions, may we be careful to seek Him first. Doing so can save us time, energy, and frustration.

Arthur Jackson

Who Needs Me?

Read 1 Kings 19:9–12, 15–18

When you get there, anoint Hazael king over Aram.

1 KINGS 19:15

While on a red-eye flight to Washington, DC, opinion writer Arthur Brooks overheard an elderly woman whisper to her husband, "It's not true that no one needs you anymore." The man murmured something about wishing he were dead, and his wife replied, "Oh, stop saying that." When the flight ended, Brooks turned around and immediately recognized the man. He was a world-famous hero. Other passengers shook his hand, and the pilot thanked him for the courage he displayed decades ago. How had this giant sunk into despair?

The prophet Elijah bravely and single-handedly defeated 450 prophets of Baal—or so he thought (1 Kings 18). Yet he hadn't really done it alone; God was there all along! But later, feeling all alone, he asked God to take his life.

God lifted Elijah's spirits by bringing him into His presence and giving him new people to serve. He must go and "anoint Hazael king over Aram," Jehu "king over Israel," and Elisha "to succeed you as prophet" (19:15–16). Invigorated with renewed purpose, Elijah found and mentored his successor.

Your great victories may lie in the rearview mirror. You may feel your life has peaked, or that it never did. No matter. Look around. The battles may seem smaller, the stakes less profound, but there are still others who need you. Serve them well for Jesus's sake, and it will count. They're your purpose—the reason you're still here. *Mike Wittmer*

2 KINGS

As might be expected, this book is about kings—lots of them: twenty-eight in all. Interspersed among the stories of the kings of the Northern Kingdom and the kings of the Southern Kingdom are stories from others such as Elijah, Elisha, and Naaman. What we see happening in 2 Kings is the demise of the great kingdom God had provided for His people. He had taken them through the wilderness and then had allowed them to establish themselves throughout the land. All of the tribes (except the Levites) were given land, and prosperity was theirs. But little by little, the whole thing came crashing down because of corrupt leaders and equally corrupt followers. From the grand kingdoms of David and Solomon to the disastrous endings of Jedekiah and Hoshea, we see this great people crash into destruction and captivity.

OUTLINE

Elijah's Ministry Ends 2 Kings 1:1–18

Elisha Makes a Difference 2 Kings 2:1–9:37

Reigns of Various Kings 2 Kings 10:1–16:20

Northern Kingdom Fall 2 Kings 17:1–41

Kings of Judah 2 Kings 18:1–23:37

Fall and Destruction of Jerusalem 2 Kings 24:1–25:30

Wearing Our Courage

Read 2 Kings 1:9–15

If I am a man of God, may fire come down from heaven.

2 KINGS 1:10

Andrew lives in a country that's closed to the gospel. When I asked how he keeps his faith a secret, he said he doesn't. He wears a button that advertises his church, and whenever he's arrested he tells the police that "they need Jesus too." Andrew has courage because he knows who's on his side.

Elijah refused to be intimidated, even when the king of Israel sent fifty soldiers to arrest him (2 Kings 1:9). The prophet knew God was with him, and he called down fire that consumed the platoon. The king sent more soldiers, and Elijah did it again (v. 12). The king sent more, but the third platoon had heard about the others. The captain begged Elijah to spare his soldiers' lives. They were more afraid of him than he'd ever been of them, so the angel of the Lord told Elijah it was safe to go with them (vv. 13–15).

Jesus doesn't want us to call down fire on our enemies. When the disciples asked if they could call down fire on a Samaritan village, Jesus rebuked them (Luke 9:51–55). We're living in a different time. But Jesus does want us to have Elijah's boldness—to be ready to tell everyone about the Savior who died for them. It may seem like one person taking on fifty, but it's actually One on fifty. Jesus provides what we need to courageously love and reach out to others.   *Mike Wittmer*

Simply Ask

Read 2 Kings 5:9–14

Before they call I will answer.
ISAIAH 65:24

Her doctor said her detached retinas couldn't be repaired. But after living without sight for fifteen years—learning Braille, and using a cane and service dog—a Montana woman's life changed when her husband asked another eye doctor a simple question: could she be helped? The answer was yes. As the doctor discovered, the woman had a common eye condition, cataracts, which the doctor removed from her right eye. When the eye patch came off the next day, her vision was 20/20. A second surgery for her left eye met with equal success.

A simple question also changed the life of Naaman, a powerful military man with leprosy. But Naaman raged arrogantly at the prophet Elisha's instructions to "wash yourself seven times in the Jordan, and your flesh will be restored" (2 Kings 5:10). Naaman's servants, however, asked the military leader a simple question: "If the prophet had told you to do some great thing, would you not have done it?" (v. 13). Persuaded, Naaman washed "and his flesh was restored and became clean" (v. 14).

In our lives, sometimes we struggle with a problem because we won't ask God. Will You help? Should I go? Will You lead? He doesn't require complicated questions from us to help. "Before they call I will answer," God promised His people (Isaiah 65:24). So today, simply ask Him.

Patricia Raybon

Lord of the Moment

Read 2 Kings 8:1–6

In their hearts humans plan their course,
but the LORD establishes their steps.

PROVERBS 16:9

Not long ago I was working on a construction project at my son's home three hours away. The job took days longer than expected, and each morning I prayed we would finish by sunset. But every evening there was more to be done.

I wondered why. Could there be a reason for the delay? An answer came the next morning. I was picking up a tool when my phone rang and a stranger's voice spoke urgently: "Your daughter was injured in an accident. You need to come immediately."

She lived near my son, so it took just fourteen minutes to reach her. If I had been home, I would have been three hours away. I followed the ambulance to the hospital and comforted her before surgery. As I sat holding her hand I realized if my project hadn't been delayed, I wouldn't have been there.

Our moments belong to God. This was the experience of a woman whose son God had resurrected through the prophet Elisha (2 Kings 4:18–37). She left the country because of famine and returned years later to beg the king for her land. At precisely that moment the king was conversing with the prophet's servant Gehazi. "Just as Gehazi was telling the king how Elisha had restored" her son, the woman walked in (8:5). Her request was granted.

We don't know what even the next second brings, but God is graciously able to use any situation for good. May God give us grace to walk with Him expectantly into His appointments for us today.

James Banks

MARCH 18

Give It to God

Read 2 Kings 19:9–19

Then [Hezekiah] went up to the temple of the
Lord and spread it out before the Lord.

2 Kings 19:14

As a teenager, when I became overwhelmed by enormous challenges or high-stakes decisions, my mother taught me the merits of putting pen to paper to gain perspective. When I was uncertain whether to take specific classes or which job to pursue, or how to cope with the frightening realities of adulthood, I learned her habit of writing out the basic facts and the possible courses of action with their likely outcomes. After pouring my heart onto the page, I was able to step back from the problem and view it more objectively than my emotions allowed.

Just as recording my thoughts on paper offered me fresh perspective, pouring our hearts out to God in prayer helps us gain His perspective and remind us of His power. King Hezekiah did just that after receiving a daunting letter from an ominous adversary. The Assyrians threatened to destroy Jerusalem as they had many other nations. Hezekiah spread out the letter before the Lord, prayerfully calling on Him to deliver the people so that the world would say to our heavenly Father: "You alone, Lord, are God" (2 Kings 19:19).

When we're faced with a situation that brings anxiety, fear, or a deep awareness that getting through it will require more than what we have, let's follow in Hezekiah's footsteps and run straight to the Lord. Like him, we too can lay our problem before God and trust Him to guide our steps and calm our uneasy hearts. *Kirsten Holmberg*

Straight Ahead

Read 2 Kings 22:1–2, 8–13

He did what was right in the eyes of the LORD . . .
not turning aside to the right or to the left.

2 KINGS 22:2

It used to take the steady eye and the firm hand of a farmer to drive a tractor or combine down straight rows. But even the best eyes would overlap rows, and by end of day even the strongest hands would be fatigued. But now there's autosteer—a GPS-based technology that allows for accuracy to within one inch when planting, cultivating, and spraying. It's incredibly efficient and hands-free. Just imagine sitting in a mammoth combine and instead of gripping the wheel, you're gripping a roast beef sandwich. An amazing tool to keep you moving straight ahead.

You may recall the name Josiah. He was crowned king when he was only eight years old (see 2 Kings 22:1). Years later, in his mid-twenties, Hilkiah the high priest found the Book of the Law in the temple. It was then read to the young king, who tore his robes in sorrow due to his ancestors' disobedience of God. Josiah set about to do what was "right in the eyes of the LORD" (v. 2). The book became a tool to steer the people so there would be no turning to the right or left. God's instructions were there to set things straight.

Allowing the Scriptures to guide us day by day keeps our lives in line with knowing God and His will. The Bible is an amazing tool that, if followed, keeps us moving straight ahead.   *John Blase*

Kossi's Courage

Read 2 Kings 23:12–14, 21–25

*You shall have no other gods before me. . . . You
shall not bow down to them or worship them.*

Exodus 20:3, 5

As he awaited his baptism in Togo's Mono River, Kossi stooped to pick up a worn wooden carving. His family had worshiped the object for generations. Now they watched as he tossed the grotesque figure into a fire prepared for the occasion. No longer would their choicest chickens be sacrificed to this god.

In the West, most Christians think of idols as metaphors for what they put in place of God. In Togo, West Africa, idols represent literal gods that must be appeased with sacrifice. Idol burning and baptism make a courageous statement about a new believer's allegiance to the one true God.

As an eight-year-old, King Josiah came to power in an idol-worshiping, sex-obsessed culture. His father and grandfather had been two of the worst kings in all of Judah's sordid history. Then the high priest discovered the book of the law. When the young king heard its words, he took them to heart (2 Kings 22:8–13). Josiah destroyed the pagan altars, burned the vile items dedicated to the goddess Asherah, and stopped the ritual prostitution (chapter 23). In place of these practices, he celebrated the Passover (23:21–23).

Whenever we look for answers apart from God—consciously or subconsciously—we pursue a false god. It would be wise to ask ourselves: What idols, literal or figurative, do we need to throw on the fire?

Tim Gustafson

1 CHRONICLES

◆

Here is another retelling of the history of Israel for the returning Hebrews after their time in Babylon had come to a close. This shortened version of the history emphasizes a more positive approach. Thus, the stories of some of the bad stories and people are not rehearsed. There is an emphasis on temple worship, which might be an encouragement for the returning people to reestablish their worship in Jerusalem. Also, they are reminded of the Davidic covenant, which could also encourage them by reminding them of God's promises to them.

OUTLINE

Facing the Battle

Read 1 Chronicles 16:1–11

Look to the LORD and his strength; seek his face always.

1 CHRONICLES 16:11

Not long ago I met up with a group of friends. As I listened to the conversation, it seemed like everyone in the room was facing some significant battle. Two of us had parents fighting cancer, one had a child with an eating disorder, another friend was experiencing chronic pain, and another was facing major surgery. It seemed a lot for a bunch of people in their thirties and forties.

First Chronicles 16 recounts a key moment in Israel's history when the ark of the covenant was brought into the City of David (Jerusalem). Samuel tells us it happened in a moment of peace between battles (2 Samuel 7:1). When the ark was in place, symbolizing God's presence, David led the people in a song (1 Chronicles 16:8–36). Together the nation sang of God's wonder-working power, His promise-keeping ways, and His past protection (vv. 12–22). "Look to the LORD and his strength," they cried out; "seek his face always" (v. 11). They'd need to, because more battles were coming.

Look to the Lord and His strength. Seek His face. That's not bad advice to follow when illness, family concerns, and other battles confront us, because we haven't been left to fight in our own waning energies. God is present; God is strong; He's looked after us in the past and will do so again.

Our God will get us through.   *Sheridan Voysey*

Who's Behind It?

Read 1 Chronicles 17:16–24

*Every good gift and perfect gift is from above, coming
down from the Father of the heavenly lights.*

JAMES 1:17

At a cultural show in Bandung, Indonesia, we enjoyed a wonderful orchestra performance. Before the finale, the two hundred people in the audience were each handed an angklung, a musical instrument made of bamboo. We were taught how to shake it in rhythm with the conductor's timing. Soon we thought we were performing like an orchestra; we felt so proud of how well we were doing! Then it dawned on me that we were not the ones who were good; it was the conductor who deserved the credit.

Similarly, when everything is going well in our lives, it's easy to feel proud. We're tempted to think that we are good and that it is by our abilities that we've achieved success. During such moments, we tend to forget that behind it all is our good God who prompts, prevents, provides, and protects.

David remembered that truth: "Then King David went in and sat before the LORD; and he said: 'Who am I, LORD God? And what is my family, that you have brought me this far?'" (1 Chronicles 17:16). David's heart swelled up in appreciation of God's goodness.

The next time we are tempted to take credit for the blessings we enjoy, let's pause and remember that it is the Lord who brings blessing.

Albert Lee

Navigating Rough Waters

Read 1 Chronicles 28:9–20

Do not be afraid or discouraged, for the LORD God, my God,
is with you. He will not fail you or forsake you.

1 CHRONICLES 28:20

I was enjoying the start of my first whitewater rafting experience—until I heard the roar of the rapids up ahead. My emotions were flooded with feelings of uncertainty, fear, and insecurity at the same time. Riding through the whitewater was a first-rate, white-knuckle experience! And then, suddenly, it was over. The guide in the back of the raft had navigated us through. I was safe—at least until the next set of rapids.

Transitions in our lives can be like whitewater experiences. The inevitable leaps from one season of life to the next—college to career, changing jobs, living with parents to living alone or with a spouse, career to retirement, youth to old age—are all marked by uncertainty and insecurity.

In one of the most significant transitions recorded in Old Testament history, Solomon assumed the throne from his father David. I'm sure he was filled with uncertainty about the future. His father's advice? "Be strong and courageous, and do the work. . . . For the LORD God, my God, is with you" (1 Chronicles 28:20).

We'll have our fair share of tough transitions in life. But with God in our raft we're not alone. Keeping our eyes on the One who is navigating the rapids brings joy and security. He's taken lots of others through before. *Joe Stowell*

The Privilege of Prayer

Read 1 Chronicles 29:11–19

Give my son Solomon the wholehearted devotion
to keep your commands, statutes and decrees.

1 CHRONICLES 29:19

Country artist Chris Stapleton's deeply personal song, "Daddy Doesn't Pray Anymore," was inspired by his own father's prayers for him. The poignant lyrics reveal the reason his father's prayers ended: not disillusionment or weariness, but his own death. Stapleton imagines that now, instead of speaking with Jesus in prayer, his dad is walking and talking face-to-face with Jesus.

Stapleton's recollection of his father's prayers for him brings to mind a biblical father's prayer for his son. As King David's life ebbed away, he made preparations for his son Solomon to take over as the next king of Israel.

After assembling the nation together to anoint Solomon, David led the people in prayer, as he'd done many times before. As David recounted God's faithfulness to Israel, he prayed for the people to remain loyal to Him. Then he included a personal prayer specifically for his son, asking God to "give my son Solomon the wholehearted devotion to keep your commands, statutes and decrees" (1 Chronicles 29:19).

We too have the remarkable privilege to faithfully pray for the people God has placed in our lives. Our example of faithfulness can make an indelible impact that will remain even after we're gone. Just as God continued to work out the answers to David's prayers for Solomon and Israel after he was gone, so too the impact of our prayers outlives us.

Lisa Samra

2 CHRONICLES

The narrative of 2 Chronicles details some key events in the life of King Solomon, including his request for wisdom and his leadership in building the temple. We see the spectacle of the visit by the Queen of Sheba, and then we read of his death after forty years of reigning in Judah. The book then turns to the stories of several other kings of Judah—stories we also read in 1 and 2 Kings. At the conclusion of the book, the fall of Jerusalem at the hands of Nebuchadnezzar is told, as well as the edict from Cyrus that would bring them back home seventy years later.

OUTLINE

The Reign of King Solomon 2 Chronicles 1:1–9:31
The Kingdom Divides 2 Chronicles 10:1–19
The Remaining Kingdoms of Judah 2 Chronicles 11:1–36:14
The Fall of Jerusalem 2 Chronicles 36:15–23

Singing in the Spirit

Read 2 Chronicles 5:12–14

Be filled with the Spirit, speaking to one another
with psalms, hymns, and songs from the Spirit.

EPHESIANS 5:18–19

During the Welsh Revivals of the early twentieth century, Bible teacher and author G. Campbell Morgan described what he observed. He believed the presence of God's Holy Spirit was moving on "billowing waves of sacred song." Morgan wrote that he had seen the unifying influence of music in meetings that encouraged voluntary prayers, confession, and spontaneous singing. If someone got carried away by their feelings and prayed too long, or spoke in a way that didn't resonate with others, someone would begin to softly sing. Others would gently join in, the chorus swelling in volume until drowning out all other sound.

The renewal in song that Morgan describes has its story in the Scriptures, where music plays a prominent role. Music was used to celebrate victories (Exodus 15:1–21); in worshipful dedication of the temple (2 Chronicles 5:12–14); and as a part of military strategy (20:21–23). At the center of the Bible we find a songbook (Psalms 1–150). And in Paul's New Testament letter to the Ephesians we read this description of life in the Spirit: "[Speak] to one another with psalms, hymns, and songs from the Spirit" (Ephesians 5:19).

In conflict, in worship, in all of life, the music of our faith can help us find one voice. In harmonies old and new we're renewed again and again, not by might, nor by power, but the Spirit and songs of our God.

Mart DeHaan

A Joyful Heart

Read 2 Chronicles 7:1–10

Shout for joy to the LORD, all the earth.

PSALM 100:1

My granddaughter's favorite tune is one of John Philip Sousa's marches. Sousa, known as "The March King," was a US composer in the late nineteenth century. Moriah isn't in a marching band; she's only twenty months old. She just loves the tune and can even hum a few notes. She associates it with joyful times. When our family gets together, we often hum this song along with claps and other boisterous noises, and the grandchildren dance or parade in circles to the beat. It always ends in dizzy children and lots of laughter.

Our joyful noise reminds me of the psalm that implores us to "worship the LORD with gladness" (Psalm 100:2). When King Solomon dedicated the temple, the Israelites celebrated with praises (2 Chronicles 7:5–6). Psalm 100 may have been one of the songs they sang. The psalm declares: "Shout for joy to the LORD, all the earth. Worship the LORD with gladness; come before him with joyful songs. . . . Enter his gates with thanksgiving and his courts with praise; give thanks to him and praise his name" (vv. 1–2, 4). Why? "For the LORD is good and his love endures forever"! (v. 5).

Our good God loves us! In grateful response, let's "shout for joy to the LORD"! (Psalm 100:1). *Alyson Kieda*

That Thing You Do

Read 2 Chronicles 13:10–18

The people of Judah were victorious because they relied on the Lord, the God of their ancestors.

2 Chronicles 13:18

As the convoy waited to roll out, a young marine rapped urgently on the window of his team leader's vehicle. Irritated, the sergeant rolled down his window. "What?"

"You gotta do that thing," the marine said. "What thing?" asked the sergeant. "You know, that thing you do," replied the marine.

Then it dawned on the sergeant. He always prayed for the convoy's safety, but this time he hadn't. So he dutifully climbed out of the Humvee and prayed for his marines. The marine understood the value of his praying leader.

In ancient Judah, Abijah doesn't stand out as a great king. First Kings 15:3 tells us, "His heart was not fully devoted to the Lord his God." But as Judah prepared for war against Israel, outnumbered two to one, Abijah knew this much: Faithful people in his kingdom of Judah had continued worshiping God (2 Chronicles 13:10–12), while the ten tribes of Israel had driven out the priests of God and worshiped pagan gods instead (vv. 8–9). So Abijah turned confidently to the one true God.

Surely Abijah's checkered history had caused grave damage. But he knew where to turn in the crisis, and his army won soundly "because they relied on the Lord, the God of their ancestors" (v. 18). Our God welcomes whoever comes to Him and relies on Him.   *Tim Gustafson*

Panic or Pray?

Read 2 Chronicles 14:1–11

*Help us, LORD our God, for we rely on you, and in
your name we have come against this vast army.*

2 CHRONICLES 14:11

An eighty-five-year-old woman, all alone in a convent, got trapped inside an elevator for four nights and three days. Fortunately, she had a jar of water, some celery sticks, and a few cough drops. After she tried unsuccessfully to open the elevator doors and get a cell phone signal, she decided to turn to God in prayer. "It was either panic or pray," she later told CNN. In her distress, she relied on God and waited till she was rescued.

Asa was also faced with the options of panic or pray (2 Chronicles 14). He was attacked by an Ethiopian army of a million men. But as he faced this huge fighting force, instead of relying on military strategy or cowering in dread, he turned to the Lord in urgent prayer. In a powerful and humble prayer, Asa confessed his total dependence on Him, asked for help, and appealed to the Lord to protect His own name: "Help us, O LORD our God, for we rest on You, and in Your name we go against this multitude" (v. 11 NKJV). The Lord responded to Asa's prayer, and he won the victory over the Ethiopian army.

When we are faced with tight spots, meager resources, a vast army of problems, or seemingly dead-end solutions, let's not panic but instead turn to God who fights for His people and gives them victory.

Marvin Williams

A Devastated Heart

Read 2 Chronicles 17:1–11; 20:32

He did what was right in the eyes of the LORD.

2 CHRONICLES 20:32

A successful Christian businessman shared his story with us at church. He was candid about his struggles with faith and abundant wealth. He declared, "Wealth scares me!"

He quoted Jesus's statement, "It is easier for a camel to go through the eye of a needle than for someone who is rich to enter the kingdom of God" (Luke 18:25). He cited Luke 16:19–31 about the rich man and Lazarus and how in this story it was the rich man who went to hell. The parable of the "rich fool" (Luke 12:16–21) disturbed him.

"But," the businessman stated, "I've learned a lesson from Solomon's verdict on the abundance of wealth. It's all 'meaningless'" (see Ecclesiastes 2:11). He determined not to let wealth get in the way of his devotion to God. Rather, he wanted to serve God with his assets and help the needy.

Throughout the centuries, God has blessed some people materially. We read of Jehoshaphat in 2 Chronicles 17:5, "The LORD established the kingdom . . . so that he had great wealth and honor." He did not become proud or bully others with his wealth. Instead, "his heart was devoted to the ways of the LORD" (v. 6). Also, "he followed the ways of his father Asa and did not stray from them; he did what was right in the eyes of the LORD" (20:32).

The Lord is not against wealth for He has blessed some with it—but He's definitely against the unethical acquisition and wrong use of it. He is worthy of devotion from all His followers. *Lawrence Darmani*

EZRA

◆

The remnant has returned to Jerusalem. However, there will be no return to the glory days of David and Solomon. The presence of other powers in the region are making that certain. However, the people need to return to their worship in the temple and they need to rebuild their city walls to provide security. So, Ezra is pivotal as it explains the returning of the people and the rebuilding of key structures in Jerusalem.

OUTLINE

Cyrus's Proclamation Ezra 1:1–11

The Jewish Exiles Return Ezra 2:1–70

The Temple Rebuild Begins Ezra 3:1–13

The Rebuild Is Halted Ezra 4:1–24

The Temple Is Completed Ezra 5:1–6:22

Ezra Arrives Ezra 7:1–8:36

Ezra Institutes Reforms Ezra 9:1–10:44

Joy in the Midst of Grief

Read Ezra 3:10–13

No one could distinguish the sound of the
shouts of joy from the sound of weeping.

EZRA 3:13

After only a few art lessons, ten-year-old Joel decided to try his hand at painting a flower. By looking at a color photograph of a Rose of Sharon, Joel was able to paint a beautiful mixture of blue, purple, red, green, and white. This made the flower, which had been photographed on the day Joel's aunt died, seem to come to life. To the family, his painting symbolized a bittersweet mixture of feelings. While it provided a lasting reminder of the loss they had suffered, it also carried a celebration of Joel's newly discovered artistic gift. The painting gave joy in the midst of grief.

When the people of Judah returned to Jerusalem from captivity in Babylon, they too had a bittersweet experience. As they began rebuilding Solomon's temple, many in the crowd sang songs of praise. At the same time, some older people, who had seen the beauty of the original temple that had been destroyed by war, wept aloud. We are told that "The people could not distinguish the sound of the shouts of joy from the sound of weeping" (Ezra 3:13).

Grieving can be like that. While there is sadness in looking back, it also includes a promise of joy in trusting God for the future. Even in a devastating loss, we have this hope: The Lord provides joy in the midst of grief. *Dennis Fisher*

Keep Calm and Carry On

Read Ezra 5:7–17

We are the servants of the God of heaven and earth.
EZRA 5:11

"Keep calm and call mom." "Keep calm and eat bacon." "Keep calm and put the kettle on." These sayings are variations of the phrase: "Keep Calm and Carry On." This message was created in Great Britain in 1939 as the government sought ways to encourage the citizenry if the country were to be attacked. While it was never used as designed, the idea resurfaced around the turn of the century and caught on as a clever slogan.

Having returned to the land of Israel after a time of captivity, the Israelites had to overcome their own fear and enemy interference as they began to rebuild the temple (Ezra 3:3). Once they finished the foundation, their opponents "bribed officials to work against them and frustrate their plans" (4:5). Israel's enemies also wrote accusing letters to government officials and successfully delayed the project (vv. 6, 24). Despite this, King Darius eventually issued a decree that allowed them to complete the temple (6:12–14).

When we are engaged in God's work and we encounter setbacks, we can calmly carry on because, like the Israelites, "We are the servants of the God of heaven and earth" (5:11). Obstacles and delays may discourage us, but we can rest in Jesus's promise: "I will build my church, and all the powers of hell will not conquer it" (Matthew 16:18 NLT). It is God's power that enables His work, not our own.

Jennifer Benson Schuldt

Seeing God's Hand

Read Ezra 7:1–10, 27–28

He arrived in Jerusalem on the first day of the fifth
month, for the gracious hand of his God was on him.

EZRA 7:9

On Jack Borden's 101st birthday, he awoke at 5 a.m., ate a hearty breakfast, and was at his law office by 6:30 ready to begin his day. When asked the secret of his long life, the practicing attorney smiled and quipped, "Not dying."

But there's more to it than that.

Mr. Borden, who was baptized at age eleven in the Clear Fork of the Trinity River in Texas, told *Fort Worth Star-Telegram* reporter David Casstevens, "I'm a firm believer that God has His hand in everything that happens. He is letting me live for some reason. I try to do the things that I believe He wants me to."

Ezra the priest experienced the "good hand of his God upon him" when he led a delegation to Jerusalem to provide spiritual leadership for the former captives who were rebuilding the temple and the city (Ezra 7:9–10 ESV). Ezra found strength and courage in knowing that the Lord was with them each step of the way. "Because the hand of the LORD my God was on me, I took courage and gathered leaders from Israel to go up with me" (v. 28).

When we see the Lord's hand in our lives, it brings forth a deep "Thank You" and a growing desire to do what He wants us to do.

David McCasland

Ripple Effect

Read Ezra 8:15–21

Because the hand of the LORD my God was on me, I took
courage and gathered leaders from Israel to go up with me.

EZRA 7:28

The little Bible college in northern Ghana didn't look impressive—just a tin-roofed cinder-block building and a handful of students. Yet Bob Hayes poured his life into those students. He gave them leadership roles and encouraged them to preach and teach, despite their occasional reluctance. Bob passed away years ago, but dozens of thriving churches, schools, and two additional Bible institutes have sprung up across Ghana—all started by graduates of that humble school.

During the reign of King Artaxerxes (465–424 BC), Ezra the scribe assembled a band of Jewish exiles to return to Jerusalem. But Ezra found no Levites among them (Ezra 8:15). He needed Levites to serve as priests. So he commissioned leaders to "bring attendants to us for the house of our God" (v. 17). They did so (vv. 18–20), and Ezra led them all in fasting and prayer (v. 21).

Ezra's name means "helper," a characteristic that resides at the heart of good leadership. Under Ezra's prayerful guidance, he and his protégés would lead a spiritual awakening in Jerusalem (see chapters 9–10). All they had needed was a little encouragement and wise direction.

That's how God's church works too. As good mentors encourage and build us up, we learn to do the same for others. Such an influence will reach far beyond our lifetime. Work done faithfully for God stretches into eternity.   *Tim Gustafson*

NEHEMIAH

It's been nearly a hundred years since the people had returned to Jeru-salem. Some lived in the old capital, and some lived in villages in the region. However, this long after the return from Babylon, the city was still vulnerable to outside attacks because the walls had not been repaired from their destruction at the hands of Nebuchadnezzar and his army in 586 BC. Thus the key event of the book is to rebuild the walls—and Nehemiah is the man to lead that project. Also, there has to be another reconstruction—a spiritual reconstruction of the nation that had become so devastated. This will be the combined work of Ezra and Nehemiah.

OUTLINE

The Prayer and the Chain Saw

Read Nehemiah 1

LORD, let your ear be attentive to the prayer of this your servant.
NEHEMIAH 1:11

I respect my Aunt Gladys's intrepid spirit, even if that very spirit concerns me sometimes. The source of my concern came in the form of news she shared in an email: "I cut down a walnut tree yesterday."

You must understand that my chainsaw-wielding aunt is seventy-six years old! The tree had grown up behind her garage. When the roots threatened to burst through the concrete, she knew it had to go. But she did tell us, "I always pray before I tackle a job like that."

While serving as butler to the king of Persia during the time of Israel's exile, Nehemiah heard news concerning the people who had returned to Jerusalem. Some work needed to be done. "The wall of Jerusalem is broken down, and its gates have been burned with fire" (Nehemiah 1:3). The broken walls left them vulnerable to attack by enemies. Nehemiah had compassion for his people and wanted to get involved. But prayer came first, especially since a new king had written a letter to stop the building efforts in Jerusalem (see Ezra 4). Nehemiah prayed for his people (Nehemiah 1:5–10), and then asked God for help before requesting permission from the king to leave (v. 11).

Is prayer your response? It's always the best way to face any task or trial in life. *Linda Washington*

How to Rebuild

Read Nehemiah 2:11–18

They replied, "Let us start rebuilding."
So they began this good work.

NEHEMIAH 2:18

It was nighttime when the leader set out by horseback to inspect the work that lay ahead. As he toured the destruction all around him, he saw city walls that had been destroyed and gates that had been burned. In some areas, the vast debris made it tough for his horse to get through. Saddened, the rider turned toward home.

When it came time to report the damage to the officials of the city, he began by saying, "You see the trouble we are in" (Nehemiah 2:17). He reported that the city was in ruins, and the protecting city wall had been rendered useless.

But then he made a statement that energized the troubled citizens: "I also told them about the gracious hand of my God on me." Immediately, the people replied, "Let us start rebuilding" (v. 18).

And they did.

With faith in God and all-out effort, despite enemy opposition and a seemingly impossible task, the people of Jerusalem—under Nehemiah's leadership—rebuilt the wall in just fifty-two days (6:15).

As you consider your circumstances, is there something that looks difficult but that you know God wants you to do? A sin you can't seem to get rid of? A relationship rift that's not God-honoring? A task for Him that looks too hard?

Ask God for guidance (2:4–5), analyze the problem (vv. 11–15), and recognize His involvement (v. 18). Then start rebuilding.

Dave Branon

Marathon Reading

Read Nehemiah 8:1–8

They read from the Book of the Law of God,
making it clear and giving the meaning so that
the people understood what was being read.

NEHEMIAH 8:8

When the sun came up on the first day of the seventh month in 444 BC, Ezra started reading the law of Moses (what we know as the first five books of the Bible). Standing on a platform in front of the people in Jerusalem, he read it straight through for the next six hours.

Men, women, and children had gathered at the entrance to the city known as the Water Gate to observe the Festival of Trumpets—one of the feasts prescribed for them by God. As they listened, four reactions stand out.

They stood up in reverence for the Book of the Law (Nehemiah 8:5). They praised God by lifting their hands and saying "Amen." They bowed down in humble worship (v. 6). Then they listened carefully as the Scriptures were both read and explained to them (v. 8). What an amazing day as the book that "the LORD had commanded for Israel" (v. 1) was read aloud inside Jerusalem's newly rebuilt walls!

Ezra's marathon reading session can remind us that God's words to us are still meant to be a source of praise, worship, and learning. When we open the Bible and learn more about Christ, let's praise God, worship Him, and seek to discover what He is saying to us now.   *Dave Branon*

APER 6

Never Too Sinful

Read Nehemiah 9:17, 27–31

You are a forgiving God . . . abounding in love.
NEHEMIAH 9:17

"If I touched a Bible, it would catch fire in my hands," said my community college English professor. My heart sank. The novel we'd been reading that morning referenced a Bible verse, and when I pulled out my Bible to look it up, she noticed and commented. My professor seemed to think she was too sinful to be forgiven. Yet I wasn't bold enough to tell her about God's love—and that the Bible tells us we can always seek God's forgiveness.

There's an example of repentance and forgiveness in Nehemiah. The Israelites had been exiled because of their sin, but now they were allowed to return to Jerusalem. When they'd "settled in," Ezra the scribe read the law to them (Nehemiah 7:73–8:3). They confessed their sins, remembering that despite their sin God "did not desert" or "abandon them" (9:17, 19). He "heard them" when they cried out; and in compassion and mercy, He was patient with them (vv. 27–31).

In a similar way, God is patient with us. He won't abandon us if we choose to confess our sin and turn to Him. I wish I could go back and tell my professor that, no matter her past, Jesus loves her and wants her to be part of His family. He feels the same way about you and me. We can approach Him seeking forgiveness—and He will give it!

Julie Schwab

ESTHER

◆

The amazing story in the book of Esther was set in motion when the king's wife, Vashti, refused to parade her beauty in front of her drunken husband and "the people and nobles" (1:11). An irate King Ahasuerus disowned Vashti and sought another queen. His search for a new queen turned up Esther, the Jewish orphan girl, and she became the new queen. Later, the king's right-hand man Haman tricked Ahasuerus into proclaiming an edict condemning all Jews to death. It was only when Esther bravely entered the king's presence and asking him to reverse his edict that the Jewish people were saved from annihilation.

OUTLINE

Ahasuerus Ousts His Queen Esther 1:1–22

Esther Becomes Queen Esther 2:1–23

Haman Plots to Kill the Jews Esther 3:1–15

Queen Esther Displays Courage; Haman Dispatched
Esther 4:1–7:10

Institution of Purim Esther 9:1–32

Honoring Mordecai Esther 10:1–3

Respect

Read Esther 1:1–5, 9–12

You have made him a little lower than the angels
and crowned him with glory and honor.

PSALM 8:5

In 1967, American vocalist Aretha Franklin topped the charts with her hit single "Respect." The song became an inspirational anthem for the civil rights movement and for others who demanded to be treated with respect.

Long before Aretha's hit record, Queen Vashti topped the Persian charts with her own version of "Respect." The book of Esther begins with King Ahasuerus hosting a great celebration. In addition to displaying his wealth and power, he also wanted to showcase his wife's beauty. So he commanded that Queen Vashti be brought before him and his guests.

If she obeyed, she would have allowed the king to degrade and disrespect her. If she refused, she risked losing her life. She refused. What courage! Vashti didn't want to compromise her character by being reduced to a piece of property. Her desire for respect led to her banishment. We have no record that Vashti feared the Lord. But her courage shows that she understood the God-given dignity accorded to every human being.

God created us in His image and crowned us with glory and honor, having made us "a little lower than the angels" (Psalm 8:5). Out of love and reverence for Him, let us treat ourselves and others with honor, dignity, and respect. *Marvin Williams*

Poetic Justice

Read Esther 3:1–11; 7:1–10

"It is mine to avenge; I will repay," says the Lord.
ROMANS 12:19

For nearly a year, a former publishing colleague lived under a cloud of fear that he would be fired. A new boss in the department, for reasons unknown, began filling his personnel file with negative comments. Then, on the day my friend expected to lose his job, the new boss was fired instead.

When the Israelites were taken as captives to Babylon, a Jew named Mordecai found himself in this kind of situation. Haman, the highest noble of King Xerxes, expected every royal official to kneel down and honor him, but Mordecai refused to bow to anyone but God (Esther 3:1–2). This outraged Haman and he set out to destroy not only Mordecai but every Jew in the whole Persian empire (vv. 5–6). Haman convinced Xerxes to sign a decree authorizing the destruction of all Jews and started building a gallows for the execution of Mordecai (5:14). But, in a startling turn of events, Haman was executed on the gallows he had built for Mordecai, and the Jewish people were spared (7:9–10; 8).

In literature, this is called poetic justice. Not everyone gets justice in such dramatic fashion, but Scripture promises that God will one day avenge all injustice (Romans 12:19). While we wait, we are to do what we can to work for justice and leave the results in God's hands.

Julie Ackerman Link

APRIL 9

Righteous among the Nations

Read Esther 4:5–14

For such a time as this.

ESTHER 4:14

At Yad Vashem, the Holocaust museum in Israel, my husband and I went to the Righteous Among the Nations garden that honors the men and women who risked their lives to save Jewish people during the Holocaust. While looking at the memorial, we met a group from the Netherlands. One woman was there to see her grandparents' names listed on the large plaques. Intrigued, we asked about her family's story.

Members of a resistance network, the woman's grandparents Rev. Pieter and Adriana Müller took in a two-year-old Jewish boy and passed him off as the youngest of their eight children from 1943 until 1945.

Moved by the story, we asked, "Did the little boy survive?" An older gentleman in the group stepped forward and proclaimed, "I am that boy!"

The bravery of many to act on behalf of the Jewish people reminds me of Queen Esther. The queen may have thought she could escape King Xerxes's decree to annihilate the Jews around 475 BC because she had concealed her ethnicity. However, she was convinced to act—even under the threat of death—when her cousin begged her to not remain silent about her Jewish heritage because she had been placed in her position "for such a time as this" (Esther 4:14).

We may never be asked to make such a dramatic decision. However, we will likely face the choice to speak out against an injustice or remain silent; to provide assistance to someone in trouble or turn away. May God grant us courage. *Lisa Samra*

Self-Destructive Hatred

Read Esther 7:1–10

Do not repay anyone evil for evil.

Romans 12:17

George Washington Carver (1864–1943) overcame terrible racial prejudice to establish himself as a renowned American educator. Spurning the temptation to give in to bitterness for the way he was treated, Carver wisely wrote, "Hate within will eventually destroy the hater."

In the book of Esther, we see how self-destructive hatred can be. Mordecai, a Jew, refused to bow down before Haman—a self-important dignitary in the Persian court. This angered Haman, who manipulated information to make Mordecai and his people appear as threats to the empire (3:8–9). When his scheming was complete, Haman called on the Persian king to kill all the Jews. The king proclaimed an edict to that effect, but before it could be carried out, Esther intervened and Haman's devious plot was revealed (7:1–6). Enraged, the king had Haman executed on gallows the schemer had built for Mordecai (7:7–10).

Carver's words and Haman's actions remind us that hatred is self-destructive. The biblical response is to turn hatred around and return good for evil. "Do not repay anyone evil for evil," Paul said (Romans 12:17). When offended, "do not take revenge" (v.19). Instead, do what is right (v.17) that you may "live at peace with everyone" (v.18).

Dennis Fisher

PART 3

◆

Poetry and Wisdom

Job, Psalms, Proverbs, Ecclesiastes, Song of Songs

While these five books are diverse in their approach, the passage as a whole is known for the wisdom it passes along to its readers. Whether through beautiful poetry, through stories, or through pithy sayings these books provide insights in how to live, how to view our relationship with God, and how to handle difficult circumstances.

JOB

---◆---

The book begins with tragedy, and it ends in triumph. In the middle we see the friends of Job—a righteous man who lost everything—counseling him about how he should view his misfortune. He never really finds out why tragedy visited him (how true this is in our lives), but the comes to terms with God's sovereignty after receiving an eye-opening visit from God himself.

OUTLINE

Job's Tragedies Job 1:1–2:13

Job's First Debate with Friends Job 3:1–14:22

Job's Second Debate with Friends Job 15:1–21:34

Job's Third Debate with Friends Job 22:1–26:14

Job Defends Himself Job 27:1–31:40

Elihu's Response Job 32:1–37:24

God Questions/Instructs Job Job 38:1–41:34

Job Replies Job 42:1–6

Job Is Restored Job 42:7–17

How Did I Get Here?

Read Job 2:1–10

Shall we accept good from God, and not trouble?
JOB 2:10

Tiffani awoke in the pitch-black darkness of an Air Canada jet. Still wearing her seat belt, she'd slept while the other passengers exited and the plane was parked. Why didn't anyone wake her? How did she get here? She shook the cobwebs from her brain and tried to remember.

Have you found yourself in a place you never expected? You're too young to have this disease, and there's no cure. Your last review was excellent; why is your position being eliminated? You were enjoying the best years of your marriage. Now you're starting over, as a single parent with a part-time job.

How did I get here? Job may have wondered as "he sat among the ashes" (Job 2:8). He'd lost his children, his wealth, and his health, in no time flat. He couldn't have guessed how he got here; he just knew he had to remember.

Job remembered his Creator and how good He'd been. He told his wife, "Shall we accept good from God, and not trouble?" (v. 10). Job remembered he could count on this good God to be faithful. So he lamented. He screamed at the heavens. And he mourned in hope, "I know that my redeemer lives," and that "in my flesh I will see God" (19:25–26). Job clung to hope as he remembered how the story began and how it ends.　　　　　　　　　　　　　　　　　　　　　　*Mike Wittmer*

Being There

Read Job 2:11-13

They sat on the ground with him for seven days and seven nights.

JOB 2:13

When Jen, a theme park employee, saw Ralph collapse in tears on the ground, she rushed to help. Ralph, a young boy with autism, was sobbing because the ride he'd waited all day to enjoy had broken down. Instead of hurrying him to his feet or simply urging him to feel better, Jen got down onto the ground with Ralph, validating his feelings and allowing him the time to cry.

Jen's actions are a beautiful example of how we can come alongside those who are grieving or suffering. The Bible tells of Job's crippling grief after the loss of his home, his herds (his income), his health, and the simultaneous deaths of his ten children. When Job's friends learned of his pain, they "set out from their homes . . . [to go] comfort him" (Job 2:11). Job sat on the ground in mourning. When they arrived, his friends sat down with him—for seven days—saying nothing because they saw the depth of his suffering.

In their humanness, Job's friends later offered Job insensitive advice. But for the first seven days, they gave him the wordless and tender gift of presence. We may not understand someone's grief, but we don't need to understand in order to love them well by simply being with them.

Kirsten Holmberg

Tried and Purified

Read Job 23:1–12

When he has tested me, I will come forth as gold.

Job 23:10

During an interview, singer and songwriter Meredith Andrews spoke about being overwhelmed as she tried to balance outreach, creative work, marital issues, and motherhood. Reflecting on her distress, she said, "I felt like God was taking me through a refining season, almost through a crushing process."

Job was overwhelmed after losing his livelihood, his health, and his family. Worse still, although Job had been a daily worshiper of God, he felt that the Lord was ignoring his pleas for help. God seemed absent from the landscape of his life. Job claimed he could not see God whether he looked to the north, south, east, or west (Job 23:2–9).

In the middle of his despair, Job had a moment of clarity. His faith flickered to life like a candle in a dark room. He said, "[God] knows the way that I take; when he has tested me, I will come forth as gold" (v. 10). Christians are tried and purified when God uses difficulty to burn away our self-reliance, pride, and earthly wisdom. If it seems as if God is silent during this process and He is not answering our cries for help, He may be giving us an opportunity to grow stronger in our faith.

Pain and problems can produce the shining, rock-solid character that comes from trusting God when life is hard.

Jennifer Benson Schuldt

Hanging on Nothing

Read Job 26:5–14

He spreads out the northern skies over empty space;
he suspends the earth over nothing.

JOB 26:7

A world map published by the National Geographic Society has this notation: "Earth's mass is 6.6 sextillion tons." And what supports all that weight? Nothing. The planet we inhabit spins on its axis at 1,000 miles per hour as it hurtles through space in its orbit around the sun. But it's easy for that to remain unnoticed in the midst of our daily concerns about health, relationships, and how to pay the bills.

The Old Testament character Job repeatedly considered God's creation in his struggle to make sense of the numbing loss of his health, his wealth, and his children. "[God] spreads out the northern skies over empty space," Job said. "He suspends the earth over nothing" (Job 26:7). Job marveled at the clouds that did not break under the heavy water inside them (v.8) and the horizon, which serves "for a boundary between light and darkness" (v.10). He called these things "the mere edges of His ways" (v. 14 NKJV).

Creation itself did not answer Job's questions, but the heavens and the earth pointed him to God the Creator, who alone could respond with help and hope.

The Lord who upholds the universe by His powerful word (Hebrews 1:3; Colossians 1:17) is in control of our everyday lives. Experiences that seem "empty places" are all undergirded by our heavenly Father's power and love. *David McCasland*

Perfectly Placed

Read Job 38:4–11

Where were you when I laid the earth's foundation?

JOB 38:4

Scientists know our planet is precisely the right distance from the sun to benefit from its heat. A little closer and all the water would evaporate, as on Venus. Only a bit farther and everything would freeze like it does on Mars. Earth is also just the right size to generate the right amount of gravity. Less would make everything weightlessly sterile like our moon, while more gravity would trap poisonous gases that suffocate life as on Jupiter.

The intricate physical, chemical, and biological interactions that comprise our world bear the imprint of a sophisticated Designer. We catch a glimpse of this complex craftsmanship when God speaks to Job about things beyond our understanding. "Where were you when I laid the earth's foundation?" God asks. "Who marked off its dimensions? Surely you know! Who stretched a measuring line across it? On what were its footings set, or who laid its cornerstone?" (Job 38:4–6).

This glimpse of creation's magnitude causes us to wonder at earth's mighty oceans bowing before the One who "shut up the sea behind doors when it burst forth from the womb, . . . [who said] 'This far you may come and no farther'" (vv. 8–11). In wonder may we sing with the morning stars and shout for joy with the angels (v. 7), for this elaborate world was made for us that we might know and trust God.

Remi Oyedele

Wonderful!

Read Job 42:1–6

I spoke of things I did not understand,
things too wonderful for me to know.

JOB 42:3

As our plane began its descent, the flight attendant read the long list of arrival information as if she were reading it for the thousandth time that day—no emotion or interest as she droned on about our impending arrival. Then, with the same tired, disinterested voice, she finished by saying, "Have a wonderful day." The dryness of her tone contrasted with her words. She said "wonderful" but in a manner completely absent of any sense of wonder.

Sometimes I fear that we approach our relationship with God in the same way: Routine. Bored. Apathetic. Disinterested. Through Christ, we have the privilege of being adopted into the family of the living God, yet often there seems to be little of the sense of wonder that should accompany that remarkable reality.

Job questioned God about his suffering, but when challenged by Him, Job was humbled by the wonder of his Creator and His creation. Job replied, "You asked, 'Who is this who hides counsel without knowledge?' Therefore I have uttered what I did not understand, things too wonderful for me, which I did not know" (Job 42:3 NKJV).

I long for the wonder of God to take hold of my heart. Adopted by God—what a wonderful reality! *Bill Crowder*

PSALMS

The variety of the Psalms is one of its most fascinating components. For instance, there are lament psalms—both corporate and individual—in which writers make complaints to God. Also, there are corporate and individual thanksgiving psalms. Many of the psalms are considered praise songs—in which the people of God sent songs of glory and adoration to God. One group of pilgrimage psalms records songs the Israelites sang on their way to worship. So, because this collection was compiled over such a long period of time by so many different people, the variety is fascinating.

OUTLINE

Asking for Help and Singing Praise, Book 1 Psalms 1:1–41:13
Psalms of Deliverance and Redemption, Book 2 Psalms 42:1–72:20
Psalms of Worship, Book 3 Psalms 73:1–89:52
Psalms of Both Confession and Praise, Book 4 Psalms 90:1–106:48
Psalms of Great Praise, Book 5 Psalms 107:1–150:6

◆

APRIL 17

Where Choices Lead

Read Psalm 1

The LORD watches over the way of the righteous.

PSALM 1:6

With no cell service and no trail map, we had just our memory of a fixed map at the trailhead to guide us. More than an hour later, we finally emerged from the woods into the parking lot. Having missed the turn-off that would have made for a half-mile hike, we took a much longer trek.

Life can be like that: we have to ask not simply if something is right or wrong, but where it will lead. Psalm 1 compares two ways of living—that of the righteous (those who love God) and that of the wicked (the enemies of those who love God). The righteous flourish like a tree, but the wicked blow away like chaff (vv. 3–4). This psalm reveals what flourishing really looks like. The person who lives it out is dependent on God for renewal and life.

So how do we become that kind of person? Among other things, Psalm 1 urges us to disengage from destructive relationships and unhealthy habits and to delight in God's instruction (v. 2). Ultimately, the reason for our flourishing is God's attentiveness to us: "The LORD watches over the way of the righteous" (v. 6).

Commit your way to God, let Him redirect you from old patterns that lead to nowhere, and allow the Scriptures to be the river that nourishes the root system of your heart.   *Glenn Packiam*

Asking God

Read Psalm 6:4–9

The LORD has heard my cry for mercy;
the LORD accepts my prayer.

PSALM 6:9

When my husband, Dan, was diagnosed with cancer, I couldn't find the "right" way to ask God to heal him. In my limited view, other people in the world had such serious problems—war, famine, poverty, natural disasters. Then one day, during our morning prayer time, I heard my husband humbly ask, "Dear Lord, please heal my disease."

It was such a simple but heartfelt plea that it reminded me to stop complicating every prayer request, because God perfectly hears our righteous cries for help. As David simply asked, "Turn, LORD, and deliver me; save me because of your unfailing love" (Psalm 6:4).

That's what David declared during a time of spiritual confusion and despair. His exact situation isn't explained in this psalm. His honest pleas, however, show deep desire for godly help and restoration. "I am worn out from my groaning," he wrote (v. 6).

Yet, David didn't let his own limits, including sin, stop him from going to God with his need. Thus, even before God answered, David was able to rejoice, "the LORD has heard my weeping. The LORD has heard my cry for mercy; the LORD accepts my prayer" (vv. 8–9).

Despite our own confusion and uncertainty, God hears and accepts the honest pleas of His children. He's ready to hear us, especially when we need Him most.   *Patricia Raybon*

Unimaginable

Read Psalm 23

Though I walk through the darkest valley,
I will fear no evil, for you are with me.

PSALM 23:4

Bart Millard penned a megahit in 2001 when he wrote, "I Can Only Imagine." The song pictures how amazing it will be to be in Christ's presence. Millard's lyrics offered comfort to our family that next year when our seventeen-year-old daughter, Melissa, died in a car accident and we imagined what it was like for her to be in God's presence.

But *imagine* spoke to me in a different way in the days following Mell's death. As fathers of Melissa's friends approached me, full of concern and pain, they said, "I can't imagine what you're going through."

Their expressions were helpful, showing that they were grappling with our loss in an empathetic way—finding it unimaginable.

David pinpointed the depth of great loss when he described walking through "the darkest valley" (Psalm 23:4). The death of a loved one certainly is that, and we sometimes have no idea how we're going to navigate the darkness. We can't imagine ever being able to come out on the other side.

But as God promised to be with us in our darkest valley now, He also provides great hope for the future by assuring us that beyond the valley we'll be in His presence. For the believer, to be "away from the body" means being present with Him (2 Corinthians 5:8). That can help us navigate the unimaginable as we imagine our future reunion with Him and others.   *Dave Branon*

The Triumph of Forgiveness

Read Psalm 32:1–7

Blessed is the one whose transgressions
are forgiven, whose sins are covered.

PSALM 32:1

Mack, having struggled with drug abuse and sexual sin, was desperate. Relationships he valued were in disarray, and his conscience was beating him up. In his misery, he found himself unannounced at a church asking to speak with a pastor. There he found relief in sharing his complicated story and in hearing about God's mercy and forgiveness.

Psalm 32 is believed to have been composed by David after his sexual sin. He compounded his wrongdoing by devising a sinister strategy that resulted in the death of the woman's husband (see 2 Samuel 11–12). While these ugly incidents were behind him, the effects of his actions remained. Psalm 32:3–4 describes the deep struggles he experienced before he acknowledged the ugliness of his deeds; the gnawing effects of unconfessed sin were undeniable. What brought relief? Relief began with confession to God and accepting the forgiveness He offers (v. 5).

What a great place for us to start—at the place of God's mercy—when we say or do things that cause hurt and harm to ourselves and others. The guilt of our sin need not be permanent. There's One whose arms are open wide to receive us when we acknowledge our wrongs and seek His forgiveness. We can join the chorus of those who sing, "Blessed is the one whose transgressions are forgiven, whose sins are covered" (v. 1).

Arthur Jackson

Strengthened in Song

Read Psalm 59:1, 14-17

I will sing of your strength, in the morning I will
sing of your love; for you are my fortress.

PSALM 59:16

When French villagers helped Jewish refugees hide from the Nazis during World War II, some sang songs in the dense forest surrounding their town—letting the refugees know it was safe to come out from hiding. These brave townspeople of Le Chambon-sur-Lignon had answered the call of local pastor André Trocmé and his wife, Magda, to offer wartime refuge to Jews on their windswept plateau known as "La Montagne Protestante." Their musical signal became just one feature of the villagers' bravery that helped save up to three thousand Jews from almost certain death.

In another dangerous time, David sang when his enemy Saul sent nighttime assassins to his house. His use of music wasn't a signal; rather, it was his song of gratitude to God his refuge. David rejoiced, "I will sing of your strength, in the morning I will sing of your love; for you are my fortress, my refuge in times of trouble" (Psalm 59:16).

Such singing isn't "whistling in the dark" during danger. Instead, David's singing conveyed his trust in the almighty God. "You, God, are my fortress, my God on whom I can rely" (v. 17).

David's praise, and the villagers' singing in Le Chambon, offer an invitation to bless God today with our singing, making melody to Him despite the worries of life. His loving presence will respond, strengthening our hearts. *Patricia Raybon*

The Man Who Couldn't Talk

Read Psalm 96

Great is the LORD and most worthy of praise.

PSALM 96:4

Sitting in his wheelchair at a senior citizens home in Belize, a man joyfully listened as a group of American high school teenagers sang about Jesus. Later, as some of the teens tried to communicate with him, they discovered he couldn't talk. A stroke had robbed him of his ability to speak.

Since they couldn't carry on a conversation with the man, the teens decided to sing to him. As they began to sing, something amazing happened. The man who couldn't talk began to sing. With enthusiasm, he belted out "How Great Thou Art" right along with his new friends.

It was a remarkable moment for everyone. This man's love for God broke through the barriers and poured out in audible worship—heartfelt, joyous worship.

We all have worship barriers from time to time. Maybe it's a relationship conflict or a money problem. Or it could be a heart that's grown a bit cold in its relationship to God.

Our non-talking friend reminds us that the greatness and majesty of our almighty God can overcome any barrier. "O Lord, my God—when I in awesome wonder, consider all the worlds Thy hands have made!"

Struggling in your worship? Reflect on how great our God is by reading a passage such as Psalm 96, and you too may find your obstacles and objections replaced by praise. *Dave Branon*

A Lifestyle of Worship

Read Psalm 100

*Worship the LORD with gladness; come
before him with joyful songs.*

PSALM 100:2

As I waited in the breakfast buffet line at a Christian conference center, a group of women entered the dining hall. I smiled, saying hello to a woman who stepped into the line behind me. Returning my greeting, she said, "I know you." We scooped scrambled eggs onto our plates and tried to figure out where we'd met. But I was pretty sure she'd mistaken me for someone else.

When we returned for lunch, the woman approached me. "Do you drive a white car?"

I shrugged. "I used to. A few years ago."

She laughed. "We stopped at the same traffic light by the elementary school almost every morning," she said. "You'd always be lifting your hands, singing joyfully. I thought you were worshiping God. That made me want to join in, even on tough days."

Praising God, we prayed together, hugged, and enjoyed lunch.

My new friend affirmed that people notice how Jesus's followers behave, even when we think no one is watching. As we embrace a lifestyle of joyful worship, we can come before our Creator anytime and anywhere. Acknowledging His enduring love and faithfulness, we can enjoy intimate communion with Him and thank Him for His ongoing care (Psalm 100). Whether we're singing praises in our cars, praying in public, or spreading God's love through kind acts, we can inspire others to "praise his name" (v. 4). Worshiping God is more than a Sunday morning event. *Xochitl Dixon*

God's Footprints

Read Psalm 104:24–35

How many are your works, LORD!
PSALM 104:24

"I know where God lives," our four-year-old grandson told my wife, Cari. "Where is that?" she asked, her curiosity piqued. "He lives in the woods beside your house," he answered.

When Cari told me about their conversation, she wondered what prompted his thinking. "I know," I responded. "When we went for a walk in the woods during his last visit, I told him that even though we can't see God, we can see the things He's done." "Do you see the footprints I'm making?" I had asked my grandson as we stepped through a sandy place by a river. "The animals and the trees and the river are like God's footprints. We know that He's been here because we can see the things He's made."

The writer of Psalm 104 also pointed to the evidence for God in creation, exclaiming "How many are your works, LORD! In wisdom you made them all; the earth is full of your creatures" (v. 24). The Hebrew word for wisdom found here is often used in the Bible to describe skillful craftsmanship. God's handiwork in nature proclaims His presence and makes us want to praise Him.

Psalm 104 begins and ends with the words: "Praise the LORD" (vv. 1, 35). From a baby's hand to an eagle's eye, our Creator's artistry all around us speaks of His consummate skill. May we take it all in with wonder today—and praise Him for it!   *James Banks*

Remembering to Sing

Read Psalm 147:1–7

How good it is to sing praises to our God.

Psalm 147:1

Nancy Gustafson, a retired opera singer, was devastated when she visited her mother and observed her decline from dementia. Her mom no longer recognized her and barely spoke. After several monthly visits, Nancy had an idea. She started singing to her. Her mother's eyes lit up at the musical sounds, and she began singing too—for twenty minutes! Then Nancy's mom laughed, joking they were "The Gustafson Family Singers!" The dramatic turnaround suggested the power of music, as some therapists conclude, to evoke lost memories. Singing "old favorites" has also been shown to boost mood, reduce falls, lessen visits to the emergency room, and decrease the need for sedative drugs.

More research is underway on a music-memory link. Yet, as the Bible reveals, the joy that comes from singing is a gift from God—and it's real. "How good it is to sing praises to our God, how pleasant and fitting to praise him!" (Psalm 147:1).

Throughout the Scriptures, in fact, God's people are urged to lift their voices in songs of praise to Him. "Sing to the Lord, for he has done glorious things" (Isaiah 12:5). "He put a new song in my mouth, a hymn of praise to our God. Many will see and fear the Lord and put their trust in him" (Psalm 40:3). Our singing inspires us but also those who hear it. May we all remember: our God is great and worthy of praise.

Patricia Raybon

PROVERBS

◆

The book of Proverbs is a compilation of wise, pithy sayings that tell us how to be wise, how to avoid being a fool, a scoffer, and a simple person. This collection of profound adages, compiled from a wide variety of sources, reflect practical information about how to live under God's rule and by His standards. While it is important when reading the Bible to consider context, Proverbs is a bit different because often the wisdom is doled out in one or two verses at a time—unrelated to each other. For instance, in reading Proverbs 20, you first get a warning about alcoholic beverages in verse one. And in verse two there is advice about how to handle a king's wrath. The two ideas seem disconnected, but both are valuable. The key to understanding the book may be Proverbs 1:7, which says, "The fear of the LORD is the beginning of knowledge, but fools despise wisdom and instruction."

OUTLINE

Introducing Wisdom Proverbs 1:1–33

Wisdom for Young People Proverbs 2:1–9:18

Solomon's Sayings about Godly Living Proverbs 10:1–24:34

Solomon's Sayings about Good Relationships Proverbs 25:1–29:27

Agur's Sayings Proverbs 30:1–33

Lemuel's Sayings Proverbs 31:1–31

Advice from My Father

Read Proverbs 3:1–7

*Trust in the LORD with all your heart
and lean not on your own understanding.*

PROVERBS 3:5

After being laid off from an editorial job, I prayed, asking for God to help me find a new one. But when weeks went by and nothing came of my attempts at networking and filling out applications, I began to pout. "Don't You know how important it is that I have a job?" I asked God, my arms folded in protest at my seemingly unanswered prayer.

When I talked to my father, who had often reminded me about believing God's promises, about my job situation, he said, "I want you to get to the point where you trust what God says."

My father's advice reminds me of Proverbs 3, which includes wise advice from a parent to a beloved child. This familiar passage was especially applicable to my situation: "Trust in the LORD with all your heart and lean not on your own understanding; in all your ways submit to him, and he will make your paths straight" (Proverbs 3:5–6). To "make . . . paths straight" means God will guide us toward His goals for our growth. His ultimate goal is that I become more like Him.

This does not mean that the paths He chooses will be easy. But I can choose to trust that His direction and timing are ultimately for my good.

Are you waiting on God for an answer? Choose to draw near to Him and trust that He will guide you.   *Linda Washington*

＊

That Was Awesome!

Read Proverbs 12:12, 24–28

Diligent hands will rule, but laziness ends in forced labor.

PROVERBS 12:24

It was the seventh-grader's first cross-country meet, but she didn't want to run. Although she'd been preparing for the event, she was afraid of doing poorly. Still, she started the race with everyone else. Later, one by one the other runners finished the two-mile course and crossed the finish line—everyone except the reluctant runner. Finally, her mom, who was watching for her daughter to finish, saw a lone figure in the distance. The mother went to the finish line, preparing to comfort a distraught competitor. Instead, when the young runner saw her mom, she exclaimed, "That was awesome!"

What can be awesome about finishing last? Finishing!

The girl had tried something difficult and had accomplished it! Scripture honors hard work and diligence, a concept often learned through sports or music or other things that require perseverance and effort.

Proverbs 12:24 says, "Diligent hands will rule, but laziness ends in forced labor." And later we read, "All hard work brings a profit, but mere talk leads only to poverty" (14:23). These wise principles—not promises—can help us serve God well.

God's plan for us always included work. Even before the fall, Adam was to "work [the Garden] and take care of it" (Genesis 2:15). And any effort we make should be done "with all [our] heart" (Colossians 3:23). Let's work in the strength He gives us—and leave the results to Him.

Dave Branon

The Two Bears

Read Proverbs 13:10–20

*Where there is strife, there is pride, but wisdom
is found in those who take advice.*

PROVERBS 13:10

Some years ago, my wife, Carolyn, and I spent a few days camping on the flanks of Mount Rainier in Washington State. When we were returning to our campsite one evening, we saw in the middle of a meadow two male bears boxing each other's ears. We stopped to watch.

There was a hiker nearby, and I asked him what the conflict was about. "A young female," he said.

"Where is she?" I asked.

"Oh, she left about twenty minutes ago," he chuckled. Thus, I gathered, the conflict at this point was not about the female bear but about being the toughest bear.

Most fights aren't about policy and principle, or about right and wrong; they're almost always about pride. The wise man of Proverbs swings his axe at the root of the problem when he writes: "Pride leads to conflict" (13:10 NLT). Quarrels are fueled by pride, by needing to be right, by wanting our way, or by defending our turf or our egos.

On the other side, wisdom resides with the well-advised—those who listen and learn, those who allow themselves to be instructed. There is wisdom in those who humble themselves—those who set aside their own selfish ambition; who acknowledge the limits of their own understanding; who listen to the other person's point of view; who allow their own ideas to be corrected. This is the wisdom from God that spreads peace wherever it goes.   *David Roper*

A Critical Reaction

Read Proverbs 15:1–2, 31–33

The one who is patient calms a quarrel.

PROVERBS 15:18

Tough words hurt. So my friend—an award-winning author—struggled with how to respond to the criticism he received. His new book had earned five-star reviews plus a major award. Then a respected magazine reviewer gave him a backhanded compliment, describing his book as well-written yet still criticizing it harshly. Turning to friends, he asked, "How should I reply?"

One friend advised, "Let it go." I shared advice from writing magazines, including tips to ignore such criticism or learn from it even while continuing to work and write.

Finally, however, I decided to see what Scripture—which has the best advice of all—has to say about how to react to strong criticism. The book of James advises, "Everyone should be quick to listen, slow to speak and slow to become angry" (1:19). The apostle Paul counsels us to "live in harmony with one another" (Romans 12:16).

An entire chapter of Proverbs, however, offers extended wisdom on reacting to disputes. "A gentle answer turns away wrath," says Proverbs 15:1. "The one who is patient calms a quarrel" (v. 18). Also, "The one who heeds correction gains understanding" (v. 32). Considering such wisdom, may God help us hold our tongues, as my friend did. More than all, however, wisdom instructs us to "fear the LORD" because "humility comes before honor" (v. 33).   *Patricia Raybon*

Biblical Perspective

Read Proverbs 17:19–22

A cheerful heart is good medicine, but a crushed spirit dries up the bones.

PROVERBS 17:22

Greg and Elizabeth have a regular "Joke Night" with their four school-age children. Each child brings several jokes they've read or heard (or made up themselves!) during the week to tell at the dinner table. This tradition has created joyful memories of fun shared around the table. Greg and Elizabeth even noticed the laughter was healthy for their children, lifting their spirits on difficult days.

The benefit of joyful conversation around the dinner table was observed by C. S. Lewis, who wrote, "The sun looks down on nothing half so good as a household laughing together over a meal."

The wisdom of fostering a joyful heart is found in Proverbs 17:22, where we read, "A cheerful heart is good medicine, but a crushed spirit dries up the bones." The proverb offers a "prescription" to stimulate health and healing—allowing joy to fill our hearts, a medicine that costs little and yields great results.

We all need this biblical prescription. When we bring joy into our conversations, it can put a disagreement into perspective. It can help us to experience peace, even after a stressful test at school or a difficult day at work. Laughter among family and friends can create a safe place where we both know and feel that we're loved.

Do you need to incorporate more laughter into your life as "good medicine" for your spirit? Remember, you have encouragement from Scripture to cultivate a cheerful heart. *Lisa Samra*

Timely Words

Read Proverbs 25:11–15

A WORD *fitly spoken is like apples of gold in settings of silver.*
PROVERBS 25:11 NKJV

You may have heard the adage, "Timing is everything." According to the Bible, good timing applies to our words and speech too. Think of a time when God used you to bring a timely word to refresh someone, or when you wanted to speak, but it was wiser for you to remain silent.

The Bible says that there is an appropriate time to speak (Ecclesiastes 3:7). Solomon compared properly timed and well-spoken words with golden apples in a silver setting—beautiful, valuable, and carefully crafted (Proverbs 25:11–12). Knowing the right time to speak is beneficial for both the speaker and hearer, whether they are words of love, encouragement, or rebuke. Keeping silent also has its place and time. When tempted to deride, belittle, or slander a neighbor, Solomon said that it is wise to hold our tongue, recognizing the appropriate time for silence (11:12–13). When talkativeness or anger tempts us to sin against God or another human being, resistance comes by being slow to speak (10:19; James 1:19).

It's often hard to know what to say and when to say it. The Spirit will help us to be discerning. He will help us use the right words at the right time and in the right manner, for the good of others and for His honor.   *Marvin Williams*

MAY 2

Windfall

Read Proverbs 30:1–9

Give us today our daily bread.
MATTHEW 6:11

Upon winning $314 million in a lottery, a happy business owner expressed noble desires. He wanted to start a charitable foundation, put laid-off workers back on the job, and do nice things for his family. Already wealthy, he told reporters the big win wouldn't change him.

A few years later, a follow-up article described a different outcome. Since winning the biggest of all lotteries, the man had run into legal problems, lost his personal reputation, and gambled away all of his money.

A thoughtful man by the name of Agur wrote words that anticipate such heartbreak. Brought low by the awareness of his own natural inclinations (Proverbs 30:2–3), Agur saw the dangers of having too much or too little. So he prayed, "Give me neither poverty nor riches, but give me only my daily bread. Otherwise, I may have too much and disown you and say, 'Who is the LORD?' Or may I become poor and steal, and so dishonor the name of my God" (vv. 8–9).

Agur saw the special challenges that come both with wealth and poverty, but also with our own tendencies. Each gives us reason for caution. Together they show our need for the One who taught us to pray, "Give us today our daily bread." *Mart DeHaan*

ECCLESIASTES

It would not be wise to read the book of Ecclesiastes as one would read the Proverbs. Whereas the aphorisms in the Proverbs can, for the most part, be read one at a time and taken from their verse moorings without damaging the meaning, Ecclesiastes cannot be read as a series of unrelated truisms. The context is all-important.

OUTLINE

A Season for Everything

Read Ecclesiastes 3:1–13

To everything there is a season.

ECCLESIASTES 3:1 NKJV

In the 1960s, the folk-rock band The Byrds popularized the song "Turn! Turn! Turn!" It climbed to the top spot on the Billboard Hot 100 chart and gained worldwide popularity. People seemed captivated by the lyrics. Interestingly, though, except for the last line, those lyrics are from the Old Testament book of Ecclesiastes.

"To everything there is a season," proclaims the writer of Ecclesiastes, "a time for every purpose under heaven" (3:1 NKJV). He then lists some of the seasons in human experience: birth and death, gain and loss, tears and laughter, mourning and dancing. Just as the seasons in nature change, so do the seasons in our lives. Our circumstances never stay the same for long.

Sometimes we welcome change in our lives. But often it is difficult, especially when it involves sorrow and loss. Yet even then we can be thankful that God does not change. "I am the LORD," He said through the prophet Malachi, "I do not change" (Malachi 3:6 NKJV).

Because God remains the same, we can rely on Him through the shifting seasons of life. His presence is always with us (Psalm 46:1), His peace has the power to guard our hearts (Philippians 4:7), and His love provides security for our souls (Romans 8:39).

Jennifer Benson Schuldt

Never Alone

Read Ecclesiastes 4:8-12

*Two are better than one . . . If either of them
falls down, one can help the other up.*

ECCLESIASTES 4:9–10

"It can be an affliction more harrowing than homelessness, hunger or disease," wrote Maggie Fergusson back in 1843 in the magazine *The Economist*. Her subject? Loneliness. Fergusson chronicled the increasing rates of loneliness, irrespective of one's social or economic status, using heart-wrenching examples of what it feels like to be lonely.

The hurt of feeling alone isn't new to our day. Indeed, the pain of isolation echoes off the pages of the ancient book of Ecclesiastes. Often attributed to King Solomon, the book captures the sorrow of those who seem to lack any meaningful relationships (4:7–8). The speaker lamented that it's possible to acquire significant wealth and yet experience no value from it because there's no one to share it with.

But the speaker also recognized the beauty of companionship, writing that friends help you accomplish more than you could achieve on your own (v. 9); companions help in times of need (v. 10); partners bring comfort (v. 11); and friends can provide protection in difficult situations (v. 12).

Loneliness is a significant struggle—God created us to offer and receive the benefits of friendship and community. If you're feeling alone, pray that God would help you form meaningful connections with others. In the meantime, find encouragement in the reality that the believer is never truly alone because Jesus's Spirit is always with us (Matthew 28:20).

Lisa Samra

Your Eulogy

Read Ecclesiastes 7:1–6

Death is the destiny of everyone;
the living should take this to heart.

ECCLESIASTES 7:2

My heart is full from attending the funeral of a faithful woman. Her life wasn't spectacular. She wasn't known widely outside her church, neighbors, and friends. But she loved Jesus, her seven children, and her twenty-five grandchildren. She laughed easily, served generously, and could hit a softball a long way.

Ecclesiastes says, "It is better to go to a house of mourning than to go to a house of feasting" (7:2). "The heart of the wise is in the house of mourning" because there we learn what matters most (7:4). *New York Times* columnist David Brooks says there are two kinds of virtues: those that look good on a résumé and those you want said at your funeral. Sometimes these overlap, though often they seem to compete. When in doubt, always choose the eulogy virtues.

The woman in the casket didn't have a résumé, but her children testified that "she rocked Proverbs 31" and its description of a godly woman. She inspired them to love Jesus and care for others. As Paul said, "Follow my example, as I follow the example of Christ" (1 Corinthians 11:1), so they challenged us to imitate their mother's life as she imitated Jesus.

What will be said at your funeral? What do you want said? It's not too late to develop eulogy virtues. Rest in Jesus. His salvation frees us to live for what matters most.   *Mike Wittmer*

SONG OF SONGS

◆

Is the book about the love relationship between a man and a woman, or is it an allegory of our relationship with God? That is the question. Some have suggested that this is the actual love story between Solomon and a woman. Others see it as allegorical as a picture of the union between Christ and the church. Or between Christ and a believer as He attempts to win that person to faith.

OUTLINE

Love Story Song of Songs 1:1–3:5

A Wedding Song Song of Songs 3:6–5:1

Marriage Realities Song of Songs 5:2–7:10

The Relationship Matures Song of Songs 7:11–8:14

No Wonder

Read Song of Songs 1:1–4

We love Him because He first loved us.

1 JOHN 4:19 NKJV

"He's perfect for you," my friend told me. She was talking about a guy she had just met. She described his kind eyes, his kind smile, and his kind heart. When I met him I had to agree. Today he's my husband, and no wonder I love him!

In the Song of Solomon the bride describes her lover. His love is better than wine and more fragrant than ointments. His name is sweeter than anything in this world. So she concludes that it's no wonder he is loved.

But there is Someone far greater than any earthly loved one, Someone whose love is also better than wine. His love satisfies our every need. His "fragrance" is better than any perfume because when He gave himself for us, His sacrifice became a sweet-smelling aroma to God (Ephesians 5:2). Finally, His name is above every name (Philippians 2:9). No wonder we love Him!

It is a privilege to love Jesus. It is the best experience in life! Do we take the time to tell Him so? Do we express with words the beauty of our Savior? If we show His beauty with our lives, others will say, "No wonder you love Him!"   *Keila Ochoa*

Indestructible Love

Read Song of Songs 8:6–7

Many waters cannot quench love;
rivers cannot sweep it away.

SONG OF SONGS 8:7

When we first saw the stream in our backyard, it was just a thin vein of water trickling through a bed of rocks in the heat of the summer. Heavy wooden planks served as a bridge we could easily cross. Months later, torrents of rain pounded our area for several days in a row. Our tame little creek swelled into a quick-moving river four-feet deep and ten-feet wide! The force of this water heaved the bridgeboards up and deposited them several feet away.

Rushing water has the potential to overwhelm almost anything that stands in its path. Yet there's something that's indestructible in the face of a flood or other forces that might threaten to destroy it—love. "Many waters cannot quench love; rivers cannot sweep it away" (Song of Songs 8:7). Love's persistent strength and intensity is often present in romantic relationships, but it's only fully expressed in the love God has for people through His Son, Jesus Christ.

When the things we consider to be sturdy and dependable are swept away, our disappointment can open the door to a new understanding of God's love for us. His affection is higher and deeper and stronger and longer lasting than anything on earth. Whatever we face, we face with Him beside us—holding us up, helping us along, and reminding us that we're loved. *Jennifer Benson Schuldt*

PART 4

The Major Prophets

Isaiah, Jeremiah, Lamentations, Ezekiel, Daniel

Although the next two sections are labeled major and minor prophets, the distinction is not one of importance but of length. The first five books are much longer (except for Lamentations, which is attached to Jeremiah because he wrote it) than the last twelve. The prophets were God's representatives, and they were called by Him to call the Hebrew people to repentance. They made it clear that if there was no repentance, judgment was in their future. While that judgment came through invasion by outsiders and exile into Babylon, the people of Judah were eventually allowed to return to their homeland.

ISAIAH

Judgment is coming, but there is hope. That is the bad news, good news message of Isaiah's prophecy. He kicks off this long prophetic book with a word of judgment on the kingdoms of Judah and Israel because of their disregard for the covenant God has made with them, accentuated by their idol worship. But in the midst of the judgment comes word of something hopeful—a branch, a child, the prospect of a mighty counselor. We now know that Isaiah was speaking of the coming Messiah, Jesus. Yet the rejection of God by his contemporaries was still on the prophet's mind, so he spoke of God's judgment on many surrounding countries. Isaiah acts heroically in helping to stop Assyria from destroying Jerusalem before he writes further about the coming Messiah. At the end, Isaiah exhorts his readers to live righteously. It is a long, complicated book, but as always, the goal of the people should be to trust God, worship Him the right way, and live according to His standards—while anticipating a coming Messiah.

OUTLINE

Hope Blossoms

Read Isaiah 35:1–4

The desert and the parched land will be glad;
the wilderness will rejoice and blossom.

ISAIAH 35:1

In the city of Philadelphia, when weedy vacant lots were cleaned up and brightened with beautiful flowers and trees, nearby residents also brightened in overall mental health. This proved especially true for those who struggled economically.

"There's a growing body of evidence that green space can have an impact on mental health," said Dr. Eugenia South, "and that's particularly important for people living in poorer neighborhoods." South, a faculty member at the University of Pennsylvania's Perelman School of Medicine, is coauthor of a study on the subject.

The downtrodden people of Israel and Judah found fresh hope in the prophet Isaiah's vision of their beautiful restoration by God. Amid all the doom and judgment Isaiah foretold, this bright promise took root: "The desert and the parched land will be glad; the wilderness will rejoice and blossom. Like the crocus, it will burst into bloom; it will rejoice greatly and shout for joy" (Isaiah 35:1–2).

No matter our situation today, we too can rejoice in the beautiful ways our heavenly Father restores us with fresh hope, including through His creation. When we feel down, reflecting on His glory and splendor will bolster us. "Strengthen the feeble hands, steady the knees that give way," Isaiah encouraged (v. 3).

Can a few flowers rekindle our hope? A prophet said yes. So does our hope-giving God. *Patricia Raybon*

Hold Steady

Read Isaiah 41:10–13

I am the LORD your God who takes hold of your right hand.
ISAIAH 41:13

Harriet Tubman was one of the great American heroes of the nineteenth century. Showing remarkable courage, she guided more than three hundred fellow slaves to freedom after she first escaped slavery by crossing into free territory in the United States North. Not content to simply enjoy her own freedom, she ventured back into slave states nineteen times to lead friends, family, and strangers to freedom, sometimes guiding people on foot all the way to Canada.

What drove Tubman to such brave action? A woman of deep faith, she at one time said this: "I always told God, I'm going to hold steady on you, and you've got to see me through." Her dependence on God's guidance as she led people out of slavery was a hallmark of her success.

What does it mean to "hold steady" to God? A verse in the prophecy of Isaiah might help us see that in reality it's He who holds us as we grab His hand. Isaiah quotes God, who said, "I am the LORD your God who takes hold of your right hand and says to you, Do not fear; I will help you" (41:13).

Harriet held tightly to God, and He saw her through. What challenges are you facing? Hold steady to God as He "takes hold" of your hand and your life. "Do not fear." He will help you.   *Dave Branon*

✦

A Road Not Traveled

Read Isaiah 42:10–17

I will lead the blind by ways they have not known,
along unfamiliar paths I will guide them.

ISAIAH 42:16

People ask me if I have a five-year plan. How can I plan five years "down the road" on a road I've never traveled?

I think back to the 1960s when I was a minister to students at Stanford University. I'd been a physical education major in college and had a lot of fun, but I left no record of being a scholar. I felt wholly inadequate in my new position. Most days I wandered around the campus, a blind man groping in the darkness, asking God to show me what to do. One day a student "out of the blue" asked me to lead a Bible study in his fraternity. It was a beginning.

God doesn't stand at a juncture and point the way: He's a guide, not a signpost. He walks with us, leading us down paths we never envisioned. All we have to do is walk alongside Him.

The path won't be easy; there'll be "rough places" along the way. But God has promised that He will "turn the darkness into light" and "will not forsake" us (Isaiah 42:16). He'll be with us all the way.

Paul said that God is "able to do immeasurably more than all we ask or imagine" (Ephesians 3:20). We can scheme and envision, but our Lord's imagination far transcends our plans. We must hold them loosely and see what God has in mind.   *David Roper*

A Wide, Sweeping Grace

Read Isaiah 44:21–23

I have swept away your offenses.

Isaiah 44:22

Alexa, Amazon's voice-controlled device, has an interesting feature: it can erase everything you say. Whatever you've asked Alexa to do, whatever information you've asked Alexa to retrieve, one simple sentence ("Delete everything I said today") sweeps it all clean, as if it never happened. It's too bad that the rest of our life doesn't have this capability. Every misspoken word, every disgraceful act, every moment we wish we could erase—we'd just speak the command, and the entire mess would disappear.

There's good news, though. God does offer each of us a clean start. Only, He goes far deeper than merely deleting our mistakes or bad behavior. God provides redemption, a deep healing that transforms us and makes us new. "Return to me," He says, "I have redeemed you" (Isaiah 44:22). Even though Israel rebelled and disobeyed, God reached out to them with lavish mercy. He "swept away [their] offenses like a cloud, [their] sins like the morning mist" (v. 22). He gathered all their shame and failures and washed them away with His wide, sweeping grace.

God will do the same with our sin and blunders. There's no mistake He can't mend, no wound He can't heal. God's mercy heals and redeems the most painful places in our soul—even the ones we've hidden for so very long. His mercy sweeps away all our guilt, washes away every regret. *Winn Collier*

Listening beyond the Stars

Read Isaiah 55:1–7

Seek the LORD while he may be found.

ISAIAH 55:6

Imagine life without mobile phones, Wi-Fi, GPS, Bluetooth devices, or microwave ovens. That's the way it is in the little town of Green Bank, West Virginia, known as "the quietest town in America." It's also the location of the Green Bank Observatory, the world's largest steerable radio telescope. The telescope needs "quiet" to "listen" to naturally occurring radio waves emitted by the movement of pulsars and galaxies in deep space. It has a surface area larger than a football field and stands in the center of the National Radio Quiet Zone, a thirteen thousand-square-mile area established to prevent electronic interference to the telescope's extreme sensitivity.

This intentional quiet enables scientists to hear "the music of the spheres." It also reminds me of our need to quiet ourselves enough to listen to the One who created the universe. God communicated to a wayward and distracted people through the prophet Isaiah, "Give ear and come to me; listen, that you may live. I will make an everlasting covenant with you" (Isaiah 55:3). God promises His faithful love to all who will seek Him and turn to Him for forgiveness.

We listen intentionally to God by turning from our distractions to meet Him in Scripture and in prayer. God isn't distant. He longs for us to make time for Him so He can be the priority of our daily lives and then for eternity. *James Banks*

JEREMIAH

In a nutshell, this book is about desolation, destruction, and depravity. There is no way to clean this up and make it shine. Jeremiah has been called by God (probably just after he grew out of his teen years) to proclaim God's good news to a nation that can't seem to keep its eyes away from idols and other useless distractions. So Jeremiah does it. He tells his people to repent, to turn to God. He dedicates himself totally to this thankless task, forsaking even marriage in order to stay focused on his message. Yet even when he promises something new to the people (chapters 30–33), they and their kings reject his message. He even tells them about the coming captivity if they don't turn things around. It is the sad story of a faithful man and a completely unfaithful kingdom.

OUTLINE

The Call of Jeremiah Jeremiah 1:1–19

Jeremiah's Twelve Sermons Jeremiah 2:1–25:38

  1. **A Nation's Sins** Jeremiah 2:1–3:5

  2. **Repent!** Jeremiah 3:6–6:30

  3. **Judgment for Hypocrisy** Jeremiah 7:1–10:25

  4. **A Broken Covenant** Jeremiah 11:1–12:17

  5. **Two Symbols** Jeremiah 13:1–27

  6. **Judgment** Jeremiah 14:1–15:21

  7. **Unmarried** Jeremiah 16:1–17:27

  8. **Potter and His Clay** Jeremiah 18:1–20:18

  9. **Two Kinds of Kings** Jeremiah 21:1–23:8

  10. **False Prophets** Jeremiah 23:9–40

  11. **Two Kinds of Figs** Jeremiah 24:1–10

  12. **Captivity** Jeremiah 25:1–38

I Am with You

Read Jeremiah 1:1–10

Do not be afraid of them, for I am with you.
JEREMIAH 1:8

When I served as an intern for a Christian magazine, I wrote a story about a person who had become a Christian. In a dramatic change, he said goodbye to his former life and embraced his new Master: Jesus. A few days after the magazine hit the street, an anonymous caller threatened, "Be careful, Darmani. We are watching you! Your life is in danger in this country if you write such stories."

That was not the only time I have been threatened for pointing people to Christ. On one occasion a man told me to vanish with the tract I was giving him or else! In both cases, I cowered. But these were only verbal threats. Many Christians have had threats carried out against them. In some cases simply living a godly lifestyle attracts mistreatment from people.

The Lord told Jeremiah, "You must go to everyone I send you to and say whatever I command you" (Jeremiah 1:7), and Jesus told His disciples, "I am sending you out like sheep among wolves" (Matthew 10:16). Yes, we may encounter threats, hardships, and even pain. But God assures us of His presence. "I am with you," He told Jeremiah (Jeremiah 1:8), and Jesus assured His followers, "I am with you always" (Matthew 28:20).

Whatever struggles we face in our attempt to live for the Lord, we can trust in the Lord's presence. *Lawrence Darmani*

Hungry for God

Read Jeremiah 15:15–21

When your WORDS came, I ate them;
they were my joy and my heart's delight.

JEREMIAH 15:16

A new believer in Jesus was desperate to read the Bible. However, he'd lost his eyesight and both hands in an explosion. When he heard about a woman who read Braille with her lips, he tried to do the same—only to discover that the nerve endings of his lips had also been destroyed. Later, he was filled with joy when he discovered that he could feel the Braille characters with his tongue! He had found a way to read and enjoy the Scriptures.

Joy and delight were the emotions the prophet Jeremiah experienced when he received God's words. "When your words came, I ate them," he said, "they were my joy and my heart's delight" (Jeremiah 15:16). Unlike the people of Judah who despised His words (8:9), Jeremiah had been obedient and rejoiced in them. His obedience, however, also led to the prophet being rejected by his own people and persecuted unfairly (15:17).

Some of us may have experienced something similar. We once read the Bible with joy, but obedience to God led to suffering and rejection from others. Like Jeremiah, we can bring our confusion to God. He answered Jeremiah by repeating the promise He gave him when He first called him to be a prophet (vv. 19–21; see 1:18–19). God reminded him that He never lets His people down. We can have this same confidence too. He's faithful and will never abandon us.   *Poh Fang Chia*

MAY 15

Don't Touch the Fence

Read Jeremiah 18:1–12

The LORD . . . sent WORD to them . . . again and again,
because he had pity on his people.
2 CHRONICLES 36:15

As a young girl I went with my parents to visit my great-grandmother, who lived near a farm. Her yard was enclosed by an electric fence, which prevented cows from grazing on her grass. When I asked my parents if I could play outside, they consented, but explained that touching the fence would result in an electric shock.

Unfortunately, I ignored their warning, put a finger to the barbed wire, and was zapped by an electrical current strong enough to teach a cow a lesson. I knew then that my parents had warned me because they loved me and didn't want me to get hurt.

When God saw the ancient Israelites in Jerusalem crafting and worshiping idols, He "sent word to them . . . again and again, because he had pity on his people" (2 Chronicles 36:15). God spoke through the prophet Jeremiah, but the people said, "We will continue with our own plans" (Jeremiah 18:12). Because of this, God allowed Nebuchadnezzar to destroy Jerusalem and capture most of its inhabitants.

Maybe God is warning you today about some sin in your life. If so, be encouraged. That is proof of His compassion for us (Hebrews 12:5–6). He sees what's ahead and wants us to avoid the problems that will come.   *Jennifer Benson Schuldt*

The Forecaster's Mistake

Read Jeremiah 23:16–22

Let the one who has my WORD *speak it faithfully.*
JEREMIAH 23:28

At noon on September 21, 1938, a young meteorologist warned the US Weather Bureau of two fronts forcing a hurricane northward toward New England. But the chief of forecasting scoffed at Charles Pierce's prediction. Surely a tropical storm wouldn't strike so far north.

Two hours later, the 1938 New England Hurricane made landfall on Long Island. By 4:00 p.m. it had reached New England, tossing ships onto land as homes crumbled into the sea. More than six hundred people died. Had the victims received Pierce's warning—based on solid data and his detailed maps—they likely would have survived.

The concept of knowing whose word to heed has precedent in Scripture. In Jeremiah's day, God warned His people against false prophets. "Do not listen [to them]," He said. "They fill you with false hopes. They speak visions from their own minds, not from the mouth of the LORD" (Jeremiah 23:16). God said of them, "If they had stood in my council, they would have proclaimed my words to my people" (v. 22).

"False prophets" are still with us. "Experts" dispense advice while ignoring God altogether or twisting His words to suit their purposes. But through His Word and Spirit, God has given us what we need to begin to discern the false from the true. As we gauge everything by the truth of His Word, our own words and lives will increasingly reflect that truth to others.   *Tim Gustafson*

Lovable!

Read Jeremiah 31:1–6

I have loved you with an everlasting love;
I have drawn you with unfailing kindness.

JEREMIAH 31:3

That exclamation came from my daughter as she got ready one morning. I didn't know what she meant. Then she tapped her shirt, a hand-me-down from a cousin. Across the front was that word: "Lovable." I gave her a big hug, and she smiled with pure joy. "You are lovable!" I echoed. Her smile grew even bigger, if that was possible, as she skipped away, repeating the word over and over again.

I'm hardly a perfect father. But that moment was perfect. In that spontaneous, beautiful interaction, I glimpsed in my girl's radiant face what receiving unconditional love looked like: It was a portrait of delight. She knew the word on her shirt corresponded completely with how her daddy felt about her.

How many of us know in our hearts that we are loved by a Father whose affection for us is limitless? Sometimes we struggle with this truth. The Israelites did. They wondered if their trials meant God no longer loved them. But in Jeremiah 31:3, the prophet reminds them of what God said in the past: "I have loved you with an everlasting love." We too long for such unconditional love. Yet the wounds, disappointments, and mistakes we experience can make us feel anything but lovable. But God opens His arms—the arms of a perfect Father—and invites us to experience and rest in His love. *Adam Holz*

The Maker of the Moon

Read Jeremiah 31:33–37

*[The LORD said,] "I will be their God,
and they will be my people."*

JEREMIAH 31:33

After astronauts set the *Eagle* down in the Sea of Tranquility, Neil Armstrong stepped off the lunar lander and said, "That's one small step for man, one giant leap for mankind." He was the first human to walk on the surface of the moon. Other space travelers followed, including the commander of the last Apollo mission, Gene Cernan. "There I was, and there you are, the Earth—dynamic, overwhelming, and I felt . . . it was just too beautiful to happen by accident," Cernan said, "There has to be somebody bigger than you and bigger than me." Even from their unique view in deep space, these men understood their smallness in comparison to the vastness of the universe.

The prophet Jeremiah also considered the immensity of God as Creator and Sustainer of the earth and beyond. The Maker of all promised to reveal himself intimately as He offered His people love, forgiveness, and hope (Jeremiah 31:33–34). Jeremiah affirms God's enormity as He who "appoints the sun to shine by day, who decrees the moon and stars to shine by night" (v. 35). Our Creator and Lord Almighty will reign above all as He works to redeem all of His people (vv. 36–37).

We'll never finish exploring the immeasurable vastness of the heavens and depths of the earth's foundations. But we can stand in awe at the complexity of the universe and trust the maker of the moon—and everything else. *Xochitl Dixon*

LAMENTATIONS

---◆---

This short book of lamentations follows the book of Jeremiah, in which he continually tried to warn the people of Jerusalem about their sin against God. But because they didn't listen, destruction fell. Thus Lamentations mourns that destruction. It is a detailing of all that was lost through the disobedience of God's people.

OUTLINE

When the Splendor Is Gone

Read Lamentations 3:13–24

*Because of the LORD's great love we are not
consumed, for his compassions never fail.*

LAMENTATIONS 3:22

I can never recapture the splendor that was our daughter Melissa. Fading from my memory are those wonderful times when we watched her joyfully playing high school volleyball. And it's sometimes hard to remember the shy smile of contentment that crossed her face when we were doing family activities. Her death at age seventeen dropped a curtain on the joy of her presence.

In the book of Lamentations, Jeremiah's words show he understood that the heart can be punctured. "My splendor is gone," he said, "and all that I had hoped from the LORD" (3:18). His situation was far different from yours and mine. He had preached God's judgment, and he saw Jerusalem defeated. The splendor was gone because he felt defeated (v. 12), isolated (v. 14), and abandoned by God (vv. 15–20).

But that's not the end of his story. Light shined through. Jeremiah, burdened and broken, stammered out "I have hope" (v. 21)—hope that comes from realizing that "because of the LORD's great love we are not consumed" (v. 22). And here is just what we need to remember when the splendor is gone: God's "compassions never fail. They are new every morning" (vv. 22–23).

Even in our darkest days, God's great faithfulness shines through.

Dave Branon

Grieving from A to Z

Read Lamentations 3:25–33

Though he brings grief, he will show compassion.
LAMENTATIONS 3:32

Jerusalem was engulfed in flames, and the prophet Jeremiah wept. His prediction of divine judgment had largely gone unheeded. Now his terrible prophecy had come to pass with horrifying vividness. The short book of Lamentations records the prophet's grieving process over the destruction of Jerusalem.

Jeremiah organized the book around the twenty-two letters of the Hebrew alphabet, using a technique of alphabetic acrostics to aid the reader in memorizing the passages more easily. But using this technique also shows that he didn't cut short his grieving process. He took deliberate and intentional time to reflect upon and even to write down his heartbreak. You might say he was learning to grieve from A to Z.

In the midst of his grief, the comfort of God surfaced. Reminders of God's sovereignty and goodness gave the prophet hope as he faced the future: "No one is cast off by the Lord forever. Though he brings grief, he will show compassion, so great is his unfailing love" (Lamentations 3:31–32).

If you've recently experienced a painful loss, remember to take adequate time to grieve and to reflect upon God's goodness. Then you will be able to experience His comfort and hope for the future.

Dennis Fisher

EZEKIEL

◆

As an eyewitness to the destruction of Jerusalem, Ezekiel is the perfect prophet to talk to the Jewish people about both the glory and presence of God. Ezekiel is in Jerusalem when he sees the glory of God in a spectacular vision—symbolizing the soon departure of that glory from the temple. God shows Ezekiel the actions (chapter 8) that will cause the glory to depart the temple. And in chapter 10, the departure is depicted. Two chapters later, Ezekiel performs a skit to show the people what is in store for them. He packs up a suitcase (or whatever they used back then) and escaped the city through a hole he has to dig through the wall. Jeremiah and Ezekiel, in their own ways, have told the people of their fate if they don't repent. After the captivity begins for the Jews, Ezekiel also pronounces judgment on neighboring countries: Ammon, Tyre, Egypt, and others. The remainder of the book looks ahead to the coming hope God will bring through His plan of redemption—extending all the way to the New Jerusalem.

OUTLINE

The Call of Ezekiel Ezekiel 1:1–3:27
Judah Faces Judgment Ezekiel 4:1–24:27
The Gentiles Face Judgment Ezekiel 25:1–32:32
Israel's Restoration Ezekiel 33:1–48:35

Choosing to Change

Read Ezekiel 18:25–32

Rid yourselves of all the offenses you have committed,
and get a new heart and a new spirit.

EZEKIEL 18:31

When my son acquired a small robot, he had fun programming it to perform simple tasks. He could make it move forward, stop, and then retrace its steps. He could even get it to beep and replay recorded noises. The robot did exactly what my son told it to do. It never laughed spontaneously or veered off in an unplanned direction. It had no choice.

When God created humans, He didn't make robots. God made us in His image, and this means we can think, reason, and make decisions. We're able to choose between right and wrong. Even if we have made a habit of disobeying God, we can decide to redirect our lives.

When the ancient Israelites found themselves in trouble with God, He spoke to them through the prophet Ezekiel. Ezekiel said, "Repent! Turn away from all your offenses; then sin will not be your downfall. . . . Get a new heart and a new spirit" (Ezekiel 18:30–31).

This kind of change can begin with just one choice, empowered by the Holy Spirit (Romans 8:13). It might mean saying no at a critical moment. No more gossip. No more greed. No more jealousy. No more _____ . (You fill in the blank.) If you know Jesus, you're not a slave to sin. You can choose to change, and with God's help, this personal revolution can start today. *Jennifer Benson Schuldt*

God Our Resource

Read Ezekiel 34:5–12

I will rescue them from all the places where they were scattered.
EZEKIEL 34:12

In the open sea, a rescuer positioned her kayak to assist panicked swimmers competing in a triathlon. "Don't grab the middle of the boat!" she called to swimmers, knowing such a move would capsize her craft. Instead, she directed weary swimmers to the bow, or front, of the kayak. There they could grab a loop, allowing the safety kayaker to help rescue them.

Whenever life or people threaten to pull us under, as believers in Jesus, we know we have a Rescuer. "For this is what the Sovereign LORD says: I myself will search for my sheep . . . I will rescue them from all the places where they were scattered" (Ezekiel 34:11–12).

This was the prophet Ezekiel's assurance to God's people when they were in exile. Their leaders had neglected and exploited them, plundering their lives and caring "for themselves rather than for [God's] flock" (v. 8). As a result, the people "were scattered over the whole earth, and no one searched or looked for them" (v. 6).

But "I will rescue my flock," declared the Lord (v. 10), and His promise still holds.

What do we need to do? Hold fast to almighty God and His promises. "I myself will search for my sheep and look after them," He says (v. 11). That's a saving promise worth holding tightly.

Patricia Raybon

Extraordinary Showers

Read Ezekiel 34:25–31

There will be showers of blessing.

EZEKIEL 34:26

What do fish, tadpoles, and spiders have in common? They have all fallen from the sky like rain in various parts of the world. Fish fell on the Australian town of Lajamanu. Tadpoles pelted areas of central Japan on multiple occasions. Spiders showered down on the San Bernardo Mountains in Argentina. Although scientists suspect that the wind plays a part in these intriguing showers, no one can fully explain them.

The prophet Ezekiel described a far more extraordinary downpour—a shower of blessing (Ezekiel 34:26). Ezekiel spoke of a time when God would send blessings like rain to refresh His people. The Israelites would be safe from enemy nations. They would have enough food, be liberated from slavery, and be freed from shame (vv. 27–29). These gifts would revive Israel's relationship with God. The people would know that God was with them, and that "they, the Israelites, [were his] people" (v. 30).

God blesses His modern-day followers too (James 1:17). Sometimes blessings abound like rain; sometimes they trickle in one by one. Whether many or few, the good things we receive come with a message from God: I see your needs. You are mine, and I will care for you.

Jennifer Benson Schuldt

How to Get a New Heart

Read Ezekiel 36:26–31

I will give you a new heart and put a new spirit in you.

EZEKIEL 36:26

A friend who is a heart transplant cardiologist has an appreciation of Ezekiel 36:26 that not many of us can understand. Mike manages the pre-operation and post-operation care for heart-transplant patients. He's often in the operating room as surgeons remove diseased, discolored hearts and replace them with vibrant, pink "new" donor hearts.

Mike explains that the process for selecting who gets a "new" physical heart is similar to who can get a "new heart" from God (Ezekiel 36:26). In both cases, need alone is the criterion.

Ezekiel's mention of the people of Israel someday getting a "new heart" is a foreshadowing of the change that takes place at salvation. Ephesians 4:24 and 2 Corinthians 5:17 refer to it as "new self" and "new creation." For the Israelites of Ezekiel's day and for those of us living today, only one criterion must be met for us to acquire a "transplant." We must need it. It matters not whether we're rich or poor, respected or scorned. Citizenship, social status, and ethnicity are inconsequential. If we need a new heart from God, we can have one through faith in Jesus Christ's death and resurrection.

What indicates that need? As sinners, all of us need a new heart. Have you had a spiritual heart transplant?   *Dave Branon*

DANIEL

◆

Babylon was a powerful country—powerful enough to send an army nine hundred miles to subdue Jerusalem and surround Judah, and transport thousands of Jews back home. It had built a magnificent city and had established its kingdom all the way from Egypt north to Assyria, west to the Mediterranean, and east to the Persian Gulf. Its strength was great and its kings were powerful. But they were no match for God, as Daniel's book shows. From Daniel's diet being better than theirs to Daniel's dream interpretations being far better than the king's wisest men's guess to Nebuchadnezzar's inability to kill three young men who wouldn't bow to him—God proved his dominance in Daniel's book. Then, at just the time God said it would happen, the captivity ended. And Daniel's grand prophecies at the end of the book showed that God has sovereignty over the leaders of great nations then and into the future. The book of Daniel leaves no doubt about God's power over even the strongest world leaders.

OUTLINE

Introducing Daniel Daniel 1:1–21

Prophecies and Stories about the Gentiles Daniel 2:1–7:28

Visions of Israel's Future Daniel 8:1–12:13

Shine On!

Read Daniel 1:1–16

We want you to know, Your Majesty, that we will not serve your gods or worship the image of gold you have set up.

DANIEL 3:18

Ashpenaz, a high court official in ancient Babylon, was committed to banishing any testimony of Israel's God from his kingdom. His strategy focused on young leadership from the captive Hebrews. Ashpenaz gave the captives new names to honor the pagan gods of Babylon. This made sense to him, because their original Hebrew names honored their God (Daniel 1:6).

But the life choices of those captives were a far more powerful witness than any label put on them. When faced with a literal trial by fire, the young men would not bow down and worship the golden idol. Instead, they accepted the punishment of being cast into the fiery furnace—confident in God's sovereignty and care (chapter 3).

Do you know unbelievers who try to pressure you to fit in with their lifestyle? If you don't party with them, follow a questionable business practice, or laugh at an offensive joke, do you get the cold shoulder? People may even call you names because you won't run with their crowd. But when you're rejected because of your loyalty to God, you can live in a way that honors the Father.

It doesn't matter what others call us. How we live our lives before God does. What's important is that we always let our light shine.

Dennis Fisher

Trusting God Even If

Read Daniel 3:13–25

The God we serve is able to deliver us.

DANIEL 3:17

Due to an injury that occurred in 1992, I suffer from chronic pain in my upper back, shoulders, and neck. During the most excruciating and disheartening moments, it's not always easy to trust or praise the Lord. But when my situation feels unbearable, God's constant presence comforts me. He strengthens me and reassures me of His unchanging goodness, limitless power, and sustaining grace. And when I'm tempted to doubt my Lord, I'm encouraged by the determined faith of Shadrach, Meshach, and Abednego. They worshiped God and trusted He was with them, even when their situation seemed hopeless.

When King Nebuchadnezzar threatened to throw them into a blazing furnace if they didn't turn away from the true God to worship his golden statue (Daniel 3:13–15), these three men displayed courageous and confident faith. They never doubted the Lord was worthy of their worship (v. 17), "even if" He didn't rescue them from their current predicament (v. 18). And God didn't leave them alone in their time of need; He joined and protected them in the furnace (vv. 24–25).

God doesn't leave us alone either. He remains with us through trials that can feel as destructive as Nebuchadnezzar's furnace. Even if our suffering doesn't end on this side of eternity, God is and always will be mighty, trustworthy, and good. We can rely on His constant and loving presence. *Xochitl Dixon*

Living with Lions

Read Daniel 6:18–28

He is the living God and he endures forever.

Daniel 6:26

When I visited a museum in Chicago, I saw one of the original Striding Lions of Babylon. It was a large mural-type image of a winged lion with a ferocious expression. Symbolizing Ishtar, the Babylonian goddess of love and war, the lion was an example of 120 similar lions that would have lined a Babylonian pathway during the years of 604–562 BC.

Historians say that after the Babylonians defeated Jerusalem, the Hebrew captives would have seen these lions during their time in Nebuchadnezzar's kingdom. Historians also say it's likely that some of the Israelites would have believed Ishtar had defeated the God of Israel.

Daniel, one of the Hebrew captives, did not share the doubts that might have troubled some of his fellow Israelites. His view of God and his commitment to God stayed steady. He prayed three times a day— with his windows open—even when he knew it would mean entering a den of lions. After God rescued Daniel from the hungry animals, King Darius said, "[Daniel's God] is the living God and he endures forever. . . . He rescues and he saves" (Daniel 6:26–27). Daniel's faithfulness allowed him to influence Babylonian leaders.

Staying faithful to God despite pressure and discouragement can inspire other people to give Him glory.   *Jennifer Benson Schuldt*

God's Answers

Read Daniel 9:20–27

While I was still in prayer, Gabriel . . . came to me.
DANIEL 9:21

Daniel poured out his heart to God (Daniel 9:2). He had read Jeremiah and rediscovered God's promise that Israel's captivity in Babylon would last seventy years. So, in an effort to represent his people before God, Daniel fasted and prayed. He pleaded with God not to delay in rescuing His people (v. 19).

When we pray, there are things we can know and other things we cannot. For instance, we have the assurance that God will hear our prayer if we know Him as our heavenly Father through faith in Jesus, and we know that His answer will come according to His will. But we don't know when the answer will come or what it will be.

For Daniel, the answer to his prayer came in miraculous fashion, and it came immediately. While he was praying, the angel Gabriel arrived to provide the answer. But the nature of the answer was as surprising as the quick reply. While Daniel asked God about "Seventy years," the answer was about a prophetic "seventy weeks of years." Daniel asked God for an answer about the here and now, but God's answer had to do with events thousands of years into the future.

Focused as we are with our immediate situation, we may be shocked by God's answer. Yet we can know that the answer will be for His glory.

Dave Branon

Behind the Scenes

Read Daniel 10:1–14

Your words were heard, and I have come in response to them.

DANIEL 10:12

My daughter sent a text message to a friend, in hopes of having a question answered quickly. Her phone's messaging service showed that the recipient had read the message, so she waited anxiously for a reply. Mere moments passed, yet she grew frustrated, groaning her annoyance at the delay. Irritation eroded into worry; she wondered whether the lack of response meant there was a problem between them. Eventually a reply came and my daughter was relieved to see their relationship was fine. Her friend had simply been sorting out the details needed to answer the question.

The Old Testament prophet Daniel also anxiously awaited a reply. After receiving a frightening vision of great war, Daniel fasted and sought God through humble prayer (10:3, 12). For three weeks, he received no reply (vv. 2, 13). Finally, an angel arrived and assured Daniel his prayers had been heard "since the first day" (10:12). In the meantime, the angel had been battling on behalf of those prayers. Though Daniel didn't know it at first, God was at work during each of the twenty-one days that elapsed between his first prayer and the angel's coming.

Our confidence that God hears our prayers (Psalm 40:1) can cause us to become anxious when His reply doesn't come when we want it to. We are prone to wonder whether He cares. Yet Daniel's experience reminds us that God is at work on behalf of those He loves even when it isn't obvious to us. *Kirsten Holmberg*

Light Up the Night

Read Daniel 12:1–3

Those who are wise will shine like the brightness of the heavens.

Daniel 12:3

On a mild fall evening when the sky was dark and the moon was full, thousands of people in my hometown gathered along the banks of the river to light sky lanterns. They released them into the darkness and watched as the lights rose to join the moon in a dazzling display that turned the night sky into a sparkling work of art.

When I saw pictures of the event, I was disappointed that I was out of town and had missed it. But a few days later I realized that what had happened in Grand Rapids could be seen as a symbol of the conference I was attending in New York City. More than one thousand people from one hundred cities around the world had gathered there to plan a "work of art"—how to light up the darkness of their own cities by planting churches and reaching thousands of people with the gospel of Christ, the Light of the world.

The prophet Daniel wrote about a time when those who turn others to the Lord will shine like stars forever (Daniel 12:3). We can all join in that great event. When we shine the light of Christ in dark places where we live and work, He is lighting up the night sky with stars that never will go out. *Julie Ackerman Link*

PART 5

◆

The Minor Prophets

Hosea, Joel, Amos, Obadiah, Jonah, Micah, Nahum, Habakkuk, Zephaniah, Haggai, Zechariah, Malachi

As was mentioned in relation to the Major Prophets, the Minor Prophets are only "minor" in that their prophecies are shorter. The cycle continues: Through the prophet, God warns His people of impending judgment as a result of their sin, calls them to repent, and promises restoration and deliverance if they turn from their sin.

HOSEA

◆

This is a jarring book because of its content. It is about a longtime prophet of God who was commanded to live in a way that seems so contrary to what we would expect God to ask of one of His people. Hosea was asked to demonstrate the faithlessness of Israel by marrying a faithless woman named Gomer. As a result of the marriage, they had three children, each of whom was given a name heavy in symbolism but clearly not a name any child would want to carry: Jezreel ("God sows"), Lo-Ruhamah ("not pitied"), and Lo-Ammi ("Not my people"). The major point God was teaching is that He desired the rebellious nation of Israel to return to His good graces.

OUTLINE

Hosea's Marriage to Gomer Hosea 1:1–11

Gomer's Infidelity Hosea 2:1–23

Restoration; Hosea's Faithfulness Hosea 3:1–5

Applying the Story: Israel's Infidelity Hosea 4:1–5:15

No Repentance Hosea 6:1–8:14

Judgment on Israel Hosea 9:1–10:15

Restoration! Hosea 11:1–14:9

God Is Here

Read Hosea 6:1–6

Let us acknowledge the LORD; let us press on to acknowledge him.

HOSEA 6:3

A plaque in our home states "Bidden or not bidden, God is present." A modern version might read, "Acknowledged or unacknowledged, God is here."

Hosea, an Old Testament prophet who lived in the late eighth century BC (755–715), wrote similar words to the Hebrew nation. He encouraged the Israelites to "press on" (Hosea 6:3) to acknowledge God because they had forgotten Him (4:1). As the people forgot God's presence, they began to turn away from Him (v. 12) and before long there was no room for God in their thoughts (see Psalm 10:4).

Hosea's simple but profound insight to acknowledge God reminds us He's near and at work in our lives, in both the joys and struggles.

To acknowledge God might mean that when we get a promotion at work, we recognize God gave us insight to finish our work on time and within budget. If our housing application is rejected, acknowledging God helps to sustain us as we trust Him to work in the situation for our good.

If we don't make it into the college of our choice, we can acknowledge God is with us and take comfort in His presence even in our disappointment. As we enjoy dinner, to acknowledge God may be to remind ourselves of God's provision of the ingredients and a kitchen to prepare the meal.

When we acknowledge God, we remember His presence in both the successes and sorrows, whether big or small, of our lives.

Lisa Samra

What Can't You Give Up?

Read Hosea 11:8–11

[Nothing] will be able to separate us from the love of God.
ROMANS 8:39

"What's one thing you can't give up?" the radio host asked. Listeners called in with some interesting answers. Some mentioned their families, including a husband who shared memories of a deceased wife. Others shared they can't give up on their dreams, such as making a living in music or becoming a mother. All of us have something we treasure dearly—a person, a passion, a possession—something we can't give up.

In the book of Hosea, God tells us that He won't give up on His chosen people Israel, His treasured possession. As Israel's loving husband, God provided her with everything she needed: land, food, drink, clothing, and security. Yet like an adulterous spouse, Israel rejected God and sought her happiness and security elsewhere. The more God pursued her, the further she drifted away (Hosea 11:2). However, though she had hurt Him deeply, He would not give her up (v. 8). He would discipline Israel so as to redeem her; His desire was to re-establish His relationship with her (v. 11).

Today, all God's children can have the same assurance: His love for us is a love that will never let us go (Romans 8:37–39). If we've wandered from Him, He yearns for us to return. When God disciplines us, we can be comforted that it's a sign of His pursuit, not of His rejection. We are His treasure; He won't give up on us. *Poh Fang Chia*

JOEL

◆

The message of Joel can be explained with two descriptions: He delivered a strong message of judgment to Judah, and he promised that someday the Holy Spirit of God would come to dwell with believers (this would be fulfilled in the book of Acts in the New Testament). In his warning to Judah in chapters one and two, he describes a great invasion of locusts.

OUTLINE

Judgment and Disaster: Locusts Joel 1:1–12

Judgment and Disaster: Drought Joel 1:13–20

Prediction: Bad News for Judah Joel 2:1–32

The Day of the Lord Joel 3:1–16

Judah Restored Joel 3:17–21

Trouble in the Land

Read Joel 1

Cry out to the LORD.

JOEL 1:14

And we think we have trouble! It's easy to lose the right perspective when we look at our world and see the way things are going. In some places people are struggling to survive, while in others they are busy killing each other.

If the difficulties of the past few years make us wistful for the good old days, we haven't read about the really old days Joel was talking about.

Here's what Judah was up against: A relentless hoard of locusts had ravaged the land. The vineyards were so damaged that the priests couldn't even squeeze out a drink offering. The fig, pomegranate, palm, and apple trees were all ruined. The entire agricultural base, which was the lifeblood of the Judean economy, was wiped out. Indeed, as Joel described it, "the people's joy is withered away" (1:12). At a time when many must have been shaking their fists at God for allowing such devastation, Joel told the people that it was time to go into the house of the Lord and cry out to Him.

That is always the answer. When there is trouble in the land, our only recourse is to turn to God, call out to Him, and trust Him without fail. No matter what calamity strikes today, that should be our number one strategy.

Do we daily "cry out to the Lord"?

Dave Branon

Restored

Read Joel 2:18–27

I will repay you for the years the locusts have eaten.

JOEL 2:25

In the early part of the century, an infestation of Mormon crickets caused more than $25 million in lost crops. The crickets came in such numbers that people couldn't so much as take a step without finding one underfoot. The grasshopper-like insect, named for attacking the crops of the Utah pioneers in 1848, can eat an astounding thirty-eight pounds of plant material in their lifetimes, despite being merely two to three inches long. The impact of infestations on farmers' livelihoods—and the overall economy of a state or country—can be devastating.

The Old Testament prophet Joel described a horde of similar insects ravaging the entire nation of Judah as a consequence for their collective disobedience. He foretold an invasion of locusts (a metaphor for a foreign army, in the minds of some Bible scholars) like nothing previous generations had seen (Joel 1:2). The locusts would lay waste to everything in their path, driving the people into famine and poverty. If, however, the people would turn from their sinful ways and ask God for forgiveness, Joel says the Lord would "repay [them] for the years the locusts have eaten" (2:25).

We too can learn from Judah's lesson: like insects, our wrongdoings eat away at the fruitful, fragrant life God intended for us. When we turn toward Him, and away from our past choices, He promises to remove our shame and restore us to an abundant life in Him.

Kirsten Holmberg

AMOS

◆

Amos prophesied during the reigns of Judah's king Uzziah and Israel's king Jeroboam I. Prosperity was found throughout the land, and the rich people kept getting richer—at the expense of the poor. Also, especially in the Northern Kingdom, worship of the one true Jehovah-God had been replaced by idol worship.

OUTLINE

Our Powerful God

Read Amos 4:12–13

*[He] who creates the wind, . . . the Lord
God Almighty is his name.*

Amos 4:13

One day by the seaside, I delighted in watching some kite surfers as they bounced along the water, moved by the force of the wind. When one came to shore, I asked him if the experience was as difficult as it looked. "No," he said, "It's actually easier than regular surfing because you harness the power of the wind."

Afterward as I walked by the sea, thinking about the wind's ability not only to propel the surfers but also to whip my hair into my face, I paused to wonder at our God the Creator. As we see in the Old Testament book of Amos, He who "forms the mountains" and "creates the wind" can turn "dawn to darkness" (4:13).

Through this prophet, the Lord reminded His people of His power as He called them back to himself. Because they had not obeyed Him, He said He would reveal himself to them (v. 13). Although we see His judgment here, we know from elsewhere in the Bible of His sacrificial love in sending His Son to save us (see John 3:16).

The power of the wind on this breezy day in the South of England reminded me of the sheer immensity of the Lord. If you feel the wind today, why not stop and ponder our all-powerful God?

Amy Boucher Pye

A Mighty Stream

Read Amos 5:21–24

*But let justice roll on like a river, righteousness
like a never-failing stream!*

Amos 5:24

Among the many exhibits and artifacts exploring the harsh reality of slavery and its aftermath in the National Museum of African American History and Culture in Washington DC, I was grateful to discover the Contemplative Court. This tranquil room features translucent walls of bronze glass, and water appears to rain down from the ceiling into a pool.

As I sat in that peaceful space, a quote on the wall from Dr. Martin Luther King Jr. caught my eye: "We are determined . . . to work and fight until justice rains down like water and righteousness like a mighty stream." These powerful words are drawn from the Old Testament book of Amos.

Amos was a prophet living among a people who were involved in religious activities, such as celebrating festivals and offering sacrifices, but whose hearts were far from God (Amos 5:21–23). God rejected their activities because they'd turned away from His commands, including those regarding justice toward the needy and oppressed.

Instead of religious ceremonies devoid of love for God and others, Amos wrote that God longed for His people to demonstrate genuine concern for the welfare of all people—a generous way of living that would be a mighty river bringing life wherever it flowed.

Jesus taught the same truth that loving God is connected with loving our neighbors (Matthew 22:37–39). As we seek to love God, may it come from hearts that also treasure justice.   *Lisa Samra*

OBADIAH

◆

In the tradition of a true prophet, Obadiah has bad news. However, most biblical prophets testify about Judah or Israel. In this book, however, the object of the prophecy is Edom. Because she has so prideful and full of sin, the country is about to be destroyed.

OUTLINE

Judgment Against Edom Obadiah 1:1–14
Results of the Judgment Obadiah 1:15–18
Israel and Edom Obadiah 1:19–21

Superman and Airplanes

Read Obadiah 1:1–7

The pride of your heart has deceived you.

OBADIAH 1:3

My daughter travels all over the world as a flight attendant and often comes home with some fascinating tales. One such story is about former heavyweight boxing champion Muhammad Ali, who was seated in an aircraft that was preparing for takeoff. A flight attendant, noticing that he did not have his seatbelt fastened, asked him kindly, "Excuse me, sir, but would you mind fastening your seatbelt?"

As the story goes, Muhammad Ali looked up with that saucy grin of his and said in a slow, gravelly voice, "Superman don't need no seatbelt!" Without missing a beat, the flight attendant packed a punch with this quick reply: "Superman don't need no airplane, so how about fastening up!"

Of course, Ali was only joking. If a person really believed he was Superman, he would be seriously deluded. He would be like the ancient Edomites in today's Scripture who had been self-deceived by their own pride. The truth is, we all have the same tendency.

A. W. Tozer aptly described the kind of Christians the Lord longs for us to be: "Men and women who have stopped being 'fooled' about their own strength and are not afraid of being 'caught' depending on their all-sufficient Lord."

Joanie Yoder

Gloating at the Enemy

Read Obadiah 1:1–14

Do not gloat when your enemy falls.

PROVERBS 24:17

Obadiah is the shortest book in the Old Testament. Yet hidden away in its brief record is a vital question that affects us all: How should we respond when we see an enemy experience misfortune?

The prophet Obadiah ministered during the time that the city of Jerusalem was under fierce attack by the armies of Babylon. The neighbors of Jerusalem, the Edomites, were actually cheering on the enemy armies to destroy and kill (Psalm 137:7–9). Ironically, these hurtful jeers were spoken by blood relatives of the Jews. They were descendants of Jacob, and the Edomites were descendants of Esau.

Obadiah condemned the Edomites for gloating: "You should not gloat over your brother in the day of his misfortune, nor rejoice over the people of Judah in the day of their destruction" (Obadiah 1:12).

If someone has repeatedly been hurtful to us, it is easy to give in to vindictive pleasure when they experience misfortune. But Scripture admonishes us, "Do not gloat when your enemy falls; when they stumble, do not let your heart rejoice" (Proverbs 24:17). Instead, we are to maintain an attitude of compassion and forgiveness and trust God to bring justice in His time.   *Dennis Fisher*

JONAH

---◆---

Nineveh, the capital of Assyria, was a city of several hundred thousand people (one hundred twenty thousand according to Jonah 4:11), and its wickedness had come to the Lord's attention (Jonah 1:2). So God told Jonah to go there and "preach against it" (1:2). Jonah, living in northern Israel, proceeded to go about as far from Nineveh as possible. It would be like living in Missouri and being told to go to New York City—but instead heading for Los Angeles. Jonah headed for Tarshish, at the western end of the Mediterranean Sea. But Nineveh was far to the north and east of where Jonah lived—across the Euphrates River and then to the Tigris River and to the north. Once Jonah got turned around with the help of a mammoth fish, he reluctantly went to Nineveh, where he proclaimed God's message of repentance. The people of the city, and even the king repented and turned to the one true God. Jonah, after such an amazing evangelistic success, became angry because of Nineveh's transformation.

OUTLINE

Jonah Rejects God's Call to Nineveh Jonah 1:1–17

Jonah's Prayer for God's Help Jonah 2:1–10

Jonah Goes to Nineveh Jonah 3:1–10

Jonah Complains; God Rebukes Him Jonah 4:1–11

When God Cleans House

Read Jonah 1

*Get rid of all bitterness, rage and anger, brawling
and slander, along with every form of malice.*

EPHESIANS 4:31

God did some fall housecleaning this week. He sent a mighty wind through our neighborhood that made the trees tremble and shake loose their dead branches. When it finished, I had a mess to clean up.

In my own life, God sometimes works in a similar way. He will send or allow stormy circumstances that shake loose the "lifeless branches" I've been refusing to release. Sometimes it's something that once was good, like an area of ministry, but is no longer bearing fruit. More often it's something that's not good, like a bad habit I've slid into or a stubborn attitude that prevents new growth.

The Old Testament prophet Jonah discovered what can happen when one refuses to get rid of a stubborn attitude. His hatred for the Ninevites was stronger than his love for God, so God sent a great storm that landed Jonah in a giant fish (Jonah 1:4, 17). God preserved the reluctant prophet in that unlikely place and gave him a second chance to obey (2:10; 3:1–3).

The lifeless limbs in my yard caused me to think of attitudes that God expects me to dispose of. Paul's letter to the Ephesians lists some of them: bitterness, anger, and slander (4:31). When God shakes things up, we need to get rid of what He shakes loose. *Julie Ackerman Link*

No More Running

Read Jonah 2

In my distress I called to the LORD, and he answered me.
From deep in the realm of the dead I called for help,
and you listened to my cry.

JONAH 2:2

On July 18, 1983, a US Air Force captain disappeared from Albuquerque, New Mexico, without a trace. Thirty-five years later, authorities found him in California. *The New York Times* reports that, "depressed about his job," he'd simply run away.

Thirty-five years on the run! Half a lifetime spent looking over his shoulder! I have to imagine that anxiety and paranoia were this man's constant companions.

But I have to admit, I also know a bit about being "on the run." No, I've never abruptly fled something in my life . . . physically. But at times I know there's something God wants me to do, something I need to face or confess. I don't want to do it. And so, in my own way, I run too.

The prophet Jonah is infamous for literally running from God's assignment to preach to the city of Nineveh (see Jonah 1:1–3). But, of course, he couldn't outrun God. You've probably heard what happened (vv. 4, 17): A storm. A fish. A swallowing. And, in the belly of the beast, a reckoning, in which Jonah faced what he'd done and cried to God for help (2:2)

Jonah wasn't a perfect prophet. But I take comfort in his remarkable story, because, even despite Jonah's stubbornness, God never let go of him. The Lord still answered the man's desperate prayer, graciously restoring His reluctant servant (v. 2)—just as He does with us.

Adam Holz

It's Not about the Fish

Read Jonah 3:10–4:4

When God saw what they did and how they
turned from their evil ways, he relented.

Jonah 3:10

Sighted numerous times off the coast of Australia's South Queensland, Migaloo is the first albino humpback whale ever documented. The splendid creature, estimated at more than forty feet long, is so rare that Australia passed a law specifically to protect him.

The Bible tells us about a "huge fish" so rare that God had provided it especially to swallow a runaway prophet (Jonah 1:17). Most know the story. God told Jonah to take a message of judgment to Nineveh. But Jonah wanted nothing to do with the Ninevites, who had a reputation for cruelty to just about everyone—including the Hebrews. So he fled. Things went badly. From inside the fish, Jonah repented. Eventually he preached to the Ninevites, and they repented too (3:5–10).

Great story, right? Except it doesn't end there. While Nineveh repented, Jonah pouted. "Isn't this what I said, Lord?" he prayed. "I knew that you are a gracious and compassionate God, slow to anger and abounding in love" (4:2). Having been rescued from certain death, Jonah's sinful anger grew until even his prayer became suicidal (v. 3).

The story of Jonah isn't about the fish. It's about our human nature and the nature of the God who pursues us. "The Lord . . . is patient with you," wrote the apostle Peter, "not wanting anyone to perish, but everyone to come to repentance" (2 Peter 3:9). God offers His love to brutal Ninevites, pouting prophets, and you and me. *Tim Gustafson*

Praying and Growing

Read Jonah 4

*Whatever you do, whether in WORD or deed, do it all in
the name of the LORD Jesus, giving thanks to God.*

COLOSSIANS 3:17

When my friend David's wife developed Alzheimer's disease, the changes
it brought to his life made him bitter. He needed to retire early to care
for her; and as the disease progressed, she required increasingly more
care.

"I was so angry at God," he told me. "But the more I prayed about
it, the more He showed me my heart and how I had been selfish for
most of our marriage." Tears welled in his eyes as he confessed, "She's
been sick ten years, but God has helped me see things differently. Now,
everything I do out of love for her, I also do for Jesus. Caring for her
has become the greatest privilege of my life."

Sometimes God answers our prayers not by giving us what we want
but by challenging us to change. When the prophet Jonah was angry
because God spared the wicked city of Nineveh from destruction, God
caused a plant to shade him from the hot sun (Jonah 4:6). Then He
made it wither. When Jonah complained, God answered, "Is it right
for you to be angry about the plant?" (vv. 7–9). Jonah, focused only on
himself, insisted it was. But God challenged him to think about others
and have compassion.

God sometimes uses our prayers in unexpected ways to help us learn
and grow. It's a change we can welcome with open hearts because He
wants to transform us with His love. *James Banks*

MICAH

◆

Micah turns his prophetic guns at both Judah and Israel, letting them know that judgment is upon them for their idolatry and for their misuse of the land God gave them. He accurately assails the leaders of the two kingdoms for their lack of justice. Despite the people's efforts to use religious rituals to make things right with God, Micah implores them to be just, merciful, and humble—which is better than sacrificing. Despite the heavy warnings, Micah does leave the people with hope at the end of the last chapter.

OUTLINE

Judgment Coming: People Micah 1:1–2:13

Judgment Coming: Leaders Micah 3:1–12

Restoration Ahead for Kingdom Micah 4:1–13

Promised Messiah Micah 5:1–15

God Appeals for Repentance Micah 6:1–7:20

A "Banana Slug" Lesson

Read Micah 6:1–8

*What does the LORD require of you? To act justly and
to love mercy and to walk humbly with your God.*

MICAH 6:8

Sports team names have a variety of origins. They come from history (Spartans, Mountaineers), nature (Cardinals, Terrapins), and even colors (Orange, Reds). One even comes from the mollusk family.

In the 1980s, the University of California at Santa Cruz was just starting to get involved in competitive sports. UCSC had a bit of disdain for the overemphasis some big-time schools place on athletics, so the student body sought a team name that would reflect a somewhat different approach. They decided on the Banana Slug, a yellow, slimy, slow, shell-less mollusk. It was a clever way for UCSC to give a balanced perspective on the relative worth of sports.

I have always loved sports, but I know that they can easily become more important than they should be. What matters most in life is what Jesus said is most vital—loving God with all of our hearts and loving our neighbors as ourselves (Matthew 22:37–39). Micah listed God's requirements this way: "act justly," "love mercy," and "walk humbly with your God" (6:8). For believers in Jesus, it is vital that nothing else takes top priority over God's expectations for us.

What matters most to you? The Spartans? The Red Sox? Or loving God in thought, word, and action?   *Bill Crowder*

Another Chance

Read Micah 7:1–3, 18–20

Once again you will have compassion on us. You will trample our sins under your feet and throw them into the depths of the ocean!

Micah 7:19 NLT

At the Second Chance Bike Shop near our neighborhood, volunteers rebuild cast-off bicycles and donate them to needy kids. Shop founder Ernie Clark also donates bikes to needy adults, including the homeless, the disabled, and military veterans struggling to make it in civilian life. Not only do the bicycles get a second chance but sometimes the recipients get a new start too. One veteran used his new bike to get to a job interview.

Second chances can transform a person's life, especially when the second chance comes from God. The prophet Micah extoled such grace during a time the nation of Israel groveled in bribery, fraud, and other despicable sins. As Micah lamented, "The godly people have all disappeared; not one honest person is left on the earth" (Micah 7:2 NLT).

God would rightly punish evil, Micah knew. But being loving, He would give those who repented another chance. Humbled by such love, Micah asked, "Where is another God like you, who pardons the guilt of the remnant, overlooking the sins of his special people?" (v. 18 NLT).

We too can rejoice that God doesn't abandon us because of our sins if we ask for forgiveness. As Micah declared of God, "Once again you will have compassion on us. You will trample our sins under your feet and throw them into the depths of the ocean!" (v. 19 NLT).

God's love gives second chances to all who seek Him.

Patricia Raybon

NAHUM

The cruelty and savagery of the nation of Assyria was well-known in the region. So his prophecy of an end to their kingdom was welcome news to surrounding countries. Look at how he ends the book: "All who hear the news about you clap their hands at your fall, for who has not felt your endless cruelty" (3:19).

OUTLINE

God's Wrath Nahum 1:1–15

Destruction of Nineveh Nahum 2:1–3:19

◆

JUNE 14

Hard Mysteries

Read Nahum 1:1–7

The LORD is slow to anger but great in power.

NAHUM 1:3

As my friend and I went for a walk, we talked about our love for the Bible. She surprised me when she said, "Oh, but I don't like the Old Testament much. All of that hard stuff and vengeance—give me Jesus!"

We might resonate with her words when we read a book like Nahum, perhaps recoiling at a statement such as, "The LORD takes vengeance and is filled with wrath" (Nahum 1:2). And yet the next verse fills us with hope: "The LORD is slow to anger but great in power" (v. 3).

When we dig more deeply into the subject of God's anger, we understand that when He exercises it, He's most often defending His people or His name. Because of His overflowing love, He seeks justice for wrongs committed and the redemption of those who have turned from Him. We see this not only in the Old Testament, as He calls His people back to himself, but also in the New, when He sends His Son to be the sacrifice for our sins.

We may not understand the mysteries of the character of God, but we can trust that He not only exercises justice but is also the source of all love. We need not fear Him, for He is "good, a refuge in times of trouble. He cares for those who trust in him" (v. 7). *Amy Boucher Pye*

215

Good News

Read Nahum 1: 7–15

Look, there on the mountains, the feet of one
who brings good news, who proclaims peace!

NAHUM 1:15

World news bombards us from the Internet, television, radio, and mobile devices. The majority seems to describe what's wrong—crime, terrorism, war, and economic problems. Yet there are times when good news invades the darkest hours of sadness and despair—stories of unselfish acts, a medical breakthrough, or steps toward peace in war-scarred places.

The words of two men recorded in the Old Testament of the Bible brought great hope to people weary of conflict.

While describing God's coming judgment on a ruthless and powerful nation, Nahum said, "Look, there on the mountains, the feet of one who brings good news, who proclaims peace!" (Nahum 1:15). That news brought hope to all those oppressed by cruelty.

A similar phrase occurs in the book of Isaiah: "How beautiful on the mountains are the feet of those who bring good news, who proclaim peace, who bring good tidings, who proclaim salvation" (Isaiah 52:7).

Nahum and Isaiah's prophetic words of hope found their ultimate fulfillment at the first Christmas when the angel told the shepherds, "Do not be afraid. I bring you good news that will cause great joy for all the people. Today in the town of David a Savior has been born to you; he is the Messiah, the Lord" (Luke 2:10–11).

The most important headline in our lives every day is the very best news ever spoken—Christ the Savior is born!   *David McCasland*

HABAKKUK

◆

Habakkuk did something different with his prophetic words. Instead of preaching to the people of Judah, he addressed God. Thus we get a glimpse into the prayer life of this prophet. And he doesn't hold back. Sounding a bit like David's complaints in the book of Psalms, he begins right off with this: "How long, O Lord, must I ask for help? But you do not listen!" (1:2 NLT). And in verse 4: "The wicked hem in the righteous, so that justice is perverted." He is writing after the reforms of Josiah had been instituted, but they were beginning to die out and the people had reverted to their sinful ways.

OUTLINE

Questions for God Habakkuk 1:1–2:20
Praises to God Habakkuk 3:1–19

Doesn't God Care?

Read Habakkuk 1:1–11

"For my thoughts are not your thoughts, neither are your ways my ways," declares the LORD.

ISAIAH 55:8

Why does the intoxicated driver escape an accident unharmed while his sober victim is seriously injured? Why do bad people prosper while good people suffer? How often have you been so confused by things going on in your life that you have cried out, "Doesn't God care?"

Habakkuk struggled with this same question as he saw the distressing situation in Judah where wickedness and injustice were running rampant (Habakkuk 1:1–4). His confusion drove him to ask God when He would act to fix the situation. God's reply was nothing short of perplexing.

God said that He would use the Chaldeans as the means of Judah's correction. The Chaldeans were notorious for their cruelty (v. 7). They were bent on violence (v. 9) and worshiped nothing but their military prowess and false gods (vv. 10–11).

In moments when we don't understand God's ways, we need to trust His unchanging character. That's exactly what Habakkuk did. He believed that God is a God of justice, mercy, and truth (Psalm 89:14). In the process, he learned to look at his circumstances from the framework of God's character instead of looking at God's character from the context of his own circumstances. He concluded, "The Sovereign LORD is my strength; he makes my feet like the feet of a deer, he enables me to tread on the heights" (Habakkuk 3:19).   *Poh Fang Chia*

Waiting for a Blessing

Read Habakkuk 1:12–2:4

Though it linger, wait for it.

HABAKKUK 2:3

A popular restaurant in Bangkok serves soup from a broth that has been cooking for forty-five years and is replenished a bit each day. The practice, called "perpetual stew," dates back to medieval times. Just as some "leftovers" taste better a few days later, the extended cooking time blends and creates unique flavors. The restaurant has won multiple awards for the most delicious broth in Thailand.

Good things often take time, but our human nature struggles with patience. The question "How long?" occurs throughout the Bible. One poignant example is from the prophet Habakkuk, who begins his book by asking, "How long, LORD, must I call for help, but you do not listen?" (Habakkuk 1:2). Habakkuk (whose name means "grappler") prophesied God's judgment on his country (Judah) through the invasion of the ruthless Babylonian Empire, and he wrestled with how God could allow corrupt people to prosper as they exploited others. But God promised hope and restoration in His own time: "For the revelation [of God's help] awaits an appointed time. . . . Though it linger, wait for it; it will certainly come and will not delay" (2:3).

The Babylonian captivity lasted seventy years. By human reckoning that's a long time, but God is always faithful and true to His Word.

Some of God's best blessings may be long in coming. Though they linger, keep looking to Him! He prepares every blessing with perfect wisdom and care—and He's always worth waiting for. *James Banks*

JUNE 18

The Voice of Faith

Read Habakkuk 3:16–19

Though the fig tree does not bud . . .
yet I will rejoice in the LORD.
HABAKKUK 3:17–18

The news was numbing. The tears came so quickly that she couldn't fight them. Her mind raced with questions, and fear threatened to overwhelm her. Life had been going along so well, when it was abruptly interrupted and forever changed without warning.

Tragedy can come in many forms—the loss of a loved one, an illness, the loss of wealth or our livelihood. And it can happen to anyone at any time.

Although the prophet Habakkuk knew that tragedy was coming, it still struck fear in his heart. As he waited for the day when Babylon would invade the kingdom of Judah, his heart pounded, his lips quivered, and his legs trembled (Habakkuk 3:16).

Fear is a legitimate emotion in the face of tragedy, but it doesn't have to immobilize us. When we don't understand the trials we are going through, we can recount how God has worked in history (vv. 3–15). That's what Habakkuk did. It didn't dispel his fear, but it gave him the courage to move on by choosing to praise the Lord (v. 18).

Our God who has proven himself faithful throughout the years is always with us. Because His character doesn't change, in our fear we can say with a confident voice of faith, "The Sovereign LORD is my strength!" (v. 19). *Poh Fang Chia*

ZEPHANIAH

◆

This book is about judgment and restoration. In the first two chapters, a variety of nations and then finally the whole world face the destruction brought on by God's judgment. And then in chapter three, we read about the restoration of Jerusalem and all nations of the world.

OUTLINE

Judgments and the Day of the Lord Zephaniah 1:1–3:8

Restoration Promised Zephaniah 3:9–20

And in Truth

Read Zephaniah 1:1–6; 2:1–3

In his love he will no longer rebuke you,
but will rejoice over you with singing.

ZEPHANIAH 3:17

Years ago, I attended a wedding where two people from different countries got married. Such a blending of cultures can be beautiful, but this ceremony included Christian traditions mixed with rituals from a faith that worshiped many gods.

Zephaniah the prophet pointedly condemned the mixing of other religions with faith in the one true God (sometimes called syncretism). Judah had become a people who bowed in worship to the true God but who also relied on the god Molek (Zephaniah 1:5). Zephaniah described their adoption of pagan culture (v. 8) and warned that as a result God would drive the people of Judah from their homeland.

Yet God never stopped loving His people. His judgment was to show them their need to turn to Him. So Zephaniah encouraged Judah to "Seek righteousness, seek humility" (2:3). Then the Lord gave them tender words promising future restoration: "At that time I will gather you; at that time I will bring you home" (3:20).

It's easy to condemn examples of obvious syncretism like the wedding I attended. But in reality, all of us easily blend God's truth with the assumptions of our culture. We need the Holy Spirit's guidance to test our beliefs against the truth of God's Word and then to stand for that truth confidently and lovingly. Our Father warmly embraces anyone who worships Him in the Spirit and in truth (see John 4:23–24).

Tim Gustafson

Our Singing Father

Read Zephaniah 3:14–20

The LORD your God is with you, the Mighty Warrior
who saves. He will take great delight in you; in his
love he will . . . rejoice over you with singing.

ZEPHANIAH 3:17

No one told me before my wife and I had children how important singing would be. My children are now six, eight, and ten. But all three had problems sleeping early on. Each night, my wife and I took turns rocking our little ones, praying they'd nod off quickly. I spent hundreds of hours rocking them, desperately crooning lullabies to (hopefully!) speed up the process. But as I sang over our children night after night, something amazing happened: It deepened my bond of love and delight for them in ways I had never dreamed.

Did you know Scripture describes our heavenly Father singing over His children too? Just as I sought to soothe my children with song, so Zephaniah concludes with a portrait of our heavenly Father singing over His people: "He will take great delight in you; in his love he will . . . rejoice over you with singing" (3:17).

Much of Zephaniah's prophetic book warns of a coming time of judgment for those who'd rejected God. Yet that's not where it ends. Zephaniah concludes not with judgment but with a description of God not only rescuing His people from all their suffering (vv. 19–20) but also tenderly loving and rejoicing over them with song (v. 17).

Our God is not only a "Mighty Warrior who saves" and restores (v. 17) but also a loving Father who tenderly sings songs of love over us.

Adam Holz

HAGGAI

◆

The people have misplaced priorities, and Haggai seeks to explain this to them. Despite the people's contention that "the time has not yet come to rebuild the Lord's house" (1:2), the Lord's response indicates that they are wrong (v. 4). They should reconcentrate their efforts on rebuilding the temple, a task that Ezra had begun about seventeen years earlier with the laying of the foundation. The project had been abandoned, and now Haggai is charged with getting the people involved in it again. As they work on the temple, they begin to notice that this new edifice is nothing like the magnificent temple of Solomon (2:3).

OUTLINE

Consider Your Ways

Read Haggai 1:1–11

Thus says the LORD of hosts: "Consider your ways!"
HAGGAI 1:7 NKJV

How long has it been since you read Haggai? If you're like me, it's been a while. Why not take a few minutes and read all thirty-eight verses of this book. Look for the word consider. It occurs four times (1:5, 7; 2:15, 18 NKJV).

God spoke through Haggai to the Israelites who had returned from exile. He said, in effect, "Think about it. You don't have enough to eat. Your clothes don't keep you warm. You're not prospering. I have commanded you to rebuild My house. When you obey, My blessing will return."

That message applies to us as well. When everything seems to be going wrong, the first step in solving our problems may be to consider our ways. Let me illustrate.

During one semester in college, my grades dropped dramatically, I got in trouble in the dorm, and I was called into the Dean's office. I went back to my room and thought seriously about my situation. The problem was not schoolwork or the guys in the dorm. I was the problem. When I changed my attitude and my behavior, things began to go better.

Not all our troubles are of our own making. But when difficulties arise, it's wise to consider our ways. Like the people of Haggai's day, we may find that our disobedience is blocking God's blessing.

David Egner

Why Am I Not Blessed?

Read Haggai 2:10–19

"I struck all the work of your hands with blight, mildew and hail, yet you did not return to me," declares the LORD.

HAGGAI 2:17

When my friends from the United States came to visit me in Singapore, I was surprised that they walked into my home without removing their shoes. Because of our cultural differences, I thought their lack of concern about tracking in dirt was strange.

As you read Haggai 2, you may think all the talk about holy meat and dead bodies is peculiar (vv. 12–15). But the Lord wasn't just concerned about physical cleanliness. He used those object lessons to help the people of Judah to remember what had happened to them after they returned from exile in Babylon.

The sinful attitudes of a few had spread and defiled the whole community. Instead of rebuilding the temple, they had focused on constructing their own homes (1:4). And because of their sin, they lost God's blessing. Then the Lord, like a father who longs for a close relationship with His child, disciplined them to encourage them to return to Him (2:17).

When Haggai came along, they renewed their commitment to God. So the prophet challenged them to remain faithful, and he said the Lord would bless them abundantly (v. 19).

Are you enjoying the blessings of a close relationship with God? Or do you need to turn from sin and renew your commitment to Him?

Albert Lee

The Signet Ring

Read Haggai 2:15–23

*"I will make you like my signet ring, for I
have chosen you," declares the LORD.*

HAGGAI 2:23

When I first made the acquaintance of a new friend from abroad, I noticed his posh English accent and that he wore a ring on his little finger. Later I learned that this wasn't just jewelry; it revealed his family's history through the family crest engraved on it.

It was a bit like a signet ring—perhaps like the one in Haggai. In this short Old Testament book, the prophet Haggai calls for the people of God to restart the rebuilding of the temple. They had been exiled and had now returned to their homeland and begun rebuilding, but enemy opposition to their project had stalled them. Haggai's message includes God's promise to Zerubbabel, Judah's leader, that he had been chosen and set apart as their leader, like a signet ring.

In ancient times, a signet ring was used as a means of identification. Instead of signing their name, people would press their ring into hot wax or soft clay to make their mark. As God's children, we too make a mark on the world as we spread the gospel, share His grace through loving our neighbors, and work to end oppression.

Each of us has our own unique stamp that reveals how we're created in God's image and expresses our particular mix of gifts, passions, and wisdom. It's our call and privilege to act as this signet ring in God's world.

Amy Boucher Pye

ZECHARIAH

◆

God reveals eight visions to Zechariah, and it is with these eight visions that Zechariah provides his message to the people. Using those visions, God is teaching about restoration, judgment, a coming Messiah, the completion of the temple, obedience, freedom from iniquity, and finally, God's future kingdom of justice and peace.

OUTLINE

Who Are You Wearing?

Read Zechariah 3

I have taken away your sin, and I will put fine garments on you.
ZECHARIAH 3:4

The Argentine women's basketball team came to their tournament game wearing the wrong uniforms. Their navy blue jerseys were too similar to Columbia's dark blue jerseys, and as the visiting team they should have worn white. With no time to find replacement uniforms and change, they had to forfeit the game. In the future, Argentina will surely double-check what they're wearing.

In the time of the prophet Zechariah, God showed him a vision in which the high priest Joshua came before God wearing smelly, filthy clothes. Satan sneered and pointed. He's disqualified! Game over! But there was time to change. God rebuked Satan and told His angel to remove Joshua's grubby garments. He turned to Joshua, "See, I have taken away your sin, and I will put fine garments on you" (Zechariah 3:4).

We came into this world wearing the stench of Adam's sin, which we layer over with sin of our own. If we stay in our filthy clothes, we'll lose the game of life. If we become disgusted with our sin and turn to Jesus, He'll dress us from head to toe with himself and His righteousness. It's time to check, Who are we wearing?

The final stanza of the hymn "The Solid Rock" explains how we win. "When He shall come with trumpet sound, / Oh, may I then in Him be found; / Dressed in His righteousness alone, / Faultless to stand before the throne." *Mike Wittmer*

By the Spirit's Power

Read Zechariah 4:1–7

What are you, mighty mountain? Before
Zerubbabel you will become level ground.

ZECHARIAH 4:7

What do you do when there is a mountain in your way? The story of Dashrath Manjhi can inspire us. When his wife died because he was unable to get her to the hospital to receive urgent medical care, Manjhi did what seemed impossible. He spent twenty-two years chiseling a massive gap in a mountain so other villagers could get to the local hospital to receive the medical care they needed. Before he died, the government of India celebrated him for his achievement.

Rebuilding the temple must have looked impossible to Zerubbabel, one of the leaders of Israel who returned from exile. The people were discouraged, faced opposition from their enemies, and lacked resources or a big army. But God sent Zechariah to remind Zerubbabel that the task would take something more powerful than military strength, individual power, or man-made resources. It would take the Spirit's power (Zechariah 4:6). With the assurance of divine aid, Zerubbabel trusted that God would level any mountain of difficulty that stood in the way of rebuilding the temple and restoring the community (v. 7).

What do we do when there is a "mountain" before us? We have two options: rely on our own strength or trust the Spirit's power. When we trust His power, He will either level the mountain or give us the strength and endurance to climb over it.   *Marvin Williams*

Returning Home

Read Zechariah 10:6–12

In distant lands they will remember me . . .
and they will return.

ZECHARIAH 10:9

Walter Dixon had five days to honeymoon before he shipped off to the Korean War. Less than a year later, troops found Dixon's jacket on the battlefield, with letters from his wife stuffed in the pockets. Military officials informed his young wife that her husband had been killed in action. Actually, Dixon was alive and spent the next two-and-a-half years as a prisoner of war. Every waking hour, he plotted to get home. Dixon escaped five times but was always recaptured. Finally, he was set free. You can imagine the shock when he returned home!

God's people knew what it was to be captured, moved far away, and to long for home. Due to their rebellion against God, they were exiles. They woke each morning yearning to return, but they had no way to rescue themselves. Thankfully, God promised He'd not forgotten them. "I will restore them because I have compassion on them" (Zechariah 10:6). He would meet the people's relentless ache for home, not because of their perseverance, but because of His mercy: "I will signal for them . . . and they will return" (vv. 8–9).

Our sense of exile may come because of our bad decisions or because of hardships beyond our control. Either way, God hasn't forgotten us. He knows our desire and will call to us. And if we'll answer, we'll find ourselves returning to Him—returning home.   *Winn Collier*

MALACHI

◆

After the people returned from exile in Babylon, they did some good things. They rebuilt the temple and restored Jerusalem to safety by reconstructing the walls. But then they did what they had been doing for generations—they grew complacent. Therefore, Malachi is called on here to let them know where they have been lacking. He told them that their sacrifices were not acceptable, that they were again marrying pagan wives, and that the priests were not behaving as they should.

OUTLINE

God Loves Israel Malachi 1:1–5
Israel Sins against God Malachi 1:6–3:18
God Makes Promises to Israel Malachi 4:1–6

◆

JUNE 27

Giving Our Best

Read Malachi 1:8–14

He will purify . . . and refine them like gold and silver.
Then the LORD will have men who will
bring offerings in righteousness.

MALACHI 3:3

We stared at the piles of donated shoes as we entered a local homeless shelter. The director had invited our youth group to help sort through the heaps of used footwear. We spent the morning searching for matches and lining them up in rows across the concrete floor. At the end of the day, we threw away more than half of the shoes because they were too damaged for others to use. Though the shelter couldn't stop people from giving poor quality items, they refused to distribute shoes that were in bad condition.

The Israelites struggled with giving God their damaged goods too. When He spoke through the prophet Malachi, He rebuked the Israelites for sacrificing blind, lame, or diseased animals when they had strong animals to offer (Malachi 1:6–8). He announced His displeasure (v. 10), affirmed His worthiness, and reprimanded the Israelites for keeping the best for themselves (v. 14). But God also promised to send the Messiah, whose love and grace would transform their hearts and ignite their desire to bring offerings that would be pleasing to Him (3:1–4).

At times, it can be tempting to give God our leftovers. We praise Him and expect Him to give us His all, yet we offer Him our crumbs. When we consider all God has done, we can rejoice in celebrating His worthiness and giving Him our very best.   *Xochitl Dixon*

An Amazing Love

Read Malachi 1:1–10; 4:5–6

"I have loved you," says the LORD.
MALACHI 1:2

The final major historic acts of the Old Testament are described in Ezra and Nehemiah as God allowed the people of Israel to return from exile and resettle in Jerusalem. The City of David was repopulated with Hebrew families, a new temple was built, and the wall was repaired.

And that brings us to Malachi. This prophet, who was most likely a contemporary of Nehemiah, brings the written portion of the Old Testament to a close. Notice the first thing he said to the people of Israel: "'I have loved you,' says the LORD." And look at their response: "How have you loved us?" (1:2).

Amazing, isn't it? Their history had proven God's faithfulness, yet after hundreds of years in which God continually provided for His chosen people in both miraculous and mundane ways, they wondered how He had shown His love. As the book continues, Malachi reminds the people of their unfaithfulness (see vv. 6–8). They had a long historical pattern of God's provision for them, followed by their disobedience, followed by God's discipline.

It was time, soon, for a new way. The prophet hints at it in Malachi 4:5–6. The Messiah would be coming. There was hope ahead for a Savior who would show us His love and pay the penalty once and for all for our sin.

That Messiah indeed has come! Malachi's hope is now a reality in Jesus.   *Dave Branon*

Fitting In

Read Malachi 3:13–18

Then those who feared the LORD talked with each
other, and the LORD listened and heard.

MALACHI 3:16

Lee is a diligent and reliable bank employee. Yet he often finds himself sticking out like a sore thumb for living out his faith. This reveals itself in practical ways, such as when he leaves the break room during an inappropriate conversation. At a Bible study, he shared with his friends, "I fear that I'm losing promotion opportunities for not fitting in."

Believers during the prophet Malachi's time faced a similar challenge. They had returned from exile and the temple had been rebuilt, but there was skepticism about God's plan for their future. Some of the Israelites were saying, "It is futile to serve God. What do we gain by carrying out his requirements . . . ? But now we call the arrogant blessed. Certainly evildoers prosper, and even when they put God to the test, they get away with it" (Malachi 3:14–15).

How can we stand firm for God in a culture that tells us we will lose out if we don't blend in? The faithful in Malachi's time responded to that challenge by meeting with like-minded believers to encourage each other. Malachi shares this important detail with us: "The LORD listened and heard" (v. 16).

God notices and cares for all who fear and honor Him. He doesn't call us to "fit in" but to draw closer to Him each day as we encourage each other. Let's stay faithful!   *Poh Fang Chia*

Sonrise

Read Malachi 4:1–6

*The Sun of Righteousness shall arise
with healing in His wings.*

MALACHI 4:2 NKJV

My state's name, "Idaho," according to one legend, comes from a Shoshone Indian word, "ee-dah-how." When translated into English, it means something like, "Behold! The sun rising over the mountain." I often think of that when the sun breaks over the eastern peaks and spills light and life into our valley.

Also, I think of Malachi's promise: "The Sun of Righteousness shall arise with healing in His wings" (Malachi 4:2). This is God's irrevocable promise that our Lord Jesus will come again and all creation "will be liberated from its bondage to decay and brought into the freedom and glory of the children of God" (Romans 8:21).

Each new sunrise is a reminder of that eternal morning when "bright heaven's Sun" will arise with healing in His wings. Then everything that has been made will be made over and made irrevocably right. There will be no throbbing backs or knees, no financial struggles, no losses, no aging. One Bible version says that when Jesus returns we will "go out and frolic like well-fed calves" (Malachi 4:2). This is my highest imagination and my hope.

Jesus said, "Surely I am coming quickly" (Revelation 22:20 NKJV). Even so, come, Lord Jesus!   *David Roper*

PART 6

◆

The Gospels

Matthew, Mark, Luke, John

The Holy Spirit inspired four different first-century followers of Jesus to tell about him—each in his own unique way. In addition, each wrote to a different audience and with a different purpose in mind. Thus we have four sketches of the life of Jesus Christ from four different perspectives. The first of the three gospels have the most unity of style and details—so we refer to Matthew, Mark, and Luke as the synoptic gospels. John's gospel leaves out many of the stories the other three tell, and his book about Jesus emphasizes important ideas such as the deity of Christ and the work of the Holy Spirit. The point is that when we read each gospel, we are rewarded with a fresh, new glimpse of who Jesus is. He is the Savior, redeemer, and Lord in all four gospels, that is for sure, but we learn different things about Him in each of the four different books.

MATTHEW

◆

Matthew's first task was to introduce his readers to who Jesus was. He wanted them to know his background (genealogy) and his birth. He introduced the concept of Jesus's virgin birth in unusual circumstances—establishing Him as a very different kind of king. Matthew then moved on to the work of Jesus—starting with His baptism and the all-important introduction at His baptism of the truth of the trinity. He told of Jesus's resistance of temptation and then His selection of His disciples. Following that, Matthew recorded Jesus's five great teaching lessons and His miracles along the way. It all led up to the reason He came—to die on the cross and to be resurrected for the sin of mankind. And at the end, Matthew records the challenge of all believers—to spread the word about Jesus.

OUTLINE

King Jesus Arrives Matthew 1:1–4:16

Jesus's Ministry and Words Matthew 4:17–16:20

Jesus and the Cross Matthew 16:21–28:20

The Only King

Read Matthew 2:1–12

They bowed down and worshiped him.

MATTHEW 2:11

As five-year-old Eldon listened to the pastor talk about Jesus leaving heaven and coming to earth, he gasped when the pastor thanked Him in prayer for dying for our sins. "Oh, no! He died?" the boy said in surprise.

From the start of Christ's life on earth, there were people who wanted Him dead. Wise men came to Jerusalem during the reign of King Herod inquiring, "Where is the one who has been born king of the Jews? We saw his star when it rose and have come to worship him" (Matthew 2:2). When the king heard this, he became fearful of one day losing his position to Jesus. So he sent soldiers to kill all the boys two years old and younger around Bethlehem. But God protected His Son and sent an angel to warn His parents to leave the area. They fled, and He was saved (vv. 13–18).

When Jesus completed His ministry, He was crucified for the sins of the world. The sign placed above His cross, though meant in mockery, read, "THIS IS JESUS, THE KING OF THE JEWS" (27:37). Yet three days later He rose in victory from the grave. After ascending to heaven, He sat down on the throne as King of kings and Lord of lords (Philippians 2:8–11).

The King died for our sins—yours, mine, and Eldon's. Let's allow Him to rule in our hearts. *Anne Cetas*

Turn On the Light

Read Matthew 5:14–16

*Let your light shine before others, that they may see
your good deeds and glorify your Father in heaven.*

Matthew 5:16

As my husband and I prepared for a cross-country move, I wanted to ensure that we kept in touch with our grown sons. I found a unique gift—friendship lamps connected by wireless internet—which can be turned on remotely. When I gave the lamps to my sons, I explained that their lamps will turn on when I touch my lamp—to provide a shining reminder of my love and ongoing prayers. No matter how great the distance between us, a tap on their lamps would trigger a light in our home too. Though we knew nothing could replace our more personal moments of connection, we could be encouraged by knowing we're loved and prayed for every time we turned on those lights.

All God's children have the privilege of being light-sharers powered by the Holy Spirit. We're designed to live as radiant beacons of God's everlasting hope and unconditional love. When we're sharing the gospel and serving others in the name of Jesus, we become brilliant spotlights and living testimonies. Every good deed, kind smile, gentle word of encouragement, and heartfelt prayer produces a beaming reminder of God's faithfulness and His unconditional and life-transforming love (Matthew 5:14–16).

Wherever God leads us, and however we serve Him, we can be used by Him to help others shine His light. As God, by His Spirit, provides the true illumination, we can reflect the light and love of His presence.

Xochitl Dixon

Taught by Turkeys

Read Matthew 6:25–34

Look at the birds of the air; they do not sow or reap or store away in barns, and yet your heavenly Father feeds them.

MATTHEW 6:26

Do you know what a group of turkeys is called? It's called a rafter. Why am I writing about turkeys? Because I've just returned from a weekend at a mountain cabin. Each day, I marveled at the train of turkeys parading past our porch.

I had never turkey-watched before. They scratched fiercely with spectacular talons. Then they hunted and pecked at the ground. Eating, I assume. (Since this was my first turkey-observation time, I wasn't one-hundred-percent positive.) The scrawny scrubs in the area didn't look like they could sustain anything. Yet here were these turkeys, a dozen of them, all of which looked delectably plump.

Watching those well-fed turkeys brought to mind Jesus's words in Matthew 6:26: "Look at the birds of the air; they do not sow or reap or store away in barns, and yet your heavenly Father feeds them. Are you not much more valuable than they?" Jesus uses God's provision for seemingly worthless birds to remind us of His care for us. If a bird's life matters, how much more does ours! Jesus then contrasts fretting about our daily needs (vv. 27–31) with a life in which we "seek first his kingdom and his righteousness" (v. 33), one in which we're confident of His rich provision for our needs. Because if God can care for that rafter of wild turkeys, He can certainly look after you and me.

Adam Holz

Deep-Rooted Faith

Read Matthew 13:18–23

The seed falling on good soil refers to someone
who hears the WORD and understands it.

MATTHEW 13:23

The Holy Oak, towering next to Basking Ridge Presbyterian Church in New Jersey for more than three hundred years, had to be removed after more than six hundred years of life. At its prime, the twisting branches spanned high and wide. Cool breezes rustled its green leaves and acorns. The sun peeked through wind-blown gaps, creating dancing glimmers of light in the shade below its canopy. But beneath the ground's surface lay its true magnificence—its root system. An oak's main root grows vertically, securing a reliable supply of nourishment. From that taproot, a mass of roots spreads horizontally to supply the tree with a lifetime of moisture and nutrients. This intricate root system often grows more massive than the tree it supports and serves as a lifeline and an anchor for stabilizing the trunk.

Like the mighty oak, most of our life-giving growth occurs beneath the surface. When Jesus explained the parable of the sower to His disciples, He emphasized the importance of being firmly planted in a personal relationship with the Father. As we grow in the knowledge of God as revealed through the Scriptures, our faith roots are sustained by His Spirit. God helps His followers thrive through ever-changing circumstances, trials, persecution, and worry (Matthew 13:18–23).

Our loving Father nourishes our hearts with His Word. As His Spirit transforms our character, He makes sure the fruit of our deep-rooted faith becomes evident to people around us. *Xochitl Dixon*

Of Loaves and Fishes

Read Matthew 14:13–21

Jesus replied, "They do not need to go away.
You give them something to eat."

MATTHEW 14:16

A young boy came home from church and announced with great excitement that the lesson had been about a boy who "loafed and fished all day." He, of course, was thinking of the little boy who offered his loaves and fish to Jesus.

Jesus had been teaching the crowds all day, and the disciples suggested He send them into the village to buy bread. Jesus replied, "You give them something to eat" (Matthew 14:16). The disciples were perplexed for there were more than five thousand people to be fed!

You may know the rest of the story: a boy gave his lunch—five small loaves of bread and two fish—and with it Jesus fed the crowd (vv. 13–21). One school of thought contends that the boy's generosity simply moved others in the crowd to share their lunches, but Matthew clearly intends us to understand that this was a miracle, and the story appears in all four gospels.

What can we learn? Family, neighbors, friends, colleagues, and others stand around us in varying degrees of need. Should we send them away to those who are more capable than we are? Certainly, some people's needs exceed our ability to help them, but not always. Whatever you have—a hug, a kind word, a listening ear, a brief prayer, some wisdom you've gathered—give it to Jesus and see what He can do. *Dave Roper*

Listening to Your Brother

Read Matthew 18:15–20

Whoever turns a sinner from the error of their way will save them from death and cover over a multitude of sins.

JAMES 5:20

"You need to listen to me, I'm your brother!" The plea came from a concerned older brother in my neighborhood and was directed to a younger sibling who was moving farther away from him than the older child was comfortable with. Clearly the older child was better able to judge what was best in the situation.

How many of us have resisted the wise counsel of a brother or sister? If you've had to face the consequences of resisting the good advice of someone more mature, you're not alone.

One of the greatest resources we can have as believers in Jesus is a family—those who are spiritually related because of a common faith in Him. This family includes mature men and women who love God and each other. Like the little brother in my neighborhood, we sometimes need a word of caution or correction to get us back on track. This is particularly true when we offend someone or someone offends us. Doing what's right can be difficult. Yet Jesus's words in Matthew 18:15–20 show us what to do when offenses happen within our spiritual family.

Thankfully, our gracious heavenly Father places in our lives people who are prepared to help us honor Him and others. And when we listen, things go better in the family (v. 15). *Arthur Jackson*

Serving the Least

Read Matthew 25:31–40

The King will reply, "Truly I tell you, whatever you did for one
of the least of these brothers and sisters of mine, you did for me."
MATTHEW 25:40

His name is Spencer. But everybody calls him "Spence." He was a state track champion in high school; then he went on to attend a prestigious university on a full academic scholarship. He lives now in one of America's largest cities and is highly respected in the field of chemical engineering. But if you were to ask Spence his greatest achievements to date, he wouldn't mention any of those things. He would excitedly tell you about the trips he makes to Nicaragua every few months to check in on the kids and teachers in the tutoring program he helped establish in one of the poorest areas of the country. And he'd tell you how enriched his life has been by serving them.

"The least of these." It's a phrase people use in a variety of ways, yet Jesus used it to describe those who, according to the world's standards, have little or nothing to offer us in return for our service. They are the men and women and children the world often overlooks—if not forgets completely. Yet it's exactly those people Jesus elevates to such a beautiful status by saying, "Whatever you did [for them], you did for me" (Matthew 25:40). You don't have to have a degree from a prestigious university to understand Christ's meaning: serving "the least" is the same as serving Him. All it really takes is a willing heart. *John Blase*

Dad at the Dentist

Read Matthew 26:36–39

*My Father, if it is possible, may this cup be taken
from me. Yet not as I will, but as you will.*

MATTHEW 26:39

I didn't expect a profound lesson about the Father's heart at the dentist's office—but I got one. I was there with my ten-year-old son. He had an adult tooth coming in under a baby tooth that hadn't fallen out yet. It had to come out. There was no other way.

My son, in tears, pleaded with me: "Dad, isn't there another way? Can't we just wait and see? Please, Dad, I don't want to have this tooth pulled!" It just about broke my heart, but I told him, "Son, it's got to come out. I'm sorry. There's no other way." And I held his hand as he wriggled and writhed while the dentist removed that stubborn molar, tears in my eyes too. I couldn't take his pain away; the best I could offer was to be present with him in it.

In that moment, I remembered Jesus in the garden of Gethsemane, asking His Father for a different way. How it must have broken the Father's heart to see His beloved Son in such agony! Yet there was no other way to save His people.

In our lives, we sometimes face unavoidable yet painful moments—just like my son did. But because of Jesus's work for us through His Spirit, even in our darkest moments our loving heavenly Father is always present with us (Matthew 28:20). *Adam Holz*

Laundry Day

Read Matthew 28:16–20

Go, then, to all peoples everywhere and make them my disciples.

MATTHEW 28:19 GNT

Driving through a low-income area near his church, Colorado pastor Chad Graham started praying for his "neighbors." When he noticed a small laundromat, he stopped to take a look inside and found it filled with customers. One asked Graham for a spare coin to operate the clothes dryer. That small request inspired a weekly "Laundry Day" sponsored by Graham's church. Members donate coins and soap to the laundromat, pray with customers, and support the owner of the laundry facility.

Their neighborhood outreach, which dares to include a laundromat, reflects Jesus's Great Commission to His disciples. As He said, "I have been given all authority in heaven and on earth. Go, then, to all peoples everywhere and make them my disciples: baptize them in the name of the Father, the Son, and the Holy Spirit" (Matthew 28:18–19 GNT).

His Holy Spirit's powerful presence enables "everywhere" outreach, including even a laundromat. Indeed, we don't go alone. As Jesus promised, "I will be with you always, to the end of the age" (v. 20 GNT).

Pastor Chad experienced that truth after praying at the laundromat for a customer named Jeff who is battling cancer. As Chad reported, "When we opened our eyes, every customer in the room was praying with us, hands stretched out toward Jeff. It was one of the most sacred moments I have experienced as a pastor."

The lesson? Let's go everywhere to proclaim Christ. *Patricia Raybon*

MARK

Without a mention of the nativity, Mark dives right into the action—beginning with Jesus's forerunner John the Baptist. We read of Jesus's baptism and His overcoming temptation in the wilderness—and the narration continues. Jesus starts accumulating His disciples and heads off with them to Capernaum. The gospel hardly lets you catch your breath as we see the Messiah drive out a demon and heal the sick and possessed. Jesus takes a brief prayer break, and then more healing. It is with breakneck speed that Mark reveals the actions of the Savior. He takes time to preach by the Sea of Galilee before He sets off to heal and feed the people. In Mark, we get a condensed version of the much longer Matthew—while getting a few new details not in the previous book.

OUTLINE

The Ministry of Jesus Mark 1–8:30
The Teaching of Jesus Mark 8:31–10:45
The Sacrifice of Jesus Mark 10:46–16:20

Join the Street Team

Read Mark 2:13–17

I have not come to call the righteous, but sinners.

MARK 2:17

City health workers in San Francisco are taking medical care to the streets. Their goal is to supply medicine for homeless people who are suffering from opioid addiction. The program began in response to the rising number of homeless who are injecting. Customarily, doctors wait for patients to come to a clinic. By taking medical care to the afflicted instead, workers free patients from the challenges of transportation or needing to remember the appointment.

The health workers' willingness to go to those in need of care reminds me of the way Jesus has come to us in our need. In His ministry, Jesus sought out those the religious elite were quick to ignore: He ate with "sinners and tax collectors" (v. 16). When asked why He would do that, Jesus replied, "It is not the healthy who need a doctor, but the sick" (v. 17). He went on to say that His intention was to call sinners, not the righteous, into relationship with Him.

When we realize that we're all "sick" and in need of a doctor (Romans 3:10), we can better appreciate Jesus's willingness to eat with the "sinners and tax collectors"—us. In turn, like the health care workers in San Francisco, Jesus appointed us as His "street team" to take His saving message to others in need. *Kirsten Holmberg*

JULY 11

Space for Me

Read Mark 3:13–19

Jesus went up on a mountainside and called to him those he wanted, and they came to him.

MARK 3:13

He was an aging military veteran, rough-edged and given to even rougher language. One day a friend cared enough about him to inquire about his spiritual beliefs. The man's dismissive response came quickly: "God doesn't have space for someone like me."

Perhaps that was just part of his "tough-guy" act, but his words couldn't be further from the truth! God creates space especially for the rough, the guilt-ridden, and the excluded to belong and thrive in His community. This was obvious from the beginning of Jesus's ministry, when He made some surprising choices for His disciples. First, He chose several fishermen from Galilee—the "wrong side of the tracks" from the perspective of those in Jerusalem. He also selected a tax collector, Matthew, whose profession included extorting from his oppressed countrymen. Then, for good measure, Jesus invited the "other" Simon—"the Zealot" (Mark 3:18).

We don't know much about this Simon (he isn't Simon Peter), but we do know about the Zealots. They hated traitors like Matthew, who got rich by collaborating with the despised Romans. Yet with divine irony, Jesus chose Simon along with Matthew, brought them together, and blended them into His team.

Don't write anyone off as too "bad" for Jesus. After all, He said, "I have not come to call the righteous, but sinners to repentance" (Luke 5:32). He has plenty of space for the tough cases—people like you and me.   *Tim Gustafson*

Servant's Heart

Read Mark 9:33–37

*Anyone who wants to be first must be the
very last, and the servant of all.*

MARK 9:35

Cook. Event Planner. Nutritionist. Nurse. These are just some of the responsibilities regularly performed by modern moms. In 2016, research estimated that moms likely worked between fifty-nine and ninety-six hours per week doing child-related tasks.

No wonder moms are always exhausted! Being a mom means giving a lot of time and energy to care for children, who need so much help as they learn to navigate the world.

When my days feel long and I need a reminder that caring for others is a worthy pursuit, I find great hope when I see Jesus affirming those who serve.

In the gospel of Mark, the disciples were having an argument about which one of them was the greatest. Jesus quietly sat down and reminded them that "anyone who wants to be first must be the very last, and the servant of all" (9:35). Then He took a child in His arms to illustrate the importance of serving others, especially the most helpless among us (vv. 36–37).

Christ's response resets the bar for what greatness looks like in His kingdom. His standard is a heart willing to care for others. And Jesus has promised that God's empowering presence will be with those who choose to serve (v. 37).

As you have opportunities to serve in your family or community, be encouraged that Jesus greatly values the time and effort you give in service to others.

Lisa Samra

Asking for Help

Read Mark 10:46–52

"What do you want me to do for you?" Jesus asked him.

MARK 10:51

Her email arrived late in a long day. In truth, I didn't open it. I was working overtime to help a family member manage his serious illness. I didn't have time, therefore, for social distractions.

The next morning, however, when I clicked on my friend's message, I saw this question: "Can I help you in any way?" Feeling embarrassed, I started to answer no. Then I took a deep breath to pause. I noticed then that her question sounded familiar—if not divine.

That's because Jesus asked it. Hearing a blind beggar call out to Him on the Jericho Road, Jesus stopped to ask this man, named Bartimaeus, a similar question. Can I help? Or as Jesus said: "What do you want me to do for you?" (Mark 10:51).

The question is stunning. It shows the Healer, Jesus, longs to help us. But first, we're invited to admit needing Him—a humbling step. The "professional" beggar Bartimaeus was needy, indeed—poor, alone, and possibly hungry and downcast. But wanting a new life, he simply told Jesus his most basic need. "Rabbi," he said, "I want to see."

For a blind man, it was an honest plea. Jesus healed him immediately. My friend sought such honesty from me too. So I promised her I'd pray to understand my basic need and, more important, I'd humbly tell her. Do you know your basic need today? When a friend asks, tell it. Then take your plea even higher. Tell God.   *Patricia Raybon*

Pure Worship

Read Mark 11:15–18

My house will be called a house of prayer.

MARK 11:17

Jose pastored a church known for its programs and theatrical productions. They were well done, yet he worried that the church's busyness had transformed into a business. Was the church growing for the right reasons or because of its activities? Jose wanted to find out, so he canceled all extra church events for one year. His congregation would focus on being a living temple where people worshiped God.

Jose's decision seems extreme, until you notice what Jesus did when He entered the temple's outer courts. The holy space that should have been full of simple prayers had become a flurry of worship business. "Get your doves here! Lily white, as God requires!" Jesus overturned the merchant's tables and stopped those who bought their merchandise. Furious at what they were doing, He quoted Isaiah 56 and Jeremiah 7: "'My house will be called a house of prayer for all nations.' But you have made it 'a den of robbers'" (Mark 11:17). The court of the gentiles, the place for outsiders to worship God, had been turned into a mundane marketplace for making money.

There's nothing wrong with business or staying busy. But that's not the point of church. We're the living temple of God, and our main task is to worship Jesus. We likely won't need to flip over any tables as Jesus did, but He may be calling us to do something equally drastic.

Mike Wittmer

JULY 15

Blocked Prayer

Read Mark 11:20–25

When you stand praying, if you hold anything
against anyone, forgive them, so that your Father
in heaven may forgive you your sins.

MARK 11:25

For fourteen years, the Mars rover *Opportunity* faithfully communicated with the people at NASA's Jet Propulsion Laboratory. After it landed in 2004, it traversed twenty-eight miles of the Martian surface, took thousands of images, and analyzed many materials. But in 2018, communication between *Opportunity* and scientists ended when a major dust storm coated its solar panels, causing the rover to lose power.

Is it possible that we can allow "dust" to block our communication with Someone outside of our world? When it comes to prayer—communicating with God—there are certain things that can get in the way.

Scripture says that sin can block our relationship with God. "If I had cherished sin in my heart, the Lord would not have listened" (Psalm 66:18). Jesus instructs, "When you stand praying, if you hold anything against anyone, forgive them, so that your Father in heaven may forgive you your sins" (Mark 11:25). Our communication with God can also be hindered by doubt and relationship problems (James 1:5–7; 1 Peter 3:7).

Opportunity's blockage of communication seems to be permanent. But our prayers don't have to be blocked. By the work of the Holy Spirit, God lovingly draws us to restored communication with Him. As we confess our sins and turn to Him, by God's grace we experience the greatest communication the universe has ever known: one-to-one prayer between us and our holy God.   *Dave Branon*

She Did What She Could

Read Mark 14:3–9

*She did what she could. She poured perfume on my
body beforehand to prepare for my burial.*

MARK 14:8

She loaded the plastic container of cupcakes onto the conveyor belt, sending it toward the cashier. Next came the birthday card and various bags of chips. Hair escaped from her ponytail, crowning her fatigued forehead. Her toddler clamored for attention. The clerk announced the total and the mom's face fell. "Oh, I guess I'll have to put something back. But these are for her party," she sighed, glancing regretfully at her child.

Standing behind her in line, another customer recognized this mother's pain. This scene is familiar in Jesus's words to Mary of Bethany: "She did what she could" (Mark 14:8). After anointing Him with a bottle of expensive nard before His death and burial, Mary was ridiculed by the disciples. Jesus corrected His followers by celebrating what she had done. He didn't say, "She did all she could," but rather, "She did what she could." The lavish cost of the perfume wasn't His point. It was Mary's investment of her love in action that mattered. A relationship with Jesus results in a response.

In that moment, before the mom could object, the second customer leaned forward and inserted her credit card into the reader, paying for the purchase. It wasn't a large expense, and she had extra funds that month. But to that mom, it was everything. A gesture of pure love poured out in her moment of need. *Elisa Morgan*

My Father Is with Me

Read Mark 14:32–50

*You will be scattered, each to your own home. You will leave
me all alone. Yet I am not alone, for my Father is with me.*

JOHN 16:32

A friend struggling with loneliness posted these words on her Facebook
page: "It's not that I feel alone because I have no friends. I have lots of
friends. I know that I have people who can hold me and reassure me
and talk to me and care for me and think of me. But they can't be with
me all the time—for all time."

Jesus understands that kind of loneliness. I imagine that during
His earthly ministry He saw loneliness in the eyes of lepers and heard
it in the voices of the blind. But above all, He must have experienced
it when His close friends deserted Him (Mark 14:50).

However, as He foretold the disciples' desertion, He also confessed
His unshaken confidence in His Father's presence. He said to His disciples: "You will leave me all alone. Yet I am not alone, for my Father is
with me" (John 16:32). Shortly after Jesus said these words, He took up
the cross for us. He made it possible for you and me to have a restored
relationship with God and to be a member of His family.

Being humans, we will all experience times of loneliness. But Jesus
helps us understand that we always have the presence of the Father
with us. God is omnipresent and eternal. Only He can be with us all
the time, for all time. *Poh Fang Chia*

LUKE

♦

Luke's purposeful recounting of the life of Jesus allows us to follow chronologically the vital information we need to know about the life of our Savior. Starting with the story of Jesus's forerunner John the Baptist and continuing on into the vital details about Jesus's incarnation, Luke creates a beautiful narrative of the Messiah's coming to earth.

OUTLINE

Introduction to Jesus, the Son of Man Luke 1:1–4:13
The Ministry and Teaching of Jesus Luke 4:14–19:27
The Death and Resurrection of Jesus Luke 19:28–24:53

Waiting in Hope

Read Luke 2:25–35

Simeon . . . was righteous and devout. He was waiting for the consolation of Israel, and the Holy Spirit was on him.

LUKE 2:25

In the movie *Hachi: A Dog's Tale*, a college professor befriended a stray Akita puppy named Hachi. The dog expressed his loyalty by waiting at the train station each day for the professor to return from work. One day, the professor suffered a fatal stroke. Hachi waited hours at the train station, and for the next ten years he returned each day—awaiting His loving master.

Luke tells the story of a man named Simeon who patiently waited for the coming of his Master (Luke 2:25). The Holy Spirit revealed to Simeon that he would not see death until he saw the Messiah (v. 26). As a result, Simeon kept waiting for the One who would provide "salvation" for God's people (v. 30). When Mary and Joseph entered the temple with Jesus, the Holy Spirit whispered to Simeon that He was the One! The wait was finally over! Simeon held Christ in his arms—the hope, salvation, and comfort for all people (vv. 28–32).

If we find ourselves in a season of waiting, may we hear the words of the prophet Isaiah with fresh ears: "Those who hope in the LORD will renew their strength. They will soar on wings like eagles; they will run and not grow weary, they will walk and not be faint" (Isaiah 40:31). As we await Jesus's return, He provides the hope and strength we need for each new day.   *Marvin Williams*

Touched by Grace

Read Luke 6:27–36

Love your enemies, do good to those who hate you.

LUKE 6:27

In Leif Enger's novel *Peace Like a River*, Jeremiah Land is a single father of three working as a janitor at a local school. He's also a man of deep, sometimes miraculous, faith. Throughout the book, his faith is often tested.

Jeremiah's school is run by Chester Holden, a mean-spirited superintendent with a skin condition. Despite Jeremiah's excellent work ethic—mopping up a sewage spill without complaint, picking up broken bottles the superintendent smashed—Holden wants him gone. One day, in front of all the students, he accuses Jeremiah of drunkenness and fires him. It's a humiliating scene.

How does Jeremiah respond? He could threaten legal action for unfair dismissal or make accusations of his own. He could slink away, accepting the injustice. Think for a moment what you might do.

"Love your enemies," Jesus says, "do good to those who hate you, bless those who curse you, pray for those who mistreat you" (Luke 6:27–28). These challenging words aren't meant to excuse evil or stop justice from being pursued. Instead, they call us to imitate God (v. 36) by asking a profound question: How can I help my enemy become all God wants him or her to be?

Jeremiah looks at Holden for a moment, then reaches up and touches his face. Holden steps back defensively, then feels his chin and cheeks in wonder. His scarred skin has been healed.

An enemy touched by grace.

Sheridan Voysey

The Kindness Man

Read Luke 7:11–17

*When the L*ORD *saw her, his heart went out to her.*

LUKE 7:13

Disillusioned and wanting a more meaningful life, Leon quit his job in finance. Then one day he saw a homeless man holding up this sign at a street corner: KINDNESS IS THE BEST MEDICINE. Leon says, "Those words rammed straight into me. It was an epiphany."

Leon decided to begin his new life by creating an international organization to promote kindness. He travels around the world, relying on strangers to provide him with food, gas, and a place to stay. Then he rewards them, through his organization, with good deeds such as feeding orphans or building on to a school for underprivileged children. He says, "It's sometimes seen as being soft. But kindness is a profound strength."

Christ's very essence as God is goodness, so kindness naturally flowed from Him. I love the story of what Jesus did when He came upon the funeral procession of a widow's only son (Luke 7:11–17). The grieving woman most likely was dependent on her son for financial support. We don't read in the story that anyone asked Jesus to intervene. Purely from the goodness of His nature (v. 13), He was concerned and brought her son back to life. The people said of Christ, "God has come to help his people" (v. 16). *Anne Cetas*

Confident Prayer

Read Luke 11:5–13

*Which of you fathers, if your son asks for a
fish, will give him a snake instead?*

Luke 11:11

Having tried for years to have a child, Richard and Susan were elated when Susan became pregnant. Her health problems, however, posed a risk to the baby, and so Richard lay awake each night praying for his wife and child. One night, Richard sensed he didn't need to pray so hard, that God had promised to take care of things. But a week later Susan miscarried. Richard was devastated. He wondered, *Had they lost the baby because he hadn't prayed hard enough?*

On first reading, we might think today's parable suggests so. In the story, a neighbor (sometimes thought to represent God) only gets out of bed to help the friend because of the friend's annoying persistence (Luke 11:5–8). Read this way, the parable suggests that God will give us what we need only if we badger Him. And if we don't pray hard enough, maybe God won't help us.

But biblical commentators like Klyne Snodgrass believe this misunderstands the parable—its real point being that if neighbors might help us for selfish reasons, how much more will our unselfish Father. We can therefore ask confidently (vv. 9–10), knowing that God is greater than flawed human beings (vv. 11–13). He isn't the neighbor in the parable, but the opposite of him.

"I don't know why you lost your baby," I told Richard, "but I know it wasn't because you didn't pray 'hard' enough. God isn't like that."

Sheridan Voysey

Priceless Lives in Christ

Read Luke 15:8-10

There is rejoicing in the presence of the angels
of God over one sinner who repents.

LUKE 15:10

Tears streamed down my cheeks during a frantic search for my lost wedding and anniversary rings. After an hour of lifting couch cushions and scouring every nook and cranny of our home, Alan said, "I'm sorry. We'll replace them."

"Thanks," I responded. "But their sentimental value surpasses their material worth. They're irreplaceable." Praying, I continued hunting for the jewelry. "Please, God. Help me find them."

Later, while reaching into the pocket of a sweater worn earlier in the week, I found the priceless jewels. "Thank You, Jesus!" I exclaimed. As my husband and I rejoiced, I slipped on the rings and recalled the parable of the woman who lost a coin (Luke 15:8–10). Like the woman who searched for her lost silver coin, I knew the worth of what had been lost. Neither of us was wrong for wanting to find our valuables. Jesus simply used that story to emphasize His desire to save every person He created. One sinner repenting results in a celebration in heaven.

What a gift it would be to become a person who prays as passionately for others as we pray for lost treasures to be found. What a privilege it is to celebrate when someone repents and surrenders his or her life to Christ. If we've placed our trust in Jesus, we can be thankful we've experienced the joy of being loved by Someone who never gave up, because He thought we were worth finding.   *Xochitl Dixon*

Sight Unseen

Read Luke 16:19–31

*If they do not listen to Moses and the Prophets, they will
not be convinced even if someone rises from the dead.*

Luke 16:31

After Yuri Gagarin became the first man in space, he parachuted into
the Russian countryside. A farmwoman spotted the orange-clad cos-
monaut, still wearing his helmet and dragging two parachutes. "Can it
be that you have come from outer space?" she asked in surprise. "As a
matter of fact, I have," he said.

Soviet leaders sadly turned the historic flight into antireligious pro-
paganda. "Gagarin went into space, but he didn't see any god there,"
their premier declared. (Gagarin himself never said such a thing.) As
C. S. Lewis observed at the time, "Those who do not find [God] on
earth are unlikely to find Him in space."

Jesus warned us about ignoring God in this life. He told a story of
two men who died—a rich man who had no time for God, and Lazarus,
a destitute man rich in faith (Luke 16:19–31). In torment, the rich man
pleaded with Abraham for his brothers still on earth. "Send Lazarus,"
he begged Abraham. "If someone from the dead goes to them, they will
repent" (vv. 27, 30). Abraham got to the heart of the problem: "If they
do not listen to Moses and the Prophets, they will not be convinced
even if someone rises from the dead" (v. 31).

"Seeing is never believing," wrote Oswald Chambers. "We interpret
what we see in the light of what we believe."   *Tim Gustafson*

Extending Mercy

Read Luke 17:1–5

If your brother or sister sins against you, rebuke them;
and if they repent, forgive them.

LUKE 17:3

Reflecting on how she forgave Manasseh, the man who killed her husband and some of her children in the Rwandan genocide, Beata said, "My forgiving is based on what Jesus did. He took the punishment for every evil act throughout all time. His cross is the place we find victory—the only place!" Manasseh had written to Beata from prison more than once, begging her—and God—for forgiveness as he detailed the regular nightmares that plagued him. At first, she could extend no mercy, saying she hated him for killing her family. But then "Jesus intruded into her thoughts," and with God's help, some two years later, she forgave him.

In this, Beata followed Jesus's instruction to His disciples to forgive those who repent. He said that even if they "sin against you seven times in a day and seven times come back to you saying 'I repent,' you must forgive them" (Luke 17:4). But to forgive can be extremely difficult, as we see by the disciples' reaction: "Increase our faith!" (v. 5).

Beata's faith increased as she wrestled in prayer over her inability to forgive. If, like her, we're struggling to forgive, we can ask God through His Holy Spirit to help us to do so. As our faith increases, He helps us to forgive.   *Amy Boucher Pye*

Found on the Edges

Read Luke 19:1–10

For the Son of Man came to seek and to save the lost.

LUKE 19:10

In the middle of the crowd at a motorcycle demonstration where riders performed breathtaking tricks, I found myself needing to stand on my tiptoes to see. Glancing around, I noticed three children perched in a nearby tree, apparently because they also couldn't get to the front of the crowd to see the action.

Watching the kids peer out from their lofty location, I couldn't help but think of Zacchaeus, who Luke identifies as a wealthy tax collector (Luke 19:2). Jews often viewed tax collectors as traitors for working for the Roman government collecting taxes from fellow Israelites, as well as frequently demanding additional money to pad their personal bank accounts. So Zacchaeus was likely shunned from his community.

As Jesus passed through Jericho, Zacchaeus longed to see Him but was unable to see over the crowd. So, perhaps feeling both desperate and lonely, he climbed into a sycamore tree to catch a glimpse (vv. 3–4). And it was there, on the outskirts of the crowd, that Jesus searched him out and announced His intention to be a guest at his home (v. 5).

Zacchaeus's story reminds us that Jesus came to "seek and to save the lost," offering His friendship and the gift of salvation (vv. 9–10). Even if we feel on the edges of our communities, pushed to the "back of the crowd," we can be assured that, even there, Jesus finds us.   *Lisa Samra*

Stronger Than Hate

Read Luke 23:32–34, 44–46

Father, forgive them, for they do not know what they are doing.
LUKE 23:34

Within twenty-four hours of his mother Sharonda's tragic death, Chris found himself uttering these powerful, grace-filled words: "Love is stronger than hate." His mother, along with eight others, had been killed at a Wednesday night Bible study in Charleston, South Carolina. What was it that had so shaped this teenager's life that these words could flow from his lips and his heart? Chris is a believer in Jesus whose mother had "loved everybody with all her heart."

In Luke 23:26–49 we get a front row seat to an execution scene that included two criminals and the innocent Jesus (v. 32). All three were crucified (v. 33). Amid the gasps and sighs and the likely groans from those hanging on the crosses, the following words of Jesus could be heard: "Father, forgive them, for they do not know what they are doing" (v. 34). The hate-filled initiative of the religious leaders had resulted in the crucifixion of the very One who championed love. Though He was in agony, Jesus's love continued to triumph.

How have you or someone you love been the target of hate, ill-will, bitterness, or ugliness? May your pain prompt your prayers, and may the example of Jesus and people like Chris encourage you by the power of the Spirit to choose love over hate.   *Arthur Jackson*

JOHN

John's Gospel is the record of someone who knew Jesus on a personal level. Some have suggested that they were cousins and may have even grown up knowing each other. But the most important thing John recognized about Jesus—and made clear in his book—was the deity of Jesus. Imagine what it was like to realize that your best friend was not just a man—but was God incarnate! So, toward the end of his life, while serving the church Paul started at Ephesus, John sat down to write Jesus's story. He saw that in the young Christian church there was a growing gap between this new faith and traditional Judaism. Through the Holy Spirit's guidance, John sets out to make sure people recognized that Jesus was God, that He was the redeemer, and that abundant life was available to all who would believe in Him. He did this by selecting the miracles and stories about Jesus that would best help people believe. After all, he had plenty of material to choose from (read John 21:25).

OUTLINE

Jesus: The Word Made Flesh John 1:1–18

Jesus Is Presented to the People John 1:19–4:54

Jesus Is Opposed in His Ministry John 5:1–12:50

Jesus Prepares for His Death John 13:1–17:26

Jesus Is Crucified, Buried, and Resurrected John 18:1–21:25

The One Who Understands

Read John 1:1–18

The WORD became flesh and made his dwelling among us.

JOHN 1:14

John Babler is the chaplain for the police and fire departments in his Texas community. During a twenty-two-week sabbatical from his job, he attended police academy training so that he could better understand the situations law enforcement officers face. Through spending time with the other cadets and learning about the intense challenges of the profession, Babler gained a new sense of humility and empathy. In the future, he hopes to be more effective as he counsels police officers who struggle with emotional stress, fatigue, and loss.

We know that God understands the situations we face because He made us and sees everything that happens to us. We also know He understands because He has been to earth and experienced life as a human being. He "became flesh and made his dwelling among us" as the person of Jesus Christ (John 1:14).

Jesus's earthly life included a wide range of difficulty. He felt the searing heat of the sun, the pain of an empty stomach, and the uncertainty of homelessness. Emotionally, He endured the tension of disagreements, the burn of betrayal, and the ongoing threat of violence.

Jesus experienced the joys of friendship and family love, as well as the worst problems that we face here on earth. He provides hope. He is the Wonderful Counselor who patiently listens to our concerns with insight and care (Isaiah 9:6). He is the One who can say, "I've been through that. I understand."   *Jennifer Benson Schuldt*

Water Where We Need It

Read John 4:7–14

Whoever drinks the water I give them will never thirst.

JOHN 4:14

Lake Baikal, the world's deepest lake, is vast and magnificent. Measuring one mile deep and nearly 400 miles (636 km) by 49 miles (79 km) across, it contains one-fifth of all the surface fresh water in the world. But this water is largely inaccessible. Lake Baikal is located in Siberia—one of the most remote areas of Russia. With water so desperately needed for much of our planet, it's ironic that such a vast supply of water is tucked away in a place where not many people can access it.

Although Lake Baikal may be remote, there is an endless source of life-giving water that is available and accessible to those who need it most. When at a well in Samaria, Jesus engaged a woman in conversation, probing at the edges of her deep spiritual thirst. The solution to her heart-need? Jesus himself.

In contrast to the water she had come to draw from the well, Jesus offered something better: "Everyone who drinks this water will be thirsty again, but whoever drinks the water I give them will never thirst. Indeed, the water I give them will become in them a spring of water welling up to eternal life" (John 4:13–14).

Many things promise satisfaction but never fully quench our thirsty hearts. Jesus alone can truly satisfy our spiritual thirst, and His provision is available to everyone, everywhere. *Bill Crowder*

The Jesus Chair

Read John 8:27-32

If you hold to my teaching, you are really my disciples.

JOHN 8:31

When my friend Marge met Tami at a Bible study meeting, she noticed that they seemed to have little in common. But Marge befriended her, and she learned a valuable lesson from her new friend.

Tami had never been to a Bible study, and she was having a hard time understanding something the other women in the study talked about: that God communicated with them—something she had never experienced.

She so desired to hear from God that she took action. Later, she told Marge, "I set aside an old wooden chair, and every time I study my Bible, I ask Jesus to come sit in it." Then Tami explained that whenever a verse stood out to her, she would write out the verse in chalk on the chair. It's become her special "Jesus chair," and she's filled it up with God's messages to her directly from the Bible.

Marge says, "[The Jesus Chair] has changed [Tami's] life. She's growing spiritually because Scripture is becoming personal."

While speaking to Jewish believers, Jesus said, "If you hold to my teaching, you are really my disciples. Then you will know the truth, and the truth will set you free" (John 8:31–32). Let's hold to His teaching, whether it means writing His words on a chair, memorizing them, or seeking to put them into action. The truth and wisdom of Christ's messages help us grow in Him and set us free.   *Dave Branon*

JULY 30

Life to the Full

Read John 10:7–15

The thief comes only to steal and kill and destroy; I have come that they may have life, and have it to the full.

JOHN 10:10

The year was 1918, near the end of World War I, and photographer Eric Enstrom was putting together a portfolio of his work. He wanted to include one that communicated a sense of fullness in a time that felt quite empty to so many people. In his now much-loved photo, a bearded old man sits at a table with his head bowed and his hands clasped in prayer. On the surface before him there is only a book, spectacles, a bowl of gruel, a loaf of bread, and a knife. Nothing more, but also nothing less.

Some might say the photograph reveals scarcity. But Enstrom's point was quite the opposite: Here is a full life, one lived in gratitude, one you and I can experience as well regardless of our circumstances. Jesus announces the good news in John 10: "life . . . to the full" (v. 10). We do a grave disservice to such good news when we equate full with many things. The fullness Jesus speaks of isn't measured in worldly categories like riches or real estate, but rather a heart, mind, soul, and strength brimming in gratitude that the Good Shepherd gave "his life for the sheep" (v. 11), and cares for us and our daily needs. This is a full life— enjoying a relationship with God—that's possible for every one of us.

John Blase

Basin of Love

Read John 13:1–17

After that, he poured water into a basin and
began to wash his disciples' feet.

JOHN 13:5

One day in physics class many years ago, our teacher asked us to tell him—without turning around—what color the back wall of the classroom was. None of us could answer, for we hadn't noticed.

Sometimes we miss or overlook the "stuff" of life simply because we can't take it all in. And sometimes we don't see what's been there all along.

It was like that for me as I recently read again the account of Jesus washing His disciples' feet. The story is a familiar one, for it is often read during Passion Week. That our Savior and King would stoop to cleanse the feet of His disciples awes us. In Jesus's day, even Jewish servants were spared this task because it was seen as beneath them. But what I hadn't noticed before was that Jesus, who was both man and God, washed the feet of Judas. Even though He knew Judas would betray Him, as we see in John 13:11, Jesus still humbled himself and washed Judas's feet.

Love poured out in a basin of water—love that He shared even with the one who would betray Him. As we ponder the events of this week leading up to the celebration of Jesus's resurrection, may we too be given the gift of humility so that we can extend Jesus's love to our friends and any enemies.   *Amy Boucher Pye*

Home Sweet Home

Read John 14:1–14

I am going there to prepare a place for you.
JOHN 14:2

"Why do we have to leave our home and move?" my son asked. It's difficult to explain what a home is, especially to a five-year-old. We were leaving a house, but not our home, in the sense that home is where our loved ones are. It's the place where we long to return after a long trip or after a full day's work.

When Jesus was in the upper room just hours before He died, He told His disciples, "Do not let your hearts be troubled" (John 14:1). The disciples were uncertain of their future because Jesus had predicted His death. But Jesus reassured them of His presence and reminded them they would see Him again. He told them, "My Father's house has many rooms. . . . I am going there to prepare a place for you" (v. 2). He could have used other words to describe heaven. However, He chose words that describe not an uncomfortable or unfamiliar place but a place where Jesus, our loved One, would be.

C. S. Lewis wrote, "Our Father refreshes us on the journey with some pleasant inns, but will not encourage us to mistake them for home." We can thank God for the "pleasant inns" in life, but let's remember that our real home is in heaven where we "will be with the Lord forever" (1 Thessalonians 4:17).   *Keila Ochoa*

Fruit Juice

Read John 15:5-8

*I am the vine; you are the branches. If you remain
in me and I in you, you will bear much fruit.*

JOHN 15:5

A thrift-store bargain, the lamp seemed perfect for my home office—the right color, size, and price. Back at home, however, when I plugged in the cord, nothing happened. No power. No juice. No light.

No problem, my husband assured me. "I can fix that. Easy." As he took the lamp apart, he saw the trouble immediately. The plug wasn't connected to anything. Without wiring to a source of power, the "perfect" pretty lamp was useless.

The same is true for us. Jesus told His disciples, "I am the vine; you are the branches. If you remain in me and I in you, you will bear much fruit." But then he added this reminder: "Apart from me you can do nothing" (John 15:5).

This teaching was given in a grape-growing region, so His disciples readily understood it. Grapevines are hardy plants, and their branches tolerate vigorous pruning. Cut off from their life source, however, the branches are worthless deadwood. So it is with us.

As we remain in Jesus and let His words dwell in us, we're wired to our life source—Christ himself. "This is to my Father's glory," said Jesus, "that you bear much fruit, showing yourselves to be my disciples" (v. 8). Such a fruitful outcome needs daily nourishment, however. Freely, God provides it through the Scriptures and His love. So plug in and let the juice flow!   *Patricia Raybon*

Is Somebody Singing?

Read John 17:20–26

[Bear] with one another in love. Make every effort to
keep the unity of the Spirit through the bond of peace.

EPHESIANS 4:2–3

From two hundred miles above Earth, Chris Hadfield, Canadian astronaut and commander of the International Space Station, joined in song with a group of students in a studio on Earth. Together they performed "Is Somebody Singing," co-written by Hadfield and Ed Robertson.

One phrase of the song caught my attention: "You can't make out borders from up here." Although we humans draw many lines to separate ourselves from one another—national, ethnic, ideological—the song reminded me that God doesn't see such distinctions. The important thing to God is that we love Him and each other (Mark 12:30–31).

Like a loving father, God wants His family united. We cannot accomplish what God has for us to do if we refuse to be reconciled with one another. In His most impassioned prayer, on the night before He was crucified, Jesus pleaded with God to unite His followers: "That they all may be one, as You, Father, are in Me, and I in You; that they also may be one in Us" (John 17:21 NKJV).

Singing illustrates unity as we agree on the lyrics, chords, and rhythms. Singing can also promote unity as it binds us together in peace, proclaims God's power through praise, and demonstrates God's glory to the world. *Julie Ackerman Link*

The Reason for Writing

Read John 20:24–31

But these are written that you may believe.

JOHN 20:31

"The Lord is my high tower. . . . We left the camp singing." On September 7, 1943, Etty Hillesum wrote those words on a postcard and threw it from a train. Those were the final recorded words we would hear from her. On November 30, 1943, she was murdered at Auschwitz. Later, Hillesum's diaries of her experiences in a concentration camp were translated and published. They chronicled her perspectives on the horrors of Nazi occupation along with the beauty of God's world. Her diaries have been translated into sixty-seven languages—a gift to all who would read and believe the good as well as the bad.

The apostle John didn't sidestep the harsh realities of Jesus's life on earth; he wrote of both the good Jesus did and the challenges He faced. The final words from his gospel give insight into the purpose behind the book that bears his name. Jesus performed "many other signs . . . which are not recorded" (20:30) by John. But these, he says, were "written that you may believe" (v. 31). John's "diary" ends on the note of triumph: "Jesus is the Messiah, the Son of God." The gift of those gospel words allows us the opportunity to believe and "have life in his name."

The gospels are diary accounts of God's love for us. They're words to read and believe and share, for they lead us to life. They lead us to Christ.   *John Blase*

No Comparison

Read John 21:17-25

A heart at peace gives life to the body, but envy rots the bones.

Proverbs 14:30

"One of these days I'm going to put it all on Facebook—not just the good stuff!"

My friend Sue's comment—made casually over lunch with her husband—caused me to laugh out loud and also to think. Social media can be a good thing, helping us stay in touch with and pray for friends across the years and miles. But if we're not careful, it can also create an unrealistic outlook on life. When much of what we see posted is a "highlight reel" of "the good stuff," we can be misled into thinking others' lives are without trouble, and we wonder where our own went wrong.

Comparing ourselves with others is a sure recipe for unhappiness. When the disciples compared themselves to each other (see Luke 9:46; 22:24), Jesus quickly discouraged it. Soon after His resurrection, Jesus told Peter how he would suffer for his faith. Peter then turned to John and asked, "Lord, what about him?" Jesus answered, "If I want him to remain alive until I return, what is that to you? You must follow me" (John 21:21–22).

Jesus pointed Peter to the best remedy for unhealthy comparisons. When our minds are focused on God and all He's done for us, self-focused thoughts fall gently away and we long to follow Him. In place of the world's competitive strain and stress, He gives us His loving presence and peace. Nothing can compare with Him.   *James Banks*

PART 7

History of the Church

Acts

The book of Acts could be seen as chapter one of the history of the church of Jesus—a history that has been two thousand years in the making. It was in this book that we see the power of the Holy Spirit falling upon the disciples, which led to the great evangelistic work of Peter and others. Right away three thousand people trusted Jesus and the church was formed. It was a time of wonders and amazing personal transformation. Churches were formed and organized, Saul's life was changed and he changed the world with his passion for Jesus. Missionaries like Paul and others went to surrounding regions to spread the gospel. By the end of the book, the gospel had reached Rome—and that was just the beginning of the worldwide spread of the message of Jesus.

ACTS

◆

Jesus's work on earth is over, and He is about to return to heaven to continue His work from there. He has promised the disciples everything they will need—included the soon coming Holy Spirit. Upon arrival, the Spirit empowered the people, and they were off and running as the New Testament church had a rousing beginning. Soon enough, officials got wind of the amazing conversions that were taking place, and they called on Peter and John to meet with officials, who told them to stop speaking out. This didn't stop the church from growing, however. The opposition to this growing faith continued, leading to the first martyr, Stephen. Attending Stephen's murder and applauding it was a man named Saul—a man who would soon become a great missionary for the gospel. Once he trusted Jesus, his mission was relentless as he crisscrossed the area around the Mediterranean to preach the gospel. He led several missionary journeys, taking some of the church's top people with him such as Luke, Barnabas, and John Mark. Those missionary journeys led to the formation of churches in Ephesus, Philippi, Corinth, and others. Paul's preaching got him into trouble, and as the book ends, he ends in Rome where he continued to teach while awaiting trial.

OUTLINE

The Holy Spirit Fills Believers Acts 1:1–2:47

Impact of the Spirit in Jerusalem Acts 3:1–7:60

Impact of the Spirit in Judea and Samaria Acts 8:1–12:25

Impact of the Spirit to the Rest of the World Acts 13:1–28:31

Don't Forget

Read Acts 1:1–11

*He was taken up before their very eyes, and
a cloud hid him from their sight.*

ACTS 1:9

My niece, her four-year-old daughter Kailyn, and I had a wonderful Saturday afternoon together. We enjoyed blowing bubbles outside, coloring in a princess coloring book, and eating peanut butter and jelly sandwiches. When they got in the car to leave, Kailyn sweetly called out the opened window, "Don't forget me, Auntie Anne." I quickly walked toward the car and whispered, "I could never forget you. I promise I will see you soon."

In Acts 1, the disciples watched as Jesus was "taken up before their very eyes" into the sky (v. 9). I wonder if they thought they might be forgotten by their Master. But He had just promised to send His Spirit to live in them and empower them to handle the persecution that was to come (v. 8). And He'd taught them He was going away to prepare a place for them and would come back and take them to be with Him (John 14:3). Yet they must have wondered how long they would have to wait. Perhaps they wanted to say, "Don't forget us, Jesus!"

For those of us who have put our faith in Jesus, He lives in us through the Holy Spirit. We still may wonder when He will come again and restore us and His creation fully. But it will happen—He won't forget us. "Therefore encourage one another and build each other up" (1 Thessalonians 5:11). *Anne Cetas*

New Humanity

Read Acts 2:1–12

*When they heard this sound, a crowd came
together in bewilderment, because each one
heard their own language being spoken.*

ACTS 2:6

While I was visiting London's Tate Modern gallery, one piece of art caught my attention. Created by Brazilian artist Cildo Meireles, it was a giant tower made of hundreds of old radios. Each radio was turned on and tuned to a different station, creating a cacophony of confusing, indecipherable speech. Meireles called the sculpture Babel.

The title is appropriate. At the original tower of Babel, God thwarted humanity's attempt to seize heaven by confusing mankind's languages (Genesis 11:1–9). No longer able to communicate with one another, humanity fractured into tribes of various dialects (vv. 10–26). Divided by language, we've struggled to understand each other ever since.

There's a second part to the story. When the Holy Spirit came upon the first Christians at Pentecost, He enabled them to praise God in the various languages of those visiting Jerusalem that day (Acts 2:1–12). Through this miracle, everyone heard the same message, no matter their nationality or language. The confusion of Babel was reversed.

In a world of ethnic and cultural division, this is good news. Through Jesus, God is forming a new humanity from every nation, tribe, and tongue (Revelation 7:9). As I stood at Tate Modern, I imagined all those radios suddenly tuning to a new signal and playing the same song to all in the room: "Amazing grace, how sweet the sound."   *Sheridan Voysey*

The Ministry of Mourning

Read Acts 7:54–8:2

Godly men buried Stephen and mourned deeply for him.
ACTS 8:2

A few months after my sister Martha and her husband, Jim, died in an accident, a friend invited me to a "Growing Through Grief" workshop at our church. I reluctantly agreed to attend the first session but had no intention of going back. To my surprise, I discovered a caring community of people trying to come to grips with a significant loss in their lives by seeking the help of God and others. It drew me back week after week as I worked toward acceptance and peace through the process of sharing our grief together.

Like the sudden loss of a loved one or friend, the death of Stephen, a dynamic witness for Jesus, brought shock and sorrow to those in the early church (Acts 7:57–60). In the face of persecution, "Godly men buried Stephen and mourned deeply for him" (8:2). These men of faith did two things together: They buried Stephen, an act of finality and loss. And they mourned deeply for him, a shared expression of their sorrow.

As followers of Jesus, we need not mourn our losses alone. In sincerity and love we can reach out to others who are hurting, and in humility we can accept the concern of those who stand beside us.

As we grieve together, we can grow in understanding and in the peace that is ours through Jesus Christ, who knows our deepest sorrow.

David McCasland

Love Changes Us

Read Acts 9:1–22

*At once he began to preach in the synagogues
that Jesus is the Son of God.*

Acts 9:20

Before I met Jesus, I had been wounded so deeply that I avoided close relationships in fear of being hurt more. My mom remained my closest friend, until I married Alan. Seven years later and on the verge of divorce, I toted our kindergartener, Xavier, into a church service. I sat near the exit door, afraid to trust but desperate for help.

Thankfully, believers reached out, prayed for our family, and taught me how to nurture a relationship with God through prayer and Bible reading. Over time, the love of Christ and His followers changed me.

Two years after that first church service, Alan, Xavier, and I asked to be baptized. Sometime later, during one of our weekly conversations, my mom said, "You're different. Tell me more about Jesus." A few months passed and she too accepted Christ as her Savior.

Jesus transforms lives . . . lives like Saul's, one of the most feared persecutors of the church until his encounter with Christ (Acts 9:1–5). Others helped Saul learn more about Jesus (vv. 17–19). His drastic transformation added to the credibility of his Spirit-empowered teaching (vv. 20–22).

Our first personal encounter with Jesus may not be as dramatic as Saul's. Our life transformation may not be as quick or drastic. Still, as people notice how Christ's love is changing us over time, we'll have opportunities to tell others what He did for us.   *Xochitl Dixon*

Living beyond the Odds

Read Acts 12:1–11

Peter was kept in prison, but the church was
earnestly praying to God for him.

ACTS 12:5

Many of us make daily decisions based on the odds. If there's a twenty-percent chance of rain, we may ignore it. If there's a ninety-percent chance, we'll take an umbrella. The greater the odds, the more our behavior is affected, because we want to choose wisely and be successful.

Acts 12:1–6 describes a situation in which Peter's odds of survival were very low. He was in prison, "sleeping between two soldiers, bound with two chains" while others guarded the door (v. 6). Herod had already executed James, one of Jesus's closest followers, and he had the same fate in mind for Peter (vv. 1–3). A gambler would not have put any money on Peter getting out of this alive.

Yet God's plan for Peter included a miraculous deliverance that even those who were interceding for him found hard to believe (vv. 13–16). They were astonished when he showed up at their prayer meeting.

God can operate outside the odds because He is all-powerful. Nothing is too hard for Him. The One who loves us and gave himself for us is in charge of our lives. In ordinary circumstances and impossible situations, God can reveal His power. Whether we are showered with success or sustained in sorrow, He is with us.   *David McCasland*

Plans Disrupted

Read Acts 16:6–10

Many are the plans in a person's heart,
but it is the LORD's purpose that prevails.

PROVERBS 19:21

Jane's plans to become a speech therapist ended when an internship revealed the job was too emotionally challenging for her. Then she was given the opportunity to write for a magazine. She'd never seen herself as an author, but years later she found herself advocating for needy families through her writing. "Looking back, I can see why God changed my plans," she says. "He had a bigger plan for me."

The Bible has many stories of disrupted plans. On his second missionary journey, Paul had sought to bring the gospel into Bithynia, but the Spirit of Jesus stopped him (Acts 16:6–7). This must have seemed mystifying: Why was Jesus disrupting plans that were in line with a God-given mission? The answer came in a dream one night: Macedonia needed him even more. There, Paul would plant the first church in Europe. Solomon also observed, "Many are the plans in a person's heart, but it is the LORD's purpose that prevails" (Proverbs 19:21).

It's sensible to make plans. A well-known adage goes, "Fail to plan, and you plan to fail." But God may disrupt our plans with His own. Our challenge is to listen and obey, knowing we can trust God. If we submit to His will, we'll find ourselves fitting into His purpose for our lives.

As we continue to make plans, we can add a new twist: Plan to listen. Listen to God's plan. *Leslie Koh*

Eloquent Yet Humble

Read Acts 18:24–28

[God] guides the humble in what is right.

PSALM 25:9

I admire people who can articulate their beliefs and persuade others with their rhetoric. Some call it "the gift of gab" or "having a way with words." Others call it "eloquence."

Apollos had that gift. We are told that he was "a learned man, with a thorough knowledge of the Scriptures" (Acts 18:24). But although he taught accurately about Christ, he preached only of the baptism of John, which was a baptism of repentance from sin (v. 25; 19:4).

Apollos knew about Jesus's teachings but may not have known about His death and resurrection and that the Spirit had arrived (Acts 2). His teaching was incomplete because he didn't know about being filled with the Spirit for daily empowerment.

So Priscilla and Aquila, a wife and husband who were friends of Paul, invited Apollos into their home to correct his teaching. Although he was highly educated and knew the Scriptures well, Apollos humbly accepted their instruction. As a result, Apollos was able to continue his ministry, but with newfound understanding.

Psalm 25:9 reminds us that God "guides the humble in what is right and teaches them his way." If we have a spirit of humility, we can be taught by God and be used to touch the lives of others.

Cindy Hess Kasper

The Faith to Endure

Read Acts 27:27–38

Suffering produces endurance.
ROMANS 5:3 ESV

Ernest Shackleton (1874–1922) led an unsuccessful expedition to cross Antarctica in 1914. When his ship, aptly named *Endurance*, became trapped in heavy ice in the Weddell Sea, it became an endurance race just to survive. With no means of communicating with the rest of the world, Shackleton and his crew used lifeboats to make the journey to the nearest shore—Elephant Island. While most of the crew stayed behind on the island, Shackleton and five crewmen spent two weeks traveling eight hundred miles across the ocean to South Georgia to get help for those left behind. The "failed" expedition became a victorious entry in the history books when all of Shackleton's men survived, thanks to their courage and endurance.

The apostle Paul knew what it meant to endure. During a stormy sea voyage to Rome to face trial for his belief in Jesus, Paul learned from an angel of God that the ship would sink. But the apostle kept the men aboard encouraged, thanks to God's promise that all would survive, despite the loss of the ship (Acts 27:23–24).

When disaster strikes, we tend to want God to immediately make everything better. But God gives us the faith to endure and grow. As Paul wrote to the Romans, "Suffering produces endurance" (Romans 5:3 ESV). Knowing that, we can encourage each other to keep trusting God in hard times. *Linda Washington*

PART 8

◆

The Letters

Romans, Corinthians, Galatians, Ephesians, Philippians, Colossians, 1 & 2 Thessalonians, 1 & 2 Timothy, Titus, Philemon, Hebrews, James, 1 & 2 Peter, 1 & 2 & 3 John, Jude

The numerous letters that were written to the new churches and to the leaders of the new churches of Christianity helped those nascent followers of Jesus—and us—know how to live. True faith in Christ is not just a creed or a confession, but it is a total life transformation. It is a life that is informed by a reading of God's guidelines, many of which are in these letters. It is a life that is lived in unity with other believers in the church, another key component of the epistles of this section. Taken together, these letters, written by such men as Paul, Peter, and John, form a trustworthy document that shows us how to live in a world that can threaten us with temptation, persecution, troubles, false teachers, and distractions. By reading these letters and carefully gleaning from them the godly standards for holy, righteous living, we can carry on the work begun by our Christian forbearers. The wisdom and instruction in these books are essential to Christlike living in any age—whether the first century or the twenty-first.

ROMANS

◆

Paul's comment in Romans 1:16 that he is not ashamed of the gospel is as much a testimony as it is a teaching. Paul clearly demonstrated through his efforts that he would take the gospel anywhere and explain it to anybody. In Romans, he takes the opportunity to record for all time the theology behind the gospel and as a result he has provided for us an abundantly clear explanation of the importance of God's solution for mankind's deadly problem of sin. In the doctrinal part of Romans, we find out about the universality of sin, the righteousness of God (with Abraham as an illustration), the advantages of justification by faith, and the results of our relationship with Jesus Christ, our Savior. Paul then moves on to spell out how we should live in light of our salvation as we interact with others.

OUTLINE

The Problem of Sin Romans 1:1–3:20

The Solution to the Problem Romans 3:21–5:21

The Sanctification of Believers Romans 6:1–8:39

Learning from Israel Romans 9:1–11:36

Putting Righteousness into Action Romans 12:1–16:27

A Blessing Bowl

Read Romans 1:1–10

I thank my God every time I remember you.

PHILIPPIANS 1:3

The familiar bing of an arriving email caught my attention while I wrote at my computer. Usually I try to resist the temptation to check every email, but the subject line was too enticing: "You are a blessing."

Eagerly, I opened it to discover a faraway friend telling me she was praying for my family. Each week, she displays one Christmas card photo in her kitchen table "Blessing Bowl" and prays for that family. She wrote, "I thank my God every time I remember you" (Philippians 1:3) and then highlighted our efforts to share God's love with others—our "partnership" in the gospel.

Through my friend's intentional gesture, the apostle Paul's words to the Philippians came trickling into my inbox, creating the same joy in my heart I suspect readers received from his first-century thank-you note. It seems Paul made it a habit to speak his gratitude to those who worked alongside him. A similar phrase opens many of his letters: "I thank my God through Jesus Christ for all of you, because your faith is being reported all over the world" (Romans 1:8).

In the first century, Paul blessed his co-laborers with a thank-you note of prayerfulness. In the twenty-first century, my friend used a Blessing Bowl to bring joy into my day. How might we thank those who serve in the mission of God with us today?   *Elisa Morgan*

Guilt and Forgiveness

Read Romans 2:12–16

*They show that the requirements of the
law are written on their hearts.*

ROMANS 2:15

In his book *Human Universals*, anthropologist Donald Brown lists more than four hundred behaviors that he considers common across humanity. He includes such things as toys, jokes, dances, and proverbs, wariness of snakes, and tying things with string! Likewise, he believes all cultures have concepts of right and wrong, where generosity is praised, promises are valued, and things like meanness and murder understood to be wrong. We all have a sense of conscience, wherever we're from.

The apostle Paul made a similar point many centuries ago. While God gave the Jewish people the Ten Commandments to clarify right from wrong, Paul noted that since gentiles could do right by obeying their conscience, God's laws were evidently written on their hearts (Romans 2:14–15). But that didn't mean people always did what was right. The gentiles rebelled against their conscience (1:32), the Jews broke the Law (2:17–24), leaving both guilty. But through faith in Jesus, God removes the death penalty from all our rule-breaking (3:23–26; 6:23).

Since God created all humans with a sense of right and wrong, each of us will likely feel some guilt over a bad thing we've done or a good thing we failed to do. When we confess those sins, God wipes away the guilt like a whiteboard wiped clean. All we have to do is ask Him—whoever we are, wherever we're from.   *Sheridan Voysey*

The Battle's Over. Really

Read Romans 6:1–11

We were . . . buried with him.

ROMANS 6:4

For twenty-nine years after World War II ended, Hiroo Onoda hid in the jungle, refusing to believe his country had surrendered. Japanese military leaders had dispatched Onoda to a remote island in the Philippines (Lubang) with orders to spy on the Allied forces. Long after a peace treaty had been signed and hostilities ceased, Onoda remained in the wilderness. In 1974, Onoda's commanding officer traveled to the island to find him and convince him the war was over.

For nearly three decades, Onoda lived a meager, isolated existence, because he refused to surrender—refused to believe the conflict was done. We can make a similar mistake. Paul proclaims the stunning truth that "all of us who were baptized into Christ Jesus were baptized into his death" (Romans 6:3). On the cross, in a powerful, mysterious way, Jesus put to death Satan's lies, death's terror, and sin's tenacious grip. Though we're "dead to sin" and "alive to God" (v. 11), we often live as though evil still holds the power. We yield to temptation, succumbing to sin's seduction. We listen to lies, failing to trust Jesus. But we don't have to yield. We don't have to live in a false narrative. By God's grace we can embrace the true story of Christ's victory.

While we'll still wrestle with sin, liberation comes as we recognize that Jesus has already won the battle. May we live out that truth in His power.   *Winn Collier*

Legally His

Read Romans 8:1–2, 10–17

The Spirit you received brought about your adoption to sonship.
ROMANS 8:15

Liz cried for joy when she and her husband received the birth certificate and passport for their child, making the adoption legally binding. Now Milena would always be their daughter, forever part of their family. As Liz pondered the legal process, she also thought of the "true exchange" that happens when we become part of Jesus's family: "No longer are we held down by our birthright of sin and brokenness." Rather, she continued, we enter into the fullness of God's kingdom legally when we are adopted as His children.

In the apostle Paul's day, if a Roman family adopted a son, his legal status would change completely. Any debts from his old life would be canceled, and he would gain all of the rights and privileges of his new family. Paul wanted the Roman believers in Jesus to understand that this new status applied to them too. No longer were they bound to sin and condemnation, but now they lived "according to the Spirit" (Romans 8:4). And those the Spirit leads are adopted as God's children (vv. 14–15). Their legal status changed when they became citizens of heaven.

If we have received the gift of salvation, we too are God's children, heirs of His kingdom and united with Christ. Our debts have been canceled by the gift of Jesus's sacrifice. We no longer need to live in fear or condemnation. *Amy Boucher Pye*

Dedicated to Love

Read Romans 9:1–5

My heart's desire and prayer to God for the
Israelites is that they may be saved.

ROMANS 10:1

As a convert to Jesus Christ, Nabeel Qureshi has written books to help his readers understand the people in the religion he left. His tone is respectful, and Qureshi always displays a heart of love for his people.

Qureshi dedicated one of his books to his sister, who has not yet put her faith in Jesus. The dedication is brief, but powerful. "I am begging God for the day that we can worship Him together," he wrote.

We get a sense of that kind of love as we read Paul's letter to the church in Rome. "My heart is filled with bitter sorrow and unending grief," he said, "for my people, my Jewish brothers and sisters. I would be willing to be forever cursed—cut off from Christ!—if that would save them" (Romans 9:2–3 NLT).

Paul loved the Jewish people so much that he would have chosen separation from God if only they would accept Christ. He understood that by rejecting Jesus, his people were rejecting the one true God. This motivated him to appeal to his readers to share the good news of Jesus with everyone (10:14–15).

Today, may we prayerfully dedicate ourselves to the love that aches for those close to us!   *Tim Gustafson*

Thinking Differently

Read Romans 12:1–3

Do not conform to the pattern of this world.
Romans 12:2

During college, I spent a good chunk of a summer in Venezuela. The food was astounding, the people delightful, the weather and hospitality beautiful. Within the first day or two, however, I recognized that my views on time management weren't shared by my new friends. If we planned to have lunch at noon, this meant anywhere between 12:00 and 1:00 p.m. The same for meetings or travel: timeframes were approximations without rigid punctuality. I learned that my idea of "being on time" was far more culturally formed than I had realized.

All of us are shaped by the cultural values that surround us, usually without ever noticing. Paul calls this cultural force the "world" (Romans 12:2). Here, "world" doesn't mean the physical universe, but rather refers to the ways of thinking pervading our existence. It refers to the unquestioned assumptions and guiding ideals handed to us simply because we live in a particular place and time.

Paul warns us to be vigilant to "not conform to the pattern of this world." Instead, we must be "transformed by the renewing of [our] mind" (v. 2). Rather than passively taking on the ways of thinking and believing that engulf us, we're called to actively pursue God's way of thinking and to learn how to understand His "good, pleasing and perfect will" (v. 2). May we learn to follow God rather than every other voice.

Winn Collier

Living on Purpose

Read Romans 12:9–21

Whatever you do, do it all for the glory of God.

1 CORINTHIANS 10:31

"We're going on vacation!" my wife enthusiastically told our three-year-old grandson Austin as we pulled out of the driveway on the first leg of our trip. Little Austin looked at her thoughtfully and responded, "I'm not going on vacation. I'm going on a mission!"

We're not sure where our grandson picked up the concept of going "on a mission," but his comment gave me something to ponder as we drove to the airport: *As I leave on this vacation and take a break for a few days, am I keeping in mind that I'm still "on a mission" to live each moment with and for God? Am I remembering to serve Him in everything I do?*

The apostle Paul encouraged the believers living in Rome, the capital city of the Roman Empire, to "never be lacking in zeal, but keep your spiritual fervor, serving the Lord" (Romans 12:11). His point was that our life in Jesus is meant to be lived intentionally and with enthusiasm. Even the most mundane moments gain new meaning as we look expectantly to God and live for His purposes.

As we settled into our seats on the plane, I prayed, "Lord, I'm yours. Whatever you have for me to do on this trip, please help me not to miss it."

Every day is a mission of eternal significance with Him!

James Banks

Living in God's Story

Read Romans 13:8–14

The night is nearly over; the day is almost here.

ROMANS 13:12

Ernest Hemingway was asked if he could write a compelling story in six words. His response: "For sale: Baby shoes. Never worn." Hemingway's story is powerful because it inspires us to fill in the details. Were the shoes simply not needed by a healthy child? Or was there a tragic loss—something requiring God's deep love and comfort?

The best stories pique our imagination, so it's no surprise that the greatest story ever told stokes the fires of our creativity. God's story has a central plot: He created all things; we (the human race) fell into sin; Jesus came to earth and died and rose again to save us from our sins; and we now await His return and the restoration of all things.

Knowing what has come before and what lies ahead, how should we now live? If Jesus is restoring His entire creation from the clutches of evil, we must "put aside the deeds of darkness and put on the armor of light" (Romans 13:12). This includes turning from sin by God's power and choosing to love Him and others well (vv. 8–10).

The specific ways we fight with Jesus against evil will depend on what gifts we have and what needs we see. Let's use our imagination and look around us. Let's seek out the wounded and weeping, and extend God's justice, love, and comfort as He guides us.   *Mike Wittmer*

All Together Now

Read Romans 15:1–7

*With one mind and one voice . . . glorify the
God and Father of our LORD Jesus Christ.*

ROMANS 15:6

While Andy was boarding a train in Perth, Australia, his leg became wedged in the gap between the platform and a commuter car. When safety officials could not free him, they coordinated the efforts of nearly fifty passengers who lined up and, on the count of three, pushed against the train. Working in unison, they shifted the weight just enough to free his leg.

The apostle Paul recognized the power of Christians working together in many of his letters to the early churches. He urged the Roman believers to accept each other the way Christ had accepted them and said, "[May God] give you the same attitude of mind toward each other that Christ Jesus had, so that with one mind and one voice you may glorify the God and Father of our Lord Jesus Christ" (Romans 15:5–6).

Unity with other believers enables us to broadcast God's greatness and also helps us to endure persecution. Knowing that the Philippians would pay a price for their faith, Paul encouraged them to strive "together as one for the faith of the gospel without being frightened in any way by those who oppose you" (Philippians 1:27–28).

Satan loves to divide and conquer, but his efforts fail when, with God's help, we "make every effort to keep the unity of the Spirit through the bond of peace" (Ephesians 4:3).   *Jennifer Benson Schuldt*

1 CORINTHIANS

◆

When whoever read this letter to the people in the church at Corinth got started, you can picture the people calmly listening and soaking up Paul's gentle beginning. A word about himself, a word about the people. A friendly, "Grace and peace to you" benediction. A thoughtful note about how thankful he was for them. And then bam! Paul gets to his point: There's trouble in Corinth, and I'm going to do something about it. As gentle as Paul was, he had to finally get to the point. Paul then explained in clear terms the problems he saw, and then he explained what the people would have to do to reverse course and follow Jesus as they should. Paul spoke prophetically (explaining what they needed to know, not foretelling the future) just as a pastor does today when a problem creeps into the local church. This was his purpose, to correct a myriad of problems that was killing the effectiveness of Christ's local body of believers in Corinth.

OUTLINE

Paul Addresses Church-Related Issues 1 Corinthians 1:1–11:34
Spiritual Gifts and the Christian 1 Corinthians 12:1–14:40
The Resurrection and the Christian 1 Corinthians 15:1–58
Personal Notes to the Church 1 Corinthians 16:1–24

Rivals or Allies?

Read 1 Corinthians 1:10-17

Be perfectly united in mind and thought.

1 CORINTHIANS 1:10

The city of Texarkana sits squarely on the state border between Texas and Arkansas. The city of 70,000 inhabitants has two mayors, two city councils, and two police and fire departments. The cross-town sporting rivalry between high schools draws an uncommonly high attendance, reflecting the deep allegiance each has to their own state's school. More significant challenges arise as well, such as disputes over the shared water system, governed by two sets of state laws. Yet the town is known for its unity despite the line that divides it. Residents gather annually for a dinner held on State Line Avenue to share a meal in celebration of their oneness as a community.

The believers in Corinth may not have drawn a line down their main thoroughfare, but they were divided. They'd been quarreling as a result of their allegiances to those who taught them about Jesus: Paul, Apollos, or Cephas (Peter). Paul called them all to oneness "in mind and thought" (1 Corinthians 1:10), reminding them it was Christ who was crucified for them, not their spiritual leaders.

We behave similarly today, don't we? We sometimes oppose even those who share our singularly important belief—Jesus's sacrifice for our wrongdoings—making them rivals instead of allies. Just as Christ himself is not divided, we, as His earthly representation—His body—mustn't allow differences over nonessentials to divide us. Instead, may we celebrate our oneness in Him.   *Kirsten Holmberg*

The "What" in Sharing Our Faith

Read 1 Corinthians 2:1–5

My message and my preaching were not with wise and persuasive
words, but with a demonstration of the Spirit's power.

1 CORINTHIANS 2:4

Alan came to me for advice on how to deal with his fear of public speaking. Like so many others, his heart would begin to race, his mouth would feel sticky and dry, and his face would flush bright red. *Glossophobia* is among the most common social fears people have—many even joke that they're more fearful of public speaking than of dying! To help Alan conquer his fear of not "performing" well, I suggested he focus on the substance of his message instead of how well he'd deliver it.

Shifting the focus to what will be shared, instead of one's ability to share it, is similar to Paul's approach to pointing others to God. When he wrote to the church at Corinth, he remarked that his message and preaching "were not with wise and persuasive words" (1 Corinthians 2:4). Instead, he'd determined to focus solely on the truth of Jesus Christ and His crucifixion (v. 2), trusting the Holy Spirit to empower his words, not his eloquence as a speaker.

When we've come to know God personally, we'll want to share about Him with those around us. Yet we sometimes shy away from it because we're afraid of not presenting it well—with the "right" or eloquent words. By focusing instead on the "what"—the truth of who God is and His amazing works—we can, like Paul, trust God to empower our words and share without fear or reluctance. *Kirsten Holmberg*

Working with God

Read 1 Corinthians 3:1–9

We are co-workers in God's service;
you are God's field, God's building.

1 Corinthians 3:9

During his 1962 visit to Mexico, Bill Ashe helped fix windmill hand pumps at an orphanage. Fifteen years later, inspired by a deep desire to serve God by helping provide clean water to villages in need, Bill founded a nonprofit organization. He said, "God awoke me to 'make the most of the time' by finding others with a desire to bring safe drinking water to the rural poor." Later, having learned about the global need for safe water through the requests of thousands of pastors and evangelists from more than one hundred countries, Bill invited others to join the ministry's efforts.

God welcomes us to team up to serve with Him and others in various ways. When the people of Corinth argued over which teachers they preferred, the apostle Paul affirmed his role as a servant of Jesus and a teammate of Apollos, fully dependent on God for spiritual growth (1 Corinthians 3:1–7). He reminds us that all work has God-given value (v. 8). Acknowledging the privilege of working with others while serving Him, Paul encourages us to build each other up as He transforms us in love (v. 9).

Though our mighty Father doesn't need our help to accomplish His great works, He equips us and invites us to partner with Him.

Xochitl Dixon

Suffering Together

Read 1 Corinthians 12:14–20

If one part suffers, every part suffers with it.
1 CORINTHIANS 12:26

Before seventy-year-old James McConnell, a British Royal Marine veteran, died, he and his family feared that no one would attend his funeral. So the man who was asked to officiate McConnell's memorial service posted a Facebook message: "In this day and age it is tragic enough that anyone has to leave this world with no one to mourn their passing, but this man was family. . . . If you can make it to the graveside . . . to pay your respects to a former brother in arms, then please try to be there." Two hundred Royal Marines packed the pews!

These British compatriots exhibited a biblical truth: we're tied to one another. "The body is not made up of one part but of many," Paul says (1 Corinthians 12:14). We're not isolated. Just the opposite: we're bound in Jesus. Scripture reveals organic interconnection: "If one member suffers, all the members suffer" (v. 26 NKJV). As believers in Jesus, members of God's new family, we move toward one another into the pain, into the sorrow, into those murky places where we would fear to go alone. But thankfully we do not go alone.

Perhaps the worst part of suffering is when we feel we're drowning in the dark all by ourselves. God, however, creates a new community that suffers together. A new community where no one should be left in the dark. *Winn Collier*

It Isn't Me

Read 1 Corinthians 15:1–11

I no longer live, but Christ lives in me.
GALATIANS 2:20

As one of the most celebrated orchestral conductors of the twentieth century, Arturo Toscanini is remembered for his desire to give credit to whom credit is due. In David Ewen's *Dictators of the Baton*, the author describes how members of the New York Philharmonic Orchestra rose to their feet and cheered Toscanini at the end of a rehearsal of Beethoven's Ninth Symphony. When there was a lull in the ovation, and with tears in his eyes, Arturo's broken voice could be heard exclaiming as he spoke: "It isn't me . . . it's Beethoven! . . . Toscanini is nothing."

In the apostle Paul's New Testament letters, he also refused to take credit for his spiritual insight and influence. He knew he was like a spiritual father and mother to many who had put their faith in Christ. He admitted he had worked hard and suffered much to encourage the faith, hope, and love of so many (1 Corinthians 15:10). But he could not, in good conscience, accept the applause of those who were inspired by his faith, love, and insight.

So for his readers' sake, and for ours, Paul said, in effect, "It isn't me, brothers and sisters. It's Christ . . . Paul is nothing." We are only messengers of the One who deserves our cheers. *Mart DeHaan*

Nothing Is Useless

Read 1 Corinthians 15:42–58

Nothing you do for the LORD is ever useless.

1 CORINTHIANS 15:58 NLT

In my third year battling discouragement and depression caused by limited mobility and chronic pain, I confided to a friend, "My body's falling apart. I feel like I have nothing of value to offer God or anyone else."

Her hand rested on mine. "Would you say it doesn't make a difference when I greet you with a smile or listen to you? Would you tell me it's worthless when I pray for you or offer a kind word?"

I settled into my recliner. "Of course not."

She frowned. "Then why are you telling yourself those lies? You do all those things for me and for others."

I thanked God for reminding me that nothing we do for Him is useless.

In 1 Corinthians 15, Paul assures us that our bodies may be weak now but they will be "raised in power" (v. 43). Because God promises we'll be resurrected through Christ, we can trust Him to use every offering, every small effort done for Him, to make a difference in His kingdom (v. 58).

Even when we're physically limited, a smile, a word of encouragement, a prayer, or a display of faith during our trial can be used to minister to the diverse and interdependent body of Christ. When we serve the Lord, no job or act of love is too menial to matter. *Xochitl Dixon*

Brave Love

Read 1 Corinthians 16:10–14

Do everything in love.
1 CORINTHIANS 16:14

The four chaplains weren't known as "heroes." But on a frigid February night in 1943, when their transport ship, the SS *Dorchester*, was torpedoed off the coast of Greenland during World War II, the four gave their all to calm hundreds of panicked soldiers. With the ship sinking and injured men jumping for overcrowded lifeboats, the four chaplains calmed the pandemonium by "preaching courage," a survivor said.

When life jackets ran out, each took his off, giving it to a frightened young man. They had determined to go down with the ship so that others might live. Said one survivor, "It was the finest thing I have seen or hope to see this side of heaven."

Linking arms as the ship began to sink, the chaplains prayed aloud together, offering encouragement to those perishing with them.

Bravery marks their saga. Love, however, defines the gift the four offered. Paul urged such love of all believers, including those in the storm-tossed church at Corinth. Roiled by conflict, corruption, and sin, Paul urged them to "be on your guard; stand firm in the faith; be courageous; be strong" (1 Corinthians 16:13). Then he added, "Do everything in love" (v. 14).

It's a sterling command for every believer in Jesus, especially during a crisis. In life, when upheaval threatens, our bravest response reflects Christ—giving to others His love. *Patrician Raybon*

2 CORINTHIANS

◆

Through no fault of his own, Paul is forced to defend himself. Certain factions in the church had begun to question his authority, and at the same time teachers had crept into the church to throw confusion about doctrine and right teaching into the mix. As he presents his case, Paul also provides teaching on subjects such as the new covenant, giving to the Lord's work, reconciliation, and warnings to those who are in rebellion.

OUTLINE

Loving Others with Prayers

Read 2 Corinthians 1:8–11

*This happened that we might not rely on
ourselves but on God, who raises the dead.*

2 CORINTHIANS 1:9

"Are people still praying for me?"

That was one of the first questions a missionary asked his wife whenever she was allowed to visit him in prison. He had been falsely accused and incarcerated for his faith for two years. His life was frequently in danger because of the conditions and hostility in the prison, and believers around the world were earnestly praying for him. He wanted to be assured they wouldn't stop, because he believed God was using their prayers in a powerful way.

Our prayers for others—especially those who are persecuted for their faith—are a vital gift. Paul made this clear when he wrote the believers in Corinth about hardships he faced during his missionary journey. He "[was] under great pressure," so much that he "despaired of life itself" (2 Corinthians 1:8). But then he told them God had delivered him and described the tool He'd used to do it: "We have set our hope that he will continue to deliver us, as you help us by your prayers" (v. 10).

God moves through our prayers to accomplish great good in the lives of His people. One of the best ways to love others is to pray for them, because through our prayers we open the door to the help only God can provide. When we pray for others, we love them in His strength. There's none greater or more loving than He.   *James Banks*

The Fragrance of Christ

Read 2 Corinthians 2:14-17

We are to God the pleasing aroma of Christ.
2 CORINTHIANS 2:15

Which of the five senses brings back your memories most sharply? For me it is definitely the sense of smell. A certain kind of sun oil takes me instantly to a French beach. The smell of chicken mash brings back childhood visits to my grandmother. A hint of pine says "Christmas," and a certain kind of aftershave reminds me of my son's teenage years.

Paul reminded the Corinthians that they were the aroma of Christ: "For we are to God the pleasing aroma of Christ" (2 Corinthians 2:15). He may have been referring to Roman victory parades. The Romans made sure everyone knew they had been victorious by burning incense on altars throughout the city. For the victors, the aroma was pleasing; for the prisoners it meant certain slavery or death. So as believers, we are victorious soldiers. And when the gospel of Christ is preached, it is a pleasing fragrance to God.

As the aroma of Christ, what perfumes do Christians bring with them as they walk into a room? It's not something that can be bought in a bottle or a jar. When we spend a lot of time with someone, we begin to think and act like that person. Spending time with Jesus will help us spread a pleasing fragrance to those around us.   *Marion Stroud*

Making His Music

Read 2 Corinthians 3:17–18

We all . . . are being transformed into his image.
2 CORINTHIANS 3:18

Choir director Arianne Abela spent her childhood sitting on her hands—to hide them. Born with fingers missing or fused together on both hands, she also had no left leg and was missing toes on her right foot. A music lover and lyric soprano, she'd planned to major in government at Smith College. But one day her choir teacher asked her to conduct the choir, which made her hands quite visible. From that moment, she found her career, going on to conduct church choirs and serving now as director of choirs at another university. "My teachers saw something in me," Abela explains.

Her inspiring story invites believers to ask, What does God, our holy Teacher, see in us, regardless of our "limits"? More than anything, He sees himself. "So God created human beings in his own image. In the image of God he created them; male and female he created them" (Genesis 1:27 NLT).

As His glorious "image bearers," when others see us, we should reflect Him. For Abela, that means Jesus, not her hands—or her lack of fingers—matters most. The same is true for all believers. "And we all, who with unveiled faces contemplate the Lord's glory, are being transformed into his image," says 2 Corinthians 3:18.

Similar to Abela, we can conduct our lives by Christ's transforming power (v. 18), offering a life song that rings out to the honor of God.

Patricia Raybon

Better Than Ever

Read 2 Corinthians 4:16–5:9

Therefore we do not lose heart. Though outwardly we are wasting away, yet inwardly we are being renewed day by day.

2 CORINTHIANS 4:16

The Notre Dame Cathedral in Paris is a spectacular building. Its architecture is spellbinding, and its stained-glass windows and beautiful interior features are breathtaking. But after centuries of towering over the Paris landscape, it needed renovation—which had begun when a devastating fire caused extensive damage to the glorious old building.

So the people who love this eight-century-old landmark are coming to its rescue. More than a billion dollars have been raised to restore the building. The stone structure must be shored up. The damaged interior and its prized artifacts need to be repaired. The effort is worthwhile, though, because for many this ancient cathedral stands as a symbol of hope.

What's true of buildings is also true of us. Our bodies, like this old church, will eventually look a bit worse for wear! But as the apostle Paul explains, there's good news: while we might gradually lose the physical vibrancy of youth, the core of who we are—our spiritual being—can be continually renewed and growing (2 Corinthians 4:16).

As "we make it our goal to please [the Lord]" (5:9), relying on the Holy Spirit to fill and transform us (3:18; Ephesians 5:18), our spiritual growth need never stop—no matter what our "building" looks like.

Dave Branon

Taking the First Step

Read 2 Corinthians 5:11–21

*God was reconciling the world to himself in Christ,
not counting people's sins against them. And he has
committed to us the message of reconciliation.*

2 CORINTHIANS 5:19

Tham Dashu sensed something was missing in his life. So he started going to church—the same church his daughter attended. But they never went together. In earlier days, he had offended her, which drove a wedge between them. So, Tham would slip in when the singing started and leave promptly after the service ended.

Church members shared the gospel story with him, but Tham always politely rejected their invitation to put his faith in Jesus. Still, he kept coming to church.

One day Tham fell gravely ill. His daughter plucked up the courage and wrote him a letter. She shared how Christ had changed her life, and she sought reconciliation with her dad. That night, Tham put his faith in Jesus and the family was reconciled. A few days later, Tham died and entered into the presence of Jesus—at peace with God and his loved ones.

The apostle Paul wrote that we are to "try to persuade others" about the truth of God's love and forgiveness (2 Corinthians 5:11). He said that it is "Christ's love [that] compels us" to carry out His work of reconciliation (v. 14).

Our willingness to forgive may help others realize that God desires to reconcile us to himself (v. 19). Would you lean on God's strength to show them His love today?   *Poh Fang Chia*

Give It All You've Got

Read 2 Corinthians 9:6–14

*Each of you should give what you have
decided in your heart to give.*

2 CORINTHIANS 9:7

Scaling. It's a term used in the world of fitness that allows room for any-one to participate. If the specific exercise is a push-up, for example, then maybe you can do ten in a row, but I can only do four. The instructor's encouragement to me would be to scale back the push-ups according to my fitness level at the time. We're not all at the same level, but we can all move in the same direction. In other words, she would say, "Do your four push-ups with all the strength you have. Don't compare yourself with anyone else. Scale the movement for now, keep doing what you can do, and you may be amazed in time you're doing seven, and even one day, ten."

When it comes to giving, the apostle Paul was clear: "God loves a cheerful giver" (2 Corinthians 9:7). But his encouragement to the believers in Corinth, and to us, is a variation of scaling. "Each of you should give what you have decided in your heart" (v. 7). We each find ourselves at different giving levels, and sometimes those levels change over time. Comparison is not beneficial, but attitude is. Based on where you are, give generously (v. 6). Our God has promised that the disciplined practice of such cheerful giving brings enrichment in every way with a blessed life that results in "thanksgiving to God" (v. 11).   *John Blase*

GALATIANS

◆

The gospel of Jesus Christ is the centerpiece of this book. Paul sets out to show that Jesus came to rescue lost sinners, and they need nothing else for salvation. He is a bit perturbed, it seems, that the people have so soon gone astray from truth and headed toward a "different gospel" (1:6). He launches into a biographical sketch to establish his faith through grace before supporting this doctrine by using numerous examples (chapter 3). He concludes by reminding his listeners about the great power of the Holy Spirit.

OUTLINE

Liberty and the Gospel Galatians 1:1–4:31

Freedom in Christ and Help from the Spirit Galatians 5:1–26

Care for Others; Legalism Galatians 6:1–18

Is It True?

Read Galatians 1:1–9

*They received the message with great eagerness and examined
the Scriptures every day to see if what Paul said true.*

ACTS 17:11

"Trust, but verify." My husband loves that quote from Ronald Reagan. During his time in office, the former US President wanted to believe everything he was told in his political dealings with others. But since the security of his country depended on the truth being told—he strived to verify everything.

Acts 17:11 tells us that the Bereans had a similar attitude about knowing the truth. "They received the message with great eagerness and examined the Scriptures every day to see if what Paul said was true." In other words, the Bereans didn't simply believe what someone else was telling them. They also verified it on their own—on a daily basis.

That's important for us to consider as well. Whether we receive our Bible teaching through church, Sunday school, a podcast, or video—we need to test what we hear against God's inspired Word (2 Timothy 3:16–17). We are to do "[our] best to present [ourselves] . . . approved, . . . who correctly handles the word of truth" (2:15). If we do this, we won't become prey to those who teach "a different gospel," and those who "are trying to pervert the gospel of Christ" (Galatians 1:6–7)—false teachers who come as wolves in sheep's clothing (Matthew 7:15).

Remember, trust—but verify!   *Cindy Hess Kasper*

No Longer Yourself

Read Galatians 2:14–21

I have been crucified with Christ and I no longer live, but Christ lives in me. The life I now live in the body, I live by faith in the Son of God, who loved me and gave himself for me.

GALATIANS 2:20

In the summer of 1859, Monsieur Charles Blondin became the first person to cross Niagara Falls on a tightrope—something he would go on to do hundreds of times. Once he did it with his manager Harry Colcord on his back. Blondin gave Colcord these instructions: "Look up, Harry . . . you are no longer Colcord, you are Blondin. . . . If I sway, sway with me. Do not attempt to do any balancing yourself. If you do, we will both go to our death."

Paul, in essence, said to the Galatian believers: You can't walk the line of living a life that is pleasing to God apart from faith in Christ. But here's the good news—you don't have to! No amount of attempting to earn our way to God will ever cut it. So are we passive in our salvation? No! Our invitation is to cling to Christ. Clinging to Jesus means putting to death an old, independent way of living; it's as if we ourselves have died. Yet, we go on living. But "the life [we] now live in the body, [we] live by faith in the Son of God, who loved [us] and gave himself for [us]" (Galatians 2:20).

Where are we trying to walk the tightrope today? God hasn't called us to walk out on the rope to Him; He's called us to cling to Him and walk this life with Him.   *Glenn Packiam*

Hosting Royalty

Read Galatians 3:26–29

So in Christ Jesus you are all children of God through faith.

GALATIANS 3:26

After meeting the Queen of England at a ball in Scotland, Sylvia and her husband received a message that the royal family would like to visit them for tea. Sylvia started cleaning and prepping, nervous about hosting the royal guests. Before they were due to arrive, she went outside to pick some flowers for the table, her heart racing. Then she sensed God reminding her that He's the King of kings and that He's with her every day. Immediately she felt peaceful and thought, "After all, it's only the Queen!"

Sylvia is right. As the apostle Paul noted, God is the "King of kings and Lord of lords" (1 Timothy 6:15) and those who follow Him are "children of God" (Galatians 3:26). When we belong to Christ, we're heirs of Abraham (v. 29). We no longer are bound by division—such as that of race, social class, or gender—for we're "all one in Christ Jesus" (v. 28). We're children of the King.

Although Sylvia and her husband had a marvelous meal with the Queen, I don't anticipate receiving an invitation from her anytime soon. But I love the reminder that the highest King of all is with me every moment. And that those who believe in Jesus wholeheartedly (v. 27) can live in unity, knowing they're God's children.

How could holding onto this truth shape the way we live today?

Amy Boucher Pye

Tight Circles

Read Galatians 5:1, 4–14

It is for freedom that Christ has set us free.

GALATIANS 5:1

A classmate gave my family a registered collie that had become too old to breed puppies. We soon learned this beautiful dog had, sadly, spent much of her life inside a small pen. She would only walk in tight circles. She couldn't fetch or run in a straight line. And even with a large yard in which to play, she thought she was fenced in.

The first Christians, many who were Jews, were used to being fenced in by the Mosaic law. Though the law was good and had been given by God to convict them of sin and lead them to Jesus (Galatians 3:19–25), it was time to live out their new faith based in God's grace and the freedom of Christ. They hesitated. After all this time, were they really free?

We may have the same problem. Perhaps we grew up in churches with rigid rules that fenced us in. Or we were raised in permissive homes and are now desperate for the security of rules. Either way, it's time to embrace our freedom in Christ (Galatians 5:1). Jesus has freed us to obey Him out of love (John 14:21) and to "serve one another humbly in love" (Galatians 5:13). An entire field of joy and love is open for those who realize "if the Son sets you free, you will be free indeed" (John 8:36).

Mike Wittmer

The Life of Peace

Read Galatians 5:16–25

The peace of God, which transcends all understanding,
will guard your hearts and your minds in Christ Jesus.

PHILIPPIANS 4:7

In Perth, Australia, there's a place called Shalom House where men struggling with addictions go to find help. At Shalom House, they'll meet caring staff members who introduce them to God's shalom (Hebrew for peace). Lives crushed under the weight of addictions to drugs, alcohol, gambling, and other destructive behaviors are being transformed by the love of God.

Central to this transformation is the message of the cross. The broken people of Shalom House discover that through the resurrection of Jesus, they can find their own lives resurrected. In Christ, we gain true peace and healing.

Peace isn't merely the absence of conflict; it's the presence of God's wholeness. All of us need this shalom, and it's only found in Christ and His Spirit. This is why Paul pointed the Galatians to the Spirit's transformational work. As the Holy Spirit operates in our lives, He generates His fruit that includes love, joy, patience, and more (Galatians 5:22–23). He gives us that vital element of true, enduring peace.

As the Spirit enables us to live in God's shalom, we learn to bring our needs and concerns to our heavenly Father. This in turn brings us "the peace of God, which transcends all understanding"—the peace that "will guard [our] hearts and [our] minds in Christ Jesus" (Philippians 4:7).

In Christ's Spirit, our hearts experience true shalom. *Bill Crowder*

EPHESIANS

It continued to be important to Paul and other leaders of the first-century church to dispel the thinking that Jews and gentiles were to be divided at all in this new faith. A new community was being formed, and it was simply the Christian church. The idea of unity of believers was vital to melding these two groups into "one new man" as Paul described it in Ephesians (2:15 ESV). The believers were then to walk in unity and holiness as they lived and worshiped together. This was the direction Paul in which was guiding the people of Ephesus and the surrounding region.

OUTLINE

Blessings of Being in Christ and Sealed by the Spirit
Ephesians 1:1–22

Alive and Unified in Christ Ephesians 2:1–22

Revealing the Mystery of the Church Ephesians 3:1–21

Church Life, Spiritual Gifts, and the New Person
Ephesians 4:1–29

Life in the Spirit Ephesians 4:30–5:21

Families and Service Ephesians 5:22–6:9

Spiritual Warfare Ephesians 6:10–24

Inheritance Isn't Earned

Read Ephesians 1:3–14

*He predestined us for adoption to sonship through Jesus
Christ, in accordance with his pleasure and will.*

EPHESIANS 1:5

"Thanks for dinner, Dad," I said as I set my napkin on the restaurant table. I was home on a break from college and, after being gone for a while, it felt strange to have my parents pay for me. "You're welcome, Julie," my dad replied, "but you don't have to thank me for everything all the time. I know you've been off on your own, but you're still my daughter and a part of the family." I smiled. "Thanks, Dad."

In my family, I haven't done anything to earn my parents' love or what they do for me. But my dad's comment reminds me that I haven't done anything to deserve to be a part of God's family either.

In the book of Ephesians, Paul tells his readers that God chose them "to be holy and blameless in his sight" (1:4), or to stand without blemish before Him (5:25–27). But this is only possible through Jesus, in whom "we have redemption through his blood, the forgiveness of sins, in accordance with the riches of God's grace" (1:7). We don't have to earn God's grace, forgiveness, or entrance into His family. We simply accept His free gift.

When we turn our lives over to Jesus, we become children of God, which means we receive eternal life and have an inheritance waiting for us in heaven. Praise God for offering such a wonderful gift!

Julie Schwab

It's All a Gift

Read Ephesians 2:1–9

For it is by grace you have been saved, through faith—
and this is not from yourselves, it is the gift of God.

EPHESIANS 2:8

West London's Café Rendezvous has nice lighting, comfortable couches, and the smell of coffee in the air. What it doesn't have are prices. Originally started as a business by a local church, the café was transformed a year after it started. The managers felt that God was calling them to do something radical—make everything on the menu free. Today you can order a coffee, cake, or sandwich without cost. It's all a gift.

I asked the manager why they were so generous. "We're just trying to treat people the way God treats us," he said. "God gives to us whether we thank Him or not. He's generous to us beyond our imaginations."

Jesus died to rescue us from our sins and reconcile us with God. He rose from the grave and is alive now. Because of this, every wrong thing we've done can be forgiven, and we can have new life today (Ephesians 2:1–5). And one of the most amazing things about this is that it is all free. We can't buy the new life Jesus offers. We can't even donate toward the cost (vv. 8–9). It's all a gift.

As the folks at Café Rendezvous serve their cakes and coffees, they give people a glimpse of God's generosity. You and I are offered eternal life for free because Jesus has paid the bill.   *Sheridan Voysey*

✦

Hand-Made for You

Read Ephesians 2:4–10

We are God's handiwork, created in Christ Jesus to do good
works, which God prepared in advance for us to do.
EPHESIANS 2:10

My grandmother was a talented seamstress who won contests in her native Texas. Throughout my life, she celebrated hallmark occasions with a hand-sewn gift. A burgundy mohair sweater for my high school graduation. A turquoise quilt for my marriage. I'd fold over a corner of each custom-crafted item to discover her signature tag reading, "Hand-made for you by Munna." With every embroidered word, I sensed my grandmother's love for me and received a powerful statement of her faith in my future.

Paul wrote to the Ephesians of their purpose in this world, describing them as "God's handiwork, created in Christ Jesus to do good works" (2:10). Here "handiwork" denotes a work of art or a masterpiece. Paul goes on to describe that God's handiwork in creating us would result in our handiwork of creating good works—or expressions of our restored relationship with Jesus—for His glory in our world. We can never be saved by our own good works, but when God hand makes us for His purposes, He can use us to bring others toward His great love.

With her head bowed over her needle, my Munna made items by hand to communicate her love for me and her passion that I discover my purpose on this planet. And with His fingers shaping the details of our days, God stitches His love and purposes in our hearts that we might experience Him for ourselves and demonstrate His handiwork to others.   *Elisa Morgan*

The Bulldog and the Sprinkler

Read Ephesians 3:14–21

*I pray that you . . . may be filled to the
measure of all the fullness of God.*
EPHESIANS 3:17, 19

Most summer mornings, a delightful drama plays out in the park behind our house. It involves a sprinkler. And a bulldog. About 6:30 or so, the sprinklers come on. Shortly thereafter, Fifi the bulldog (yes, they named her Fifi) arrives.

Fifi's owner lets her off her leash. The bulldog sprints with all her might to the nearest sprinkler, attacking the stream of water as it douses her face. If Fifi could eat the sprinkler, I think she would. It's a portrait of utter exuberance, of Fifi's seemingly infinite desire to be drenched by the liquid she can never get enough of.

There are no bulldogs in the Bible, or sprinklers. Yet, in a way, Paul's prayer in Ephesians 3 reminds me of Fifi. There, Paul prays that the Ephesian believers might be filled with God's love and "have power, together with all the Lord's holy people, to grasp how wide and long and high and deep is the love of Christ." He prayed that we might be "filled to the measure of all the fullness of God" (vv. 18–19).

Still today, we're invited to experience a God whose infinite love exceeds anything we can comprehend, that we too might be drenched, saturated, and utterly satisfied by His goodness. We're free to plunge with abandon, relish, and delight into a relationship with the One who alone can fill our hearts and lives with love, meaning, and purpose.

Adam Holz

SEPTEMBER 14

Gentleness

Read Ephesians 4:1–6

Be completely humble and gentle.

Ephesians 4:2

The troubles of life can make us cranky and out of sorts, but we should never excuse these bouts of bad behavior, for they can wither the hearts of those we love and spread misery all around us. We have not fulfilled our duty to others until we have learned to be pleasant.

The New Testament has a word for the virtue that corrects our unpleasantness—*gentleness*, a term that suggests a kind and gracious soul. Ephesians 4:2 reminds us, "Be completely humble and gentle."

Gentleness is a willingness to accept limitations and ailments without taking out our aggravation on others. It shows gratitude for the smallest service rendered and tolerance for those who do not serve us well. It puts up with bothersome people—especially noisy, boisterous little people; for kindness to children is a crowning mark of a good and gentle person. It speaks softly in the face of provocation. It can be silent; for calm, unruffled silence is often the most eloquent response to unkind words.

Jesus is "gentle and humble in heart" (Matthew 11:29). If we ask Him, He will, in time, recreate us in His image. Scottish author George MacDonald says, "[God] would not hear from [us] a tone to jar the heart of another, a word to make it ache. . . . From such, as from all other sins, Jesus was born to deliver us." *David Roper*

Life Changes

Read Ephesians 4:20–24

Put on the new self, created to be like God
in true righteousness and holiness.

EPHESIANS 4:24

Stephen grew up in a rough part of East London and fell into crime by the age of ten. He said, "If everyone's selling drugs and doing robberies and fraud, then you're going to get involved. It's just a way of life." But when he was twenty, he had a dream that changed him: "I heard God saying, 'Stephen, you're going to prison for murder.'" This vivid dream served as a warning, and he turned to God and received Jesus as his Savior—and the Holy Spirit transformed his life.

Stephen set up an organization that teaches inner-city kids discipline, morality, and respect through sports. He credits God with the success he has seen as he prays with and trains the kids. "Rebuilding misguided dreams," he says.

In pursuing God and leaving behind our past, we—like Stephen—follow Paul's charge to the Ephesians to embrace a new way of life. Although our old self is "corrupted by its deceitful desires," we can daily seek to "put on the new self" that's created to be like God (Ephesians 4:22, 24). All believers embrace this continual process as we ask God through His Holy Spirit to make us more like Him.

Stephen said, "Faith was a crucial foundation for me changing my life around." How has this been true for you?   *Amy Boucher Pye*

Removing the Intruder

Read Ephesians 5:25–33

Husbands, love your wives, just as Christ loved
the church and gave himself up for her.

EPHESIANS 5:25

It wasn't quite dawn when my husband rose from bed and went into the kitchen. I saw the light flip on and off and wondered at his action. Then I recalled that the previous morning I'd yelped at the sight of an "intruder" on our kitchen counter. Translated: an undesirable creature of the six-legged variety. My husband knew my paranoia and immediately arrived to remove it. This morning he'd risen early to ensure our kitchen was bug-free so I could enter without concern. What a guy!

My husband awoke with me on his mind, putting my need before his own. To me, his action illustrates the love Paul describes in Ephesians 5:25, "Husbands, love your wives, just as Christ loved the church and gave himself up for her." Paul goes on, "Husbands ought to love their wives as their own bodies. He who loves his wife loves himself" (v. 28). Paul's comparison of a husband's love to the love of Christ pivots on how Jesus put our needs before His own. My husband knows I'm afraid of certain intruders, and so he made my concern his priority.

That principle doesn't apply to husbands only. After the example of Jesus, each of us can lovingly sacrifice to help remove an intruder of stress, fear, shame, or anxiety so that someone can move more freely in the world. *Elisa Morgan*

It's Time to Pray Again

Read Ephesians 6:10–20

*Pray in the Spirit on all occasions with all
kinds of prayers and requests.*

EPHESIANS 6:18

I pulled into my driveway, waving at my neighbor Myriam and her little girl Elizabeth. Over the years, Elizabeth had grown accustomed to our spontaneous chats lasting longer than the promised "few minutes" and morphing into prayer meetings. She climbed the tree planted in the center of their front yard, dangled her legs over a branch, and busied herself while her mother and I spoke. After a while, Elizabeth hopped down from her roost and ran to where we stood. Grabbing our hands, she smiled and almost sang, "It's time to pray . . . again." Even at an early age, Elizabeth seemed to understand how important prayer was in our friendship.

After encouraging believers to "be strong in the Lord and in his mighty power" (Ephesians 6:10), the apostle Paul offered special insight on the crucial role of continual prayer. He described the necessary armor God's people would need during their spiritual walk with the Lord, who provides protection, discernment, and confidence in His truth (vv. 11–17). However, the apostle emphasized that this God-given strength grew from deliberate immersion in the life-giving gift of prayer (vv. 18–20).

God hears and cares about our concerns, whether they're spoken boldly, sobbed silently, or secured deep in a hurting heart. He's always ready to make us strong in His power, as He invites us to pray again and again and again.   *Xochitl Dixon*

PHILIPPIANS

◆

Paul's first order of business in this letter was to convey a hearty thank you to his friends and fellow believers in Philippi. There seems to be a great deal of mutual admiration going on. He recognizes that he has suffered, but he rejoices nonetheless. He requests that his friends live in unity and conduct themselves in a worthy manner. One of the key passages for them—and for us—is the beginning of chapter two when he pleads for humility in the light of Jesus's great example of setting aside heaven's glories to come to earth. Paul tells his friends to press on, and he gives them the hope of finding God's peace.

OUTLINE

SEPTEMBER 18

The Shrinking Piano

Read Philippians 1:1–11

*He who began a good work in you will carry it on
to completion until the day of Christ Jesus.*

PHILIPPIANS 1:6

For three consecutive years, my son participated in a piano recital. The last year he played, I watched him mount the steps and set up his music. He played two songs and then sat down next to me and whispered, "Mom, this year the piano was smaller." I said, "No, it's the same piano you played last year. You're bigger! You've grown."

Spiritual growth, like physical growth, often happens slowly over time. It is an ongoing process that involves becoming more like Jesus, and it happens as we are transformed through the renewing of our minds (Romans 12:2).

When the Holy Spirit is at work in us, we may become aware of sin in our lives. Wanting to honor God, we make an effort to change. Sometimes we experience success, but at other times, we try and fail. If it seems like nothing changes, we get discouraged. We may equate failure with a lack of progress, when it's often proof that we are in the middle of the process.

Spiritual growth involves the Holy Spirit, our willingness to change, and time. At certain points in our lives, we may look back and see that we have grown spiritually. May God give us the faith to continue to believe that "He who began a good work in [us] will carry it on to completion until the day of Christ Jesus" (Philippians 1:6).

Jennifer Benson Schuldt

Every Moment Matters

Read Philippians 1:12–24

For to me, to live is Christ and to die is gain.
PHILIPPIANS 1:21

When I met Ada, she had outlived her entire group of friends and family and was living in a nursing home. "It's the hardest part of getting old," she told me "watching everyone else move on and leave you behind." One day I asked Ada what kept her interest and how she spent her time. She answered me with a Scripture passage from the apostle Paul (Philippians 1:21): "For to me, to live is Christ and to die is gain." Then she said, "While I'm still around, I have work to do. On my good days, I get to talk to the people here about Jesus; on the hard days, I can still pray."

Significantly, Paul wrote Philippians while in prison. And he acknowledged a reality many Christians understand as they face their mortality: Even though heaven seems so inviting, the time we have left on earth matters to God.

Like Paul, Ada recognized that every breath she took was an opportunity to serve and glorify God. So Ada spent her days loving others and introducing them to her Savior.

Even in our darkest moments, Christians can hold on to the promise of permanent joy in the company of God. And while we live, we enjoy relationship with Him. He fills all our moments with significance.

Randy Kilgore

Singing with Violet

Read Philippians 1:21–26

I desire to depart and be with Christ, which is better by far;
but it is more necessary for you that I remain in the body.

PHILIPPIANS 1:23–24

An elderly woman named Violet sat on her bed in a Jamaican infirmary and smiled as some teenagers stopped to visit with her. The hot, sticky, midday air came into her little group home unabated, but she didn't complain. Instead, she began wracking her mind for a song to sing. Then a huge smile appeared and she sang, "I am running, skipping, jumping, praising the Lord!" As she sang, she swung her arms back and forth as if she were running. Tears came to those around her, for Violet had no legs. She was singing because, she said, "Jesus loves me—and in heaven I will have legs to run with."

Violet's joy and hopeful anticipation of heaven give new vibrancy to Paul's words in Philippians 1 when he referred to life-and-death issues. "If I am to go on living in the body, this will mean fruitful labor for me," he said. "I am torn between the two: I desire to depart and be with Christ, which is better by far" (vv. 22–23).

Each of us faces tough times that may cause us to long for the promise of heavenly relief. But as Violet showed us joy despite her current circumstances, we too can keep "running, skipping, praising the Lord"—both for the abundant life He gives us here and for the ultimate joy that awaits us. *Dave Branon*

Easy Does It

Read Philippians 2:2–18

*It is God who works in you to will and to act
in ORDer to fulfill his good purpose.*

PHILIPPIANS 2:13

My father and I used to fell trees and cut them to size with a two-man crosscut saw. Being young and energetic, I tried to force the saw into the cut. "Easy does it," my father would say. "Let the saw do the work."

I think of Paul's words in Philippians: "It is God who works in you" (2:13). Easy does it. Let Him do the work of changing us.

C. S. Lewis said that growth is much more than reading what Christ said and carrying it out. He explained, "A real Person, Christ, . . . is doing things to you . . . gradually turning you permanently into . . . a new little Christ, a being which . . . shares in His power, joy, knowledge and eternity."

God is at that process today. Sit at the feet of Jesus and take in what He has to say. Pray. "Keep yourselves in God's love" (Jude v. 21), reminding yourself all day long that you are His. Rest in the assurance that He's gradually changing you.

"But shouldn't we hunger and thirst for righteousness?" you ask. Picture a small child trying to get a gift high on a shelf, his eyes glittering with desire. His father, sensing that desire, brings the gift down to him.

The work is God's; the joy is ours. Easy does it. We shall get there some day.

David Roper

False Confidence

Read Philippians 3:2–8

I consider everything a loss because of the
surpassing worth of knowing Christ Jesus my
LORD, for whose sake I have lost all things.

PHILIPPIANS 3:8

A few years ago, my doctor gave me a stern talk about my health. I took his words to heart and began going to the gym and adjusting my diet. Over time, both my cholesterol and my weight went down, and my self-esteem went up. But then something not so good happened: I began noticing other people's dietary choices and judging them. Isn't it funny that often when we find a scoring system that grades us well, we use it to lift ourselves up and put others down? It seems to be an innate human tendency to cling to self-made standards in an attempt to justify ourselves—systems of self-justification and guilt-management.

Paul warned the Philippians about doing such things. Some were putting their confidence in religious performance or cultural conformity, and Paul told them he had more reason to boast of such things: "If someone else thinks they have reasons to put confidence in the flesh, I have more" (3:4). Yet Paul knew his pedigree and performance was "garbage" compared to "knowing Christ" (v. 8). Only Jesus loves us as we are, rescues us, and gives us the power to become more like Him. No earning required; no scorekeeping possible.

Boasting is bad in itself, but a boast based on false confidence is tragic. The gospel calls us away from misplaced confidence and into communion with a Savior who loves us and gave himself for us.

Glenn Packiam

It's Who You Know

Read Philippians 3:7–11

*I consider everything a loss because of the surpassing
worth of knowing Christ Jesus my LORD.*

PHILIPPIANS 3:8

In early 2019, Charlie VanderMeer died at the age of eighty-four. For many decades, he was known to thousands and thousands of people as Uncle Charlie, the host of the national radio broadcast Children's Bible Hour. The day before Uncle Charlie slipped into eternity, he told a good friend, "It's not what you know, it's who you know. Of course, I'm talking about Jesus Christ."

Even as he faced the end of his life, Uncle Charlie couldn't help but talk about Jesus and the necessity for people to receive Him as their Savior.

The apostle Paul considered knowing Jesus his most important task: "I consider everything a loss because of the surpassing worth of knowing Christ Jesus my Lord, for whose sake I have lost all things. I consider them garbage, that I may gain Christ and be found in him" (Philippians 3:8–9). And how do we know Jesus? "If you declare with your mouth, 'Jesus is Lord,' and believe in your heart that God raised him from the dead, you will be saved" (Romans 10:9).

We may know facts about Jesus, we may know all about the church, and we may even be familiar with the Bible. But the only way to know Jesus as Savior is to accept His free gift of salvation. He's the Who we need to know. *Dave Branon*

The Cure for Anxiety

Read Philippians 4:1–9

Do not be anxious about anything, but in every situation, by prayer and petition, with thanksgiving, present your requests to God.

PHILIPPIANS 4:6

We were excited about moving for my husband's job. But the unknowns and challenges left me feeling anxious. Thoughts of sorting and packing up belongings. Looking for a place to live. My finding a new job too. Making my way around a new city, and getting settled. It was all . . . unsettling. As I thought about my "to-do" list, words written by the apostle Paul echoed in my mind: Don't worry, but pray (Philippians 4:6–7).

If anyone could have been anxious about unknowns and challenges, it would have been Paul. He was shipwrecked. He was beaten. He was jailed. In his letter to the Philippian church, he encouraged his friends who also were facing unknowns, telling them, "Do not be anxious about anything, but in every situation, by prayer and petition, with thanksgiving, present your requests to God" (v. 6).

Paul's words encourage me. Life is not without uncertainties—whether they come in the form of a major life transition, family issues, health scares, or financial trouble. What I continue to learn is that God cares. He invites us to let go of our fears of the unknown by giving them to Him. When we do, He, who knows all things, promises that His peace, "which transcends all understanding, will guard" our heart and mind in Christ Jesus (v. 7). *Karen Wolfe*

Front-Porch Relief

Read Philippians 4:10–20

*I have learned the secret of being content
in any and every situation.*

PHILIPPIANS 4:12

On a particularly hot day, eight-year-old Carmine McDaniel wanted to make sure his neighborhood mail carrier stayed cool and hydrated. So he left a cooler filled with a sports drink and water bottles on their front step. The family security camera recorded the mail carrier's reaction: "Oh man, water and Gatorade. Thank God; thank you!"

Carmine's mom says, "Carmine feels that it's his 'duty' to supply the mailman with a cool beverage even if we're not home."

This story warms our hearts, but it also reminds us that there is One who will "meet all your needs," as the apostle Paul phrased it. Though Paul was languishing in jail and uncertain about his future, he expressed joy for the Christians in Philippi because God had met his needs through their financial gift to him. The Philippian church was not wealthy, but they were generous, giving to Paul and others out of their poverty (see 2 Corinthians 8:1–4). As the Philippians had met Paul's needs, so God would meet theirs, "according to the riches of his glory in Christ Jesus" (Philippians 4:19).

God often sends vertical help through horizontal means. Put another way, He sends us what we need through the help of others. When we trust Him for what we need, we learn, as Paul did, the secret of true contentment (vv. 12–13).   *Marvin Williams*

COLOSSIANS

In order to counter an erroneous argument, Paul takes the right tack. He doesn't call names and accuse; he simply explains the right doctrine and expects his hearers to understand what he is refuting. The key element to getting people back on track is to explain fundamental truths such as the supremacy of Jesus Christ and the fullness of Christ. To remain strong, he told the Colossians, they were to stay connected to the Head: Jesus. He followed the teaching on doctrine with some teaching on Christian living.

OUTLINE

The Greatest Mystery

Read Colossians 1:15–22

The Son is the image of the invisible God,
the firstborn over all creation.

COLOSSIANS 1:15

Before I came to faith in Jesus, I'd heard the gospel preached but wrestled with His identity. How could He offer forgiveness for my sins when the Bible says only God can forgive sins? I discovered I wasn't alone in my struggles after reading J. I. Packer's *Knowing God*. Packer suggests that for many unbelievers the "really staggering Christian claim is that Jesus of Nazareth was God made man . . . as truly and fully divine as He was human." Yet this is the truth that makes salvation possible.

When the apostle Paul refers to Christ as "the image of the invisible God," he's saying Jesus is completely and perfectly God—Creator and Sustainer of all things in heaven and earth–but also fully human (Colossians 1:15–17). Because of this truth, we can be confident that through Christ's death and resurrection, He's not only carried the consequences for our sins but has also redeemed human nature, so that we—and all of creation—can be reconciled to God (vv. 20–22).

In an amazing, initiating act of love, God the Father reveals himself in and through Scripture by the power of God the Holy Spirit and through the life of God the Son. Those who believe in Jesus are saved because He is Emmanuel—God with us. Hallelujah!   *Xochitl Dixon*

It's Jesus

Read Colossians 1:27–29; 2:6–10

*God has chosen to make known . . . the glorious riches of
this mystery, which is Christ in you, the hope of glory.*

COLOSSIANS 1:27

During an episode of the popular US television talent competition
America's Got Talent, a five-year-old girl sang with such exuberance that
a judge compared her to a famous child singer and dancer in the 1930s.
He remarked, "I think Shirley Temple is living somewhere inside of
you." Her unexpected response: "Not Shirley Temple. Jesus!"

I marveled at the young girl's deep awareness that her joy came from
Jesus living in her. Scripture assures us of the amazing reality that all
who trust in Him not only receive the promise of eternal life with God
but also Jesus's presence living in them through His Spirit—our hearts
become Jesus's home (Colossians 1:27; Ephesians 3:17).

Jesus's presence in our hearts fills us with countless reasons for gratitude (Colossians 2:6–7). He brings the ability to live with purpose
and energy (1:28–29). He cultivates joy in our hearts in the midst of
all circumstances, in both times of celebration and times of struggle
(Philippians 4:12–13). Christ's Spirit provides hope to our hearts that
God is working all things together for good, even when we can't see it
(Romans 8:28). And the Spirit gives a peace that persists regardless of
the chaos swirling around us (Colossians 3:15).

With the confidence that comes from Jesus living in our hearts, we
can allow His presence to shine through so that others can't help but
notice.   *Lisa Samra*

Doing the Opposite

Read Colossians 2:20–3:4

For you died, and your life is now hidden with Christ in God.

COLOSSIANS 3:3

A wilderness excursion can seem daunting, but for outdoor enthusiasts this only adds to the appeal. Because hikers need more water than they can carry, they purchase bottles with built-in filters so they can use water sources along the way. But the process of drinking from such a container is counterintuitive. Tipping the bottle does nothing. A thirsty hiker has to blow into it to force the water through the filter. Reality is contrary to what seems natural.

As we follow Jesus, we find much that is counterintuitive. Paul pointed out one example: Keeping rules won't draw us closer to God. He asked, "Why, as though you still belonged to the world, do you submit to its rules: 'Do not handle! Do not taste! Do not touch!'? These rules . . . are based on merely human commands and teachings" (Colossians 2:20–22).

So what are we to do? Paul gave the answer. "Since, then, you have been raised with Christ, set your hearts on things above" (3:1). "You died," he told people who were still very much alive, "and your life is now hidden with Christ in God" (v. 3).

We are to consider ourselves "dead" to the values of this world and alive to Christ. We now aspire to a way of life demonstrated by the One who said, "Whoever wants to become great among you must be your servant" (Matthew 20:26). *Tim Gustafson*

The Best Is Yet to Come

Read Colossians 3:1–11

Set your minds on things above, not on earthly things.
COLOSSIANS 3:2

In our family, March means more than the end of winter. It means that the college basketball extravaganza called "March Madness" has arrived. As avid fans, we watch the tournament and enthusiastically root for our favorite teams. If we tune in early we get a chance to listen to the broadcasters talk about the upcoming game and to enjoy some of the pre-game drills where players shoot practice shots and warm up with teammates.

Our life on earth is like the pre-game in basketball. Life is interesting and full of promise, but it doesn't compare to what lies ahead. Just think of the pleasure of knowing that even when life is good, the best is yet to come! Or that when we give cheerfully to those in need, it's an investment in heavenly treasure. In times of suffering and sorrow, we can find hope as we reflect on the truth that a pain-free, tearless eternity awaits us. It's no wonder that Paul exhorts: "Set your minds on things above" (Colossians 3:2).

The future God has promised us enables us to see all of life in new dimensions. While this may be a great life, the best life is still to come. It is a wonderful privilege to live here in the light of there. *Joe Stowell*

Thriving Together

Read Colossians 3:5–16

*Let the peace of Christ rule in your hearts, since as
members of one body you were called to peace.*

COLOSSIANS 3:15

My husband, Alan, stood below the towering lights illuminating the athletic field, as a member of the opposing team hit a ball into the air. With his eyes fixed on the ball, Alan ran full speed toward the darkest corner of the field—and slammed into the chain link fence.

Later that night, I handed him an ice pack. "Are you feeling okay?" I asked. He rubbed his shoulder. "I'd feel better if my buddies had warned me that I was getting near the fence," he said.

Teams function best when they work together. Alan's injury could have been avoided, if only one of his teammates had yelled out a warning as he approached the fence.

Scripture reminds us that members of the church are designed to work together and watch out for each other like a team. The apostle Paul tells us that God cares about how we interact with each other, because the actions of one person can impact the whole community of believers (Colossians 3:13–14). When we all embrace opportunities to serve each other, fully devoted to unity and peace, the church flourishes (v. 15).

Paul instructed his readers to "let the message of Christ dwell among you richly as you teach and admonish one another with all wisdom through psalms, hymns, and songs from the Spirit" (v. 16). In this way we can inspire and protect one another through loving and honest relationships, obeying and praising God with grateful hearts—thriving together. *Xochitl Dixon*

Attitude of Gratitude

Read Colossians 3:12–25

Let the peace of Christ rule in your hearts, since as members
of one body you were called to peace. And be thankful.

COLOSSIANS 3:15

In Michigan, where I lived for many years, the winters can be brutal, with sub-zero temperatures and never-ending snow. One bitterly cold day, as I shoveled snow for what seemed like the thousandth time, our postman paused in his rounds to ask how I was doing. I told him that I disliked winter and was weary of all the heavy snow. I then commented that his job must be pretty rough during these extreme weather conditions. He responded, "Yeah, but at least I have a job. A lot of people don't. I'm thankful to be working."

I have to admit that I felt quite convicted by his attitude of gratitude. How easily we can lose sight of everything we have to be thankful for when the circumstances of life become unpleasant.

Paul told the followers of Christ at Colossae, "Let the peace of Christ rule in your hearts, since as members of one body you were called to peace. And be thankful" (Colossians 3:15). He wrote to the Thessalonians, "Give thanks in all circumstances; for this is God's will for you in Christ Jesus" (1 Thessalonians 5:18).

Even in our times of genuine struggle and pain, we can know God's peace and permit it to rule our hearts. And in that peace, we'll find reminders of all that we've been given in Christ. In that, we can truly be thankful.   *Bill Crowder*

Speak Up!

Read Colossians 4:2–6

Pray . . . that God may open a door for our message,
so that we may proclaim the mystery of Christ.

COLOSSIANS 4:3

Brittany exclaimed to her coworker at the restaurant, "There's that man! There's that man!" She was referring to Melvin, who first encountered her under different circumstances. While he was tending to the lawn of his church, the Spirit prompted him to start a conversation with a woman who appeared to be a prostitute. Her reply when he invited her to church was: "Do you know what I do? They wouldn't want me in there." As Melvin told her about the love of Jesus and assured her of His power to change her life, tears streamed down her face. Now, some weeks later, Brittany was working in a new environment, living proof of the power of Jesus to change lives.

In the context of encouraging believers to be devoted to prayer, the apostle Paul made a twofold request: "Pray for us, too, that God may open a door for our message, so that we may proclaim the mystery of Christ, for which I am in chains. Pray that I may proclaim it clearly, as I should" (Colossians 4:3–4).

Have you prayed for opportunities to speak boldly and clearly for Jesus? What a fitting prayer! Such prayers can lead His followers, like Melvin, to speak about Him in unexpected places and to unexpected people. Speaking up for Jesus can seem uncomfortable, but the rewards—changed lives—have a way of compensating for our discomforts.

Arthur Jackson

Didn't Get Credit

Read Colossians 4:7–18

Let your light shine before others, that they may see
your good deeds and glorify your Father in heaven.

MATTHEW 5:16

Hollywood musicals were wildly popular during the 1950s and 1960s, and three actresses in particular—Audrey Hepburn, Natalie Wood, and Deborah Kerr—thrilled viewers with their compelling performances. But a huge part of the appeal of these actresses was the breathtaking singing that enhanced their acting. In fact, the classic films' successes were actually due in large part to Marni Nixon, who dubbed the voices for each of those leading ladies and who for a long time went completely uncredited for her vital contribution.

In the body of Christ there are often people that faithfully support others who take a more public role. The apostle Paul depended on exactly that kind of person in his ministry. Tertius's work as a scribe gave Paul his powerful written voice (Romans 16:22). Epaphras's consistent behind-the-scene prayers were an essential foundation for Paul and the early church (Colossians 4:12–13). Lydia generously opened her home when the weary apostle needed restoration (Acts 16:15). Paul's work could not have been possible without the support he received from these fellow servants in Christ (vv. 7–18).

We may not always have highly visible roles, yet we know that God is pleased when we obediently play our essential part in His plan. When we "give [ourselves] fully to the work of the Lord" (1 Corinthians 15:58), we will find value and meaning in our service as it brings glory to God and draws others to Him (Matthew 5:16). *Cindy Hess Kasper*

1 THESSALONIANS

During Paul's short visit in Thessalonica, his message of the gospel turned the lives of these new Christians upside down. Because they embraced this new faith, their lives were affected; they even faced persecution. And he had left town when things got tough. So, some people wondered about Paul—whether he was the real deal or not. Therefore, the first thing he did in his initial letter was to defend his ministry, which he did in 1 Thessalonians 2:1–16. Second, he gave the people guidelines on how to live a holy life as believers. Also, the people were concerned about how things worked regarding death and the return of Christ. So, he addressed that in 4:13–5:11.

OUTLINE

Building a Bridge

Read 1 Thessalonians 1:1–10

Your faith toward God has gone out, so that
we do not need to say anything.

1 THESSALONIANS 1:8 NKJV

James Michener's *Centennial* is a fictional account of the history and set-tlement of the American West. Through the eyes of a French-Canadian trader named Pasquinel, Michener converges the stories of the Arapaho of the Great Plains and the European-based community of St. Louis. As this rugged adventurer moves between the growing clutter of the city and the wide-open spaces of the plains, he becomes a bridge between two drastically different worlds.

Followers of Christ also have the opportunity to build bridges between two very different worlds—those who know and follow Jesus and those who do not know Him. Early Christians in Thessalonica had been building bridges to their idol-worshiping culture, so Paul said of them, "The Lord's message rang out from you not only in Macedo-nia and Achaia—your faith in God has become known everywhere" (1 Thessalonians 1:8). The bridge they were building had two compo-nents: the "the Lord's message" and the example of their faith. It was clear to everyone that they had "turned to God from idols to serve the living and true God" (v. 9).

As God declares himself to those around us by His Word and through our lives, we can become a bridge to those who do not yet know the love of Christ. *Bill Crowder*

The Approval of One

Read 1 Thessalonians 2:1–4

We are not trying to please people but God, who tests our hearts.

1 THESSALONIANS 2:4

When the legendary composer Giuseppe Verdi (1813–1901) was young, a hunger for approval drove him toward success. Warren Wiersbe wrote of him: "When Verdi produced his first opera in Florence, the composer stood by himself in the shadows and kept his eye on the face of one man in the audience—the great Rossini. It mattered not to Verdi whether the people in the hall were cheering him or jeering him; all he wanted was a smile of approval from the master musician."

Whose approval do we seek? A parent's? A boss's? A love interest's? For Paul, there was but one answer. He wrote, "We speak as those approved by God to be entrusted with the gospel. We are not trying to please people but God, who tests our hearts" (1 Thessalonians 2:4).

What does it mean to seek God's approval? At the very least, it involves two things: turning from the desire for the applause of others and allowing His Spirit to make us more like Christ—the One who loved us and gave himself for us. As we yield to His perfect purposes in us and through us, we can anticipate a day when we will experience the smile of His approval—the approval of the One who matters most.

Bill Crowder

God's Doing Something New

Read 1 Thessalonians 3:6–13

*May the LORD make your love increase and overflow for
each other and for everyone else, just as ours does for you.*

1 THESSALONIANS 3:12

"Is God doing something new in your life?" was the question the leader
asked in a group I was in recently. My friend Mindy, who is dealing
with some difficult situations, responded. She told of needing patience
with aging parents, stamina for her husband's health issues, and understanding of her children and grandchildren who have not yet chosen to
follow Jesus. Then she made an insightful comment that runs contrary
to what we might normally think: "I believe the new thing God is doing
is He's expanding my capacity and opportunities to love."

That fits nicely with the apostle Paul's prayer for new believers in
Thessalonica: "May the Lord make your love increase and overflow
for each other and for everyone else" (1 Thessalonians 3:12). He had
taught them about Jesus but had to leave abruptly because of rioting
(Acts 17:1–9). Now in his letter he encouraged them to continue to
stand firm in their faith (1 Thessalonians 3:7–8). And he prayed that
the Lord would increase their love for all.

During difficulties, we often choose to complain and ask, *Why?* Or
wonder, *Why me?* Another way to handle those times could be to ask
the Lord to expand His love in our hearts and to help us take the new
opportunities that come to love others. *Anne Cetas*

Finding a Quiet Life

Read 1 Thessalonians 4:9–12

Make it your ambition to lead a quiet life.

1 THESSALONIANS 4:11

"What do you want to be when you grow up?" We all heard that question as children and sometimes even as adults. The question is born in curiosity, and the answer is often heard as an indication of ambition. My answers morphed over the years, starting with a cowboy, then a truck driver, followed by a soldier, and I entered college set on becoming a doctor. However, I can't recall one time that someone suggested or I consciously considered pursuing "a quiet life."

Yet that's exactly what Paul told the Thessalonians. First, he urged them to love one another and all of God's family even more (1 Thessalonians 4:10). Then he gave them a general admonition that would cover whatever specific plow they put their hand to. "Make it your ambition to lead a quiet life" (v. 11). Now, what did Paul mean by that exactly? He clarified: "You should mind your own business and work with your hands" so outsiders respect you and you're not a burden on anyone (vv. 11–12). We don't want to discourage children from pursuing their giftedness or passions but maybe we could encourage them that whatever they choose to do, they do with a quiet spirit.

Considering the world we live in, the words *ambitious* and *quiet* couldn't seem further apart. But the Scriptures are always relevant, so perhaps we should consider what it might look like to begin living quieter. *John Blase*

Hope in Grief

Read 1 Thessalonians 4:13–18

*We do not want you to be uninformed about those
who sleep in death, so that you do not grieve like
the rest of mankind, who have no hope.*

1 THESSALONIANS 4:13

As the cabbie drove us to London's Heathrow Airport, he told us his story. He had come alone to the United Kingdom at age fifteen, seeking to escape war and deprivation. Now, eleven years later, he has a family of his own and is able to provide for them in ways unavailable in his native land. But he laments that he's still separated from his parents and siblings. He told us that he has had a hard journey that won't be complete until he's reunited with his family.

Being separated from our loved ones in this life is hard, but losing a loved one in death is much harder and creates a sense of loss that won't be made right until we're reunited with them. When the new believers at Thessalonica wondered about such losses, Paul wrote, "Brothers and sisters, we do not want you to be uninformed about those who sleep in death, so that you do not grieve like the rest of mankind, who have no hope" (1 Thessalonians 4:13). He explained that as believers in Jesus, we can live in expectation of a wonderful reunion—together forever in the presence of Christ (v. 17).

Few experiences mark us as deeply as the separations we endure, but in Jesus we have hope of being reunited. And in the midst of grief and loss we can find the comfort we need in that enduring promise (v. 18).

Bill Crowder

On the Same Team

Read 1 Thessalonians 5:1–11, 16–18

Encourage one another and build each other up.

1 THESSALONIANS 5:11

A few years ago, when Philadelphia Eagles quarterback Carson Wentz returned to the field after healing from a severe injury, the NFL team's backup quarterback, Nick Foles, graciously returned to the bench. Although competing for the same position, the two men chose to support each other and remained confident in their roles. One reporter observed that the two athletes have a "unique relationship rooted in their faith in Christ" shown through their ongoing prayers for each other. As others watched, they brought honor to God by remembering they were on the same team—not just as Eagles quarterbacks, but as believers in Jesus representing Him.

The apostle Paul reminds believers to live as "children of the light" awaiting Jesus's return (1 Thessalonians 5:5–6). With our hope secure in the salvation Christ has provided, we can shrug off any temptations to compete out of jealousy, insecurity, fear, or envy. Instead, we can "encourage one another and build each other up" (v. 11). We can respect spiritual leaders who honor God and "live in peace" as we serve together to accomplish our shared goal—telling people about the gospel and encouraging others to live for Jesus (vv. 12–15).

As we serve on the same team, we can heed Paul's command: "Rejoice always, pray continually, give thanks in all circumstances; for this is God's will for you in Christ Jesus" (vv. 16–18). *Xochitl Dixon*

OCTOBER 10

Wise Aid

Read 1 Thessalonians 5:12–15

Encourage the disheartened, help the
weak, be patient with everyone.

1 Thessalonians 5:14

As I stopped my car at a red light, I saw the same man standing beside the road again. He held a cardboard sign: "Need money for food. Anything helps." I looked away and sighed. Was I the kind of person who ignored the needy?

Some people pretend to have needs but are actually con artists. Others have legitimate needs but face difficulties overcoming destructive habits. Social workers tell us it's better to give money to the aid ministries in our city. I swallowed hard and drove past. I felt bad, but I may have acted wisely.

God commands us to "warn those who are idle and disruptive, encourage the disheartened, help the weak" (1 Thessalonians 5:14). To do this well, we must know who belongs in which category. If we warn a weak or disheartened person, we may break her spirit; if we help an idle person, we may encourage laziness. Consequently, we help best from up close, when we know the person well enough to know what he needs.

Has God burdened your heart to help someone? Great! Now the work begins. Don't assume you know what that person needs. Ask her to share her story, and listen. Prayerfully give as seems wise and not merely to feel better. When we truly aim "to do what is good for each other," we will more readily "be patient with everyone," even when they stumble (vv. 14–15).

Mike Wittmer

Prayer Marathon

Read 1 Thessalonians 5:16–28

Pray continually.

1 THESSALONIANS 5:17

Do you struggle to maintain a consistent prayer life? Many of us do. We know that prayer is important, but it can also be downright difficult. We have moments of deep communion with God, and then we have times when it feels like we're just going through the motions. Why do we struggle so in our prayers?

The life of faith is a marathon. The ups, the downs, and the plateaus in our prayer life are reflections of this race. And just as in a marathon we need to keep running, so we keep praying. The point is: Don't give up!

That is God's encouragement too. The apostle Paul said, "pray continually" (1 Thessalonians 5:17), "keep on praying" (Romans 12:12 NLT), and "devote yourselves to prayer" (Colossians 4:2). All of these statements carry the idea of remaining steadfast and continuing in the work of prayer.

And because God, our heavenly Father, is a personal being, we can develop a time of close communion with Him, just as we do with our close human relationships. A. W. Tozer writes that as we learn to pray, our prayer life can grow "from the initial most casual brush to the fullest, most intimate communion of which the human soul is capable." And that's what we really want—deep communication with God. It happens when we keep praying. *Poh Fang Chia*

2 THESSALONIANS

It didn't take long for people to try to mislead the new Christians about what was true. Once Paul heard about this, he sat down while in Corinth and wrote another encouraging, edifying, teaching letter to guide the people about doctrine and practice as they followed their Savior, the Lord Jesus Christ.

OUTLINE

Relief for the Troubled

Read 2 Thessalonians 1:3–12

[God will] give relief to you who are troubled.

2 Thessalonians 1:7

One of my favorite scenes in literature occurs when a feisty aunt confronts an evil stepfather over the abuse of her nephew, David Copperfield. This scene takes place in Charles Dickens' novel named after the main character.

When David Copperfield shows up at his aunt's house, his stepfather is not far behind. Aunt Betsy Trotwood is not pleased to see the malicious Mr. Murdstone. She recounts a list of offenses and does not let him slither out of his responsibility for each act of cruelty. Her charges are so forceful and truthful that Mr. Murdstone—a normally aggressive person—finally leaves without a word. Through the strength and goodness of Aunt Betsy's character, David finally receives justice.

There is Someone else who is strong and good, and who will one day right the wrongs in our world. When Jesus returns, He will come down from heaven with a group of powerful angels. He will "give relief to you who are troubled," and He will not ignore those who have created problems for His children (2 Thessalonians 1:6–7). Until that day, Jesus wants us to stand firm and have courage. No matter what we endure on earth, we are safe for eternity. *Jennifer Benson Schuldt*

Servant-Friendship

Read 2 Thessalonians 2:1–8

We were gentle among you, just as a nursing
mother cherishes her own children.

1 THESSALONIANS 2:7 NKJV

Don Tack wanted to know what life was like for homeless people. So he concealed his identity and went to live on the streets of his city. He found out that food and shelter were offered by many organizations. At one shelter he could spend the night if he listened to a sermon beforehand. He appreciated the guest speaker's message and wanted to talk with him afterward. But as Don reached out to shake the man's hand and asked if he could talk with him, the speaker walked right past him as if he didn't exist.

Don learned that what was missing most in ministry to the homeless in his area were people who were willing to build relationships. So he began an organization called Servants Center to offer help through friendship.

What Don encountered at the shelter was the opposite of what the people who heard the apostle Paul experienced. When he shared the gospel, he gave himself too. He testified in his letter to the Thessalonians, "Because we loved you so much, we were delighted to share with you not only the gospel of God but our lives as well" (1 Thessalonians 2:8). He said, "We were gentle among you," like a mother (v. 7 NKJV).

In our service for the Lord, do we share not just our words or money but our time and friendship? *Anne Cetas*

Not Again!

Read 2 Thessalonians 2:13–17

God chose you as firstfruits to be saved through the sanctifying work of the Spirit and through belief in the truth.

2 THESSALONIANS 2:13

As I was reading the text message on my mobile phone, my temperature started to rise and my blood began to boil. I was on the verge of shooting back a nasty message when an inner voice told me to cool down and reply tomorrow. The next morning after a good night's sleep, the issue that had upset me so greatly seemed so trivial. I had blown it out of proportion because I didn't want to put another person's interest before my own. I was unwilling to inconvenience myself so I could help someone.

Regretfully, I am tempted to respond in anger more often than I would like to admit. I constantly find myself having to put into practice familiar Bible truths, such as "In your anger do not sin" (Ephesians 4:26) and don't look "to your own interests but each of you to the interests of the others" (Philippians 2:4).

Thankfully, God has given us His Spirit, who will assist us in our battle with our sin. The apostles Paul and Peter called it the "sanctifying work of the Spirit" (2 Thessalonians 2:13; 1 Peter 1:2). Without His power, we are helpless and defeated; but with His power, we can have victory.   *Poh Fang Chia*

A Plea for Prayer

Read 2 Thessalonians 3:1–5

Brothers and sisters, pray for us.
2 THESSALONIANS 3:1

A missionary recently visited the Bible study I was attending. She described what it had been like to pack up her household, part with friends, and relocate to a distant country. When she and her family arrived, they were greeted with a flourishing drug-trade and hazardous roadways. The language barrier brought on bouts of loneliness. They contracted four different stomach viruses. And her oldest daughter narrowly escaped death after falling through a railing on an unsafe stairwell. They needed prayer.

The apostle Paul experienced danger and hardship as a missionary. He was imprisoned, shipwrecked, and beaten. It's no surprise that his letters contained pleas for prayer. He asked the believers in Thessalonica to pray for success in spreading the gospel—that God's Word would "spread rapidly and be honored" (2 Thessalonians 3:1) and that God would deliver him from "wicked and evil people" (v. 2). Paul knew he would need to "open [his] mouth boldly" and declare the gospel (Ephesians 6:19 NKJV), which was yet another prayer request.

Do you know people who need supernatural help as they spread the good news of Christ? Remember Paul's appeal, "Brothers and sisters, pray for us" (2 Thessalonians 3:1), and intercede for them before the throne of our powerful God. *Jennifer Benson Schuldt*

Hard Labor

Read 2 Thessalonians 3:7–13

Whatever you do, work at it with all your heart, as working for the LORD, not for human masters.

COLOSSIANS 3:23

Think back to Labor Day this year. Did you get the day off? Pretty ironic, isn't it, that on Labor Day many of us don't have to labor. What better way to reward a hard-working populace than to give the laborers a holiday!

As we think about our work—our careers—we might need to take a closer look at what it takes to offer our employers our best.

1. No matter what our task, it's our duty to work for God's glory (Colossians 3:23). In this sense, no job is better than another. Each should result in honor to God.
2. The way we work can earn the respect of those who do not follow Christ (1 Thessalonians 4:11–12). A boss shouldn't have to tell a Christian to use time well or to work hard.
3. Our work is one way to fulfill our dual purpose: to love God and others. Showing love to our co-workers is a good way to show that we love God (Matthew 22:37–40).
4. We must work to provide for those who depend on us. Harsh words of criticism are reserved for those who don't take care of their family (1 Timothy 5:8).

Having a job can be hard work. Even for those who truly enjoy their jobs, it's nice to have a breather. But until the day comes when our work is over, our task is to make our labor a testimony to God's glory.

Dave Branon

The Secret of Peace

Read 2 Thessalonians 3:16–18

The LORD of peace himself give you peace.

2 THESSALONIANS 3:16

Grace is a very special lady. One word comes to mind when I think of her: peace. The quiet and restful expression on her face has seldom changed in the six months I have known her, even though her husband was diagnosed with a rare disease and then hospitalized.

When I asked Grace the secret of her peace, she said, "It's not a secret, it's a person. It's Jesus in me. There is no other way I can explain the quietness I feel in the midst of this storm."

The secret of peace is our relationship to Jesus Christ. He is our peace. When Jesus is our Savior and Lord, and as we become more like Him, peace becomes real. Things like sickness, financial difficulties, or danger may be present, but peace reassures us that God holds our lives in His hands (Daniel 5:23), and we can trust that things will work together for good.

Have we experienced this peace that goes beyond logic and understanding? Do we have the inner confidence that God is in control? My wish for all of us today echoes the words of the apostle Paul: "May the Lord of peace himself give you peace." And may we feel this peace "at all times and in every way" (2 Thessalonians 3:16).   *Keila Ochoa*

1 TIMOTHY

Paul's first directive to Timothy was to get him to stop false teachers from teaching and causing controversies in the church. Paul even named names—pinpointing Hymenaeus and Alexander as men who had to be extracted from the church. Paul's next admonition was about prayer and its importance in the church. He then mentions women and their situation in the worship services. He continues by giving guidelines for selecting church leadership, the dangers of error in the church, and the absolute value of simply preaching the Word of God.

OUTLINE

What's Wrong with the World?

Read 1 Timothy 1:12–17

Christ Jesus came into the world to save
sinners—of whom I am the worst.

1 TIMOTHY 1:15

There is an oft-heard story that *The London Times* posed a question to readers at the turn of the twentieth century: What's wrong with the world?

That's quite the question, isn't it? Someone might quickly respond, "Well, how much time do you have for me to tell you?" And that would be fair, as there seems to be so much that's wrong with our world. As the story goes, The Times received a number of responses, but one in particular has endured in its brief brilliance. The English writer, poet, and philosopher G. K. Chesterton penned this four-word response, a refreshing surprise to the usual passing-of-the-buck: "Dear Sirs, I am."

Whether the story is factual or not is up for debate. But that response? It's nothing but true. Long before Chesterton came along, there was an apostle named Paul. Far from a lifelong model citizen, Paul confessed his past shortcomings: "I was once a blasphemer and a persecutor and a violent man" (1 Timothy 1:13). After naming who Jesus came to save ("sinners"), he goes on to make a very Chesterton-like qualification: "of whom I am the worst" (v. 15). Paul knew exactly what was and is wrong with the world. And he further knew the only hope of making things right—"the grace of our Lord" (v.14). What an amazing reality! This enduring truth lifts our eyes to the light of Christ's saving love.

John Blase

Prompted to Pray

Read 1 Timothy 2:1-8

I constantly remember you in my prayers.

2 TIMOTHY 1:3

"Several years ago I was prompted to pray for you often, and I wonder why."

That text message from an old friend came with a photo of a note she'd kept in her Bible: "Pray for James. Cover mind, thoughts, words." Beside my name she'd recorded three separate years.

I looked at the years and caught my breath. I wrote back and asked what month she began to pray. She responded, "Sometime around July."

That was the month I was preparing to leave home for extended study abroad. I would be facing an unfamiliar culture and language and have my faith challenged like never before. As I looked at the note, I realized I'd received the precious gift of generous prayer.

My friend's kindness reminded me of another "prompting" to pray, Paul's instruction to his young missionary friend Timothy: "I urge, then, first of all, that petitions, prayers, intercession and thanksgiving be made for all people" (1 Timothy 2:1). The phrase "first of all" indicates highest priority. Our prayers matter, Paul explains, because God "wants all people to be saved and to come to a knowledge of the truth" about Jesus (v. 4).

God moves through faithful prayer in countless ways to encourage others and draw them near to himself. We may not know someone's circumstances when he or she comes to mind, but God does. And He'll help that person as we pray! *James Banks*

In the Spotlight

Read 1 Timothy 3:1–10

He must . . . have a good reputation . . ., so that he
will not fall into disgrace and into the devil's trap.

1 TIMOTHY 3:7

Rosa Parks's refusal in 1955 to give her bus seat to a white man in Montgomery, Alabama, was a turning point in the civil rights struggle. So in 1994, the public was stunned when eighty-year-old Rosa was robbed and mugged in her home by an intruder. A short time later, an alert citizen recognized the suspect from a police photo, and with a friend he subdued Rosa's mugger until police could arrive.

But the public spotlight was not good for the new hero. After he gave a TV interview, FBI agents recognized him as a fugitive from the law. They arrested him for driving the getaway car in a 1991 robbery of an automatic teller machine.

This incident illustrates the truth that unresolved sin can rob a person of the honor of being known for doing good. This is why Paul emphasized in 1 Timothy 3 how important it is for church leaders to have a good conscience and a blameless record of dealing with their own sin. Those who want to be known for walking with Christ must face and deal with anything that would disqualify them from receiving that honor.

Living with a good conscience isn't just a religious and moral obligation. It's the only way to be able to walk with Christ in the spotlight of a watching world.   *Mart DeHaan*

First Things First

Read 1 Timothy 4:12–16

Watch your life and doctrine closely.
1 TIMOTHY 4:16

When you travel by air, before the flight takes off an airline employee presents a safety briefing, which explains what to do if there is a loss of cabin pressure. Passengers are told that oxygen masks will drop from the compartment above, and they are to put one on themselves before helping others. Why? Because before you can help anyone else, you need to be physically alert yourself.

When Paul wrote to Timothy, he stressed the importance of maintaining his own spiritual health before helping and serving others. He reminded Timothy of his many responsibilities as a pastor: There were false teachings to contend with (1 Timothy 4:1–5) and wrong doctrines to correct (vv. 6–8). But to discharge his duties well, what was most important was to "watch [his] life and doctrine closely [and] persevere in them" (v. 16). He needed to take care of his own relationship with the Lord first before he could attend to others.

What Paul told Timothy applies to us too. Each day we encounter people who do not know the Lord. When we tank up on our spiritual oxygen first through time in God's Word, prayer, and the enabling of the Holy Spirit, we keep our relationship right with God. Then we will be spiritually alert to help others. *C. P. Hia*

Lifework

Read 1 Timothy 5:1–8

*Anyone [who] does not provide for his own, and
especially for those of his household, he has denied
the faith and is worse than an unbeliever.*

1 Timothy 5:8 nkjv

Some of our friends have chosen to curtail or leave their ministries for a while. They did so in order to care for family members—for aging parents, ill spouses, siblings, or children with special needs. All were involved in fruitful works for which they were uniquely gifted. All believed that there was much to be done.

Some have chosen to reduce the time and energy they spend on those ministries; others have left their work completely. These adjustments have been difficult because ministry has been their lifework—a work for which they spent years in preparation and had many years yet to serve.

It occurs to me, however, that they have not given up their lifework but rather have assumed another. Loving and caring for others is our life's work, and caring for those of our "own house" is the highest and holiest work of all. To deny love is to align ourselves with a cold, uncaring world.

Not everyone can leave a career or calling to care for others. Financial realities and obligations may dictate otherwise. But is not such love the mark of one who does the work of God? Did not Jesus promise that one who gives a cup of cold water to one of His children "shall by no means lose his reward"? (Matthew 10:42 nkjv).   *David Roper*

Roughing the Pastor

Read 1 Timothy 5:17–25

*The elders who direct the affairs of the church
well are worthy of double honor, especially those
whose work is preaching and teaching.*

1 TIMOTHY 5:17

I was at my grandson's eighth-grade football game when the referee indicated there was a penalty and stopped play. Apparently, after the ball was thrown, the boy who passed it was tackled, prompting a penalty flag. The announcer from the press box said: "There is a flag on the field. The penalty is roughing the pastor . . . I mean, roughing the passer." As soon as he said it, I thought to myself, God could give that penalty to some churches today!

It's not that pastors are perfect. If that is what we are looking for, then pastorless churches would be the norm. It's that God calls on us to honor those who lead us spiritually, particularly "those who labor in preaching and teaching" (1 Timothy 5:17 ESV). In my opinion, pastoring is one of the hardest occupations on the planet. We live in a sophisticated, fast-paced, and complex world, and our expectations for "high-performance" pastors often set the bar at unattainable heights.

So, let's switch the focus and become high-performance church members who honor our pastors with words of encouragement and prayer. A supportive note or a "thank you" in the foyer will go a long way to stimulate pastors to serve with joy and efficiency. *Joe Stowell*

Rich toward God

Read 1 Timothy 6:6–11

Godliness with contentment is great gain.

1 TIMOTHY 6:6

Growing up during the Great Depression, my parents knew deep hardship as children. As a result, they were thrifty adults—hard-working and grateful money stewards. At the same time, they were never greedy. They gave time, talent, and treasury to their church, charity groups, and the needy. Indeed, they handled their money wisely and gave cheerfully.

As believers in Jesus, my parents took to heart the apostle Paul's warning: "Those who want to get rich fall into temptation and a trap and into many foolish and harmful desires that plunge people into ruin and destruction" (1 Timothy 6:9).

Paul gave this advice to Timothy, the young pastor of the city of Ephesus, a wealthy city where riches tempted rich and poor alike.

"The love of money is a root of all kinds of evil," Paul warned. "Some people, eager for money, have wandered from the faith and pierced themselves with many griefs" (v. 10).

What, then, is the antidote to greed? Being "rich toward God," said Jesus (see Luke 12:13–21). By pursuing, appreciating, and loving our heavenly Father above all, He remains our chief delight. As the psalmist wrote, "Satisfy us in the morning with your unfailing love, that we may sing for joy and be glad all our days" (Psalm 90:14).

Rejoicing in Him daily relieves us of coveting, leaving us contented. May Jesus redeem our heart's desires, making us rich toward God!

Patricia Raybon

An Open, Generous Heart

Read 1 Timothy 6:17–19

Be generous and willing to share.
1 Timothy 6:18

After Vicki's old car broke down with no option for repair, she started scraping together money for another vehicle. Chris, a frequent customer of the restaurant where Vicki works at the drive-thru window, one day heard her mention she needed a car. "I couldn't stop thinking about it," Chris said. "I [had] to do something." So he bought his son's used car (his son had just put it up for sale), shined it up, and handed Vicki the keys. Vicki was shocked. "Who . . . does that?" she said in amazement and gratitude.

The Scriptures call us to live with open hands, giving freely as we can—providing what's truly best for those in need. As Paul says: "Command [those who are rich] to do good, to be rich in good deeds" (1 Timothy 6:18). We don't merely perform a benevolent act here or there, but rather live out a cheerful spirit of giving. Big-heartedness is our normal way of life. "Be generous and willing to share," we're told (v. 18).

As we live with an open, generous heart, we don't need to fear running out of what we need. Rather, the Bible tells us that in our compassionate generosity, we're taking "hold of [true] life" (v. 19). With God, genuine living means loosening our grip on what we have and giving to others freely. *Winn Collier*

2 TIMOTHY

◆

Despite the discouraging situation Paul found himself in—imagine being arrested again after thinking you were now a free man—Paul encouraged Timothy. In this note to his "dear son" (1:2), Paul reminded Timothy of his heritage, encouraged him not to be ashamed, and exhorted him to keep preaching what Paul had modeled. He told him to be bold in the grace of Jesus. In 2 Timothy 2, Paul gave some pastor-to-pastor advice about dealing with false teaching and foolish arguments. He told Timothy that hard times would come but to persevere.

OUTLINE

The Frosting of Faith

Read 2 Timothy 1:1–5

*I am reminded of your sincere faith, which first lived
in your grandmother Lois and in your mother Eunice
and, I am persuaded, now lives in you also.*

2 Timothy 1:5

Hand in hand, my grandson and I skipped across the parking lot to find a special back-to-school outfit. A preschooler now, he was excited about everything, and I was determined to ignite his happiness into joy. I'd just seen a coffee mug with the inscription, "Grandmas are moms with lots of frosting." Frosting equals fun, glitter, joy! That's my job description as his grandma, right? That . . . and more.

In his second letter to his spiritual son Timothy, Paul calls out his sincere faith—and then credits its lineage both to Timothy's grandmother, Lois, and his mother, Eunice (2 Timothy 1:5). These women lived out their faith in such a way that Timothy also came to believe in Jesus. Surely, Lois and Eunice loved Timothy and provided for his needs. But clearly, they did more. Paul points to the faith living in them as the source of the faith later living in Timothy.

My job as a grandmother includes the "frosting" moment of a back-to-school outfit. But even more, I'm called to the frosting moments when I share my faith: Bowing our heads over chicken nuggets. Noticing angelic cloud formations in the sky as God's works of art. Chirping along with a song about Jesus on the radio. Let's be wooed by the example of moms and grandmas like Eunice and Lois to let our faith become the frosting in life so others will want what we have. *Elisa Morgan*

◆

OCTOBER 27

Trusting God in Sorrow

Read 2 Timothy 1:6–12

I know whom I have believed.

2 TIMOTHY 1:12

When a man known as "Papa John" learned he had terminal cancer, he and his wife, Carol, sensed God calling them to share their illness journey online. Believing that God would minister through their vulnerability, they posted their moments of joy and their sorrow and pain for two years.

When Carol wrote that her husband "went into the outstretched arms of Jesus," hundreds of people responded, with many thanking Carol for their openness. One person remarked that hearing about dying from a Christian point of view was healthy, for "we all have to die" someday. Another said that although she'd never met the couple personally, she couldn't express how much encouragement she'd received through their witness of trusting God.

Although Papa John sometimes felt excruciating pain, he and Carol shared their story so they could demonstrate how God upheld them. They knew their testimony would bear fruit for God, echoing what Paul wrote to Timothy when he suffered: "I know whom I have believed, and am convinced that he is able to guard what I have entrusted to him until that day" (2 Timothy 1:12).

God can use even the death of a loved one to strengthen our faith in Him (and the faith of others) through the grace we receive in Christ Jesus (v. 9). If you're experiencing anguish and difficulty, know that He can bring comfort and peace. *Amy Boucher Pye*

Faithful Service

Read 2 Timothy 2:1–10

*You therefore must endure hardship as
a good soldier of Jesus Christ.*

2 Timothy 2:3 nkjv

Having served in World War I, C. S. Lewis was no stranger to the stresses of military service. In a public address during World War II, he eloquently described the hardships a soldier has to face: "All that we fear from all the kinds of adversity . . . is collected together in the life of the soldier on active service. Like sickness, it threatens pain and death. Like poverty, it threatens ill lodging, cold, heat, thirst, and hunger. Like slavery, it threatens toil, humiliation, injustice, and arbitrary rule. Like exile, it separates you from all you love."

The apostle Paul used the analogy of a soldier suffering hardship to describe the trials a believer may experience in service to Christ. Paul—now at the end of his life—had faithfully endured suffering for the sake of the gospel. He encourages Timothy to do the same: "You therefore must endure hardship as a good soldier of Jesus Christ" (2 Timothy 2:3 nkjv).

Serving Christ requires perseverance. We may encounter obstacles of poor health, troubled relationships, or difficult circumstances. But as a good soldier we press on—with God's strength—because we serve the King of Kings and Lord of Lords who sacrificed himself for us!

Dennis Fisher

Gentle Speech

Read 2 Timothy 2:22–26

The LORD's servant must not be quarrelsome.

2 TIMOTHY 2:24

I was on Facebook, arguing. Bad move. What made me think I was obligated to "correct" a stranger on a hot topic—especially a divisive one? The results were heated words, hurt feelings (on my part anyway), and a broken opportunity to witness well for Jesus. That's the sum outcome of "internet anger." It's the term for the harsh words flung daily across the blogosphere. As one ethics expert explained, people wrongly conclude that rage "is how public ideas are talked about."

Paul's wise advice to Timothy gave the same caution. "Don't have anything to do with foolish and stupid arguments, because you know they produce quarrels. And the Lord's servant must not be quarrelsome but must be kind to everyone" (2 Timothy 2:23–24).

Paul's good counsel, written to Timothy from a Roman prison, was sent to prepare the young pastor for teaching God's truth. The apostle's advice is just as timely for us today, especially when the conversation turns to our faith. "Opponents must be gently instructed, in the hope that God will grant them repentance leading them to a knowledge of the truth" (v. 25).

Speaking kindly to others is part of this challenge, but not just for pastors. For all who love God and seek to tell others about Him, may we speak His truth in love. With every word, the Holy Spirit will help us.

Patricia Raybon

Spray-on Mud

Read 2 Timothy 3:1–7

Having a form of godliness but denying its power.
Have nothing to do with such people.

2 Timothy 3:5

A British company has developed a product called "spray-on mud" so city dwellers can give their expensive 4x4 vehicles the appearance of having been off-road for a day of hunting or fishing without ever leaving town. The mud is even filtered to remove stones and debris that might scratch the paint. According to the company, sales are going well.

There is something within each of us that values how we look on the outside more than who we are on the inside. It causes some people to pad their résumés or embellish their memoirs. But it has no place in our lives as followers of Jesus.

Paul warned Timothy about people in the church who had a form of godliness but denied its power. "They will maintain a façade of 'religion,' but their conduct will deny its validity. You must keep clear of people like this" (2 Timothy 3:5 Phillips). The inward reality of Christ is what counts, because it will produce the outward signs of faith.

Paul's authority to instruct the church about spiritual authenticity came through his suffering, not by "spraying on mud." "I bear on my body the marks of Jesus," said the apostle (Galatians 6:17).

God calls us to authentic living today.   *David McCasland*

Guiding Children to God

Read 2 Timothy 3:10–15

*Continue in what you have learned . . . how from
infancy you have known the Holy Scriptures.*
2 TIMOTHY 3:14–15

An outspoken atheist believes it's immoral for parents to teach their children religion as though it were actually true. He even claims that parents who pass along their faith to their children are committing child abuse. Though these views are extreme, I do hear from parents who are hesitant to boldly encourage their children toward faith. While most of us readily hope to influence our children with our view of politics or nutrition or sports, for some reason some of us treat our convictions about God differently.

In contrast, Paul wrote of how Timothy had been taught "from infancy . . . the Holy Scriptures, which are able to make you wise for salvation through faith in Christ Jesus" (2 Timothy 3:15). Timothy didn't arrive at faith as an adult through the power of his own, unaided reason. Rather, his mother nurtured his heart toward God; then he continued in what he had learned (v. 14). If God is life, the source of true wisdom, then it's vital for us to tenderly cultivate a love for God in our families.

There are many belief systems that are influencing our children. TV shows, movies, music, teachers, friends, the media—each of these carry assumptions (either obvious or under the radar) about faith that exert real influence. May we choose not to be silent. The beauty and grace we've experienced compels us to guide our children toward God.

Winn Collier

Joyful Reunion

Read 2 Timothy 4:1–8

*He who testifies to these things says, "Yes, I am
coming soon." Amen. Come, LORD Jesus!*
REVELATION 22:20

Some years ago when our children were still small, I flew home after a ten-day ministry trip. In those days people were allowed to visit the airport boarding area to greet incoming passengers. When my flight landed, I came out of the jet-bridge and was greeted by our little ones— so happy to see me that they were screaming and crying. I looked at my wife, whose eyes were teary. I couldn't speak. Strangers in the gate area also teared up as our children hugged my legs and cried their greetings. It was a wonderful moment.

The memory of the intensity of that greeting serves as a gentle rebuke to the priorities of my own heart. The apostle John, eagerly desiring Jesus's return, wrote, "He who testifies to these things says, 'Yes, I am coming soon.' Amen. Come, Lord Jesus!" (Revelation 22:20). In another passage, Paul even spoke of a crown awaiting those who have "longed for his appearing" (2 Timothy 4:8). Yet sometimes I don't feel as eager for Christ's return as my children were for mine.

Jesus is worthy of the very best of our love and devotion—and nothing on earth should compare to the thought of seeing Him face-to-face. May our love for our Savior deepen as we anticipate our joyful reunion with Him.   *Bill Crowder*

From Pity to Praise

Read 2 Timothy 4:9–18

But the LORD stood at my side and gave me strength.

2 TIMOTHY 4:17

At a coat drive for children, excited kids searched gratefully for their favorite colors and proper sizes. They also gained self-esteem, an organizer said, with new coats boosting their acceptance by peers and school attendance on winter days.

The apostle Paul seemed to need a coat, as well, when he wrote Timothy, "Bring the cloak that I left with Carpus at Troas" (2 Timothy 4:13). Held in a cold Roman prison, Paul needed warmth but also companionship. "No one came to my support, but everyone deserted me," he lamented, when he faced a Roman judge (v. 16). His words pierce our hearts with the honesty of this great missionary's pain.

Yet in these final words of Paul's last recorded letter—his closing thoughts after an astounding ministry—he moves from pity to praise. "But the Lord stood at my side," he adds (v. 17), and his words rally our hearts. As Paul declared, "[God] gave me strength so that I might preach the Good News in its entirety for all the Gentiles to hear. And he rescued me from certain death" (v. 17 NLT).

If you're facing a crisis, lacking even the right clothing for warmth or close friends to help, remember God. He's faithful to revive, provide, and deliver. Why? For His glory and for our purpose in His kingdom.

Patricia Raybon

TITUS

◆

While a group of Christians had been established on Crete, they had not yet been organized into a true New Testament church. So Paul left Titus there to appoint elders and give the church a framework. Paul recognized that it was a tough crowd in Crete ("many rebellious people" Titus 1:10), so he made it clear the kind of person who would serve as an elder (1:7–9). Beyond that, Titus was given help with how to handle various groups in the church (older people, younger people, slaves). Paul also spoke about encouraging good works and good behavior among the people.

OUTLINE

Smooth Talkers

Read Titus 1:5–16

Teach what is appropriate to sound doctrine.

Titus 2:1

A man who was trying to explain the meaning of the word *oratory* commented with tongue in cheek, "If you say black is white, that's foolishness. But if while you say black is white you roar like a bull, pound on the table with both fists, and race from one end of the platform to another, that's oratory!"

We can quickly be swept off our feet by the way people express themselves, even though we have some questions about their message. Jude warned us about those whose mouths speak "great swelling words" (v. 16 NKJV). The masses are often moved more by style than by content.

According to Paul, the time will come when people will turn away from the truth of sound doctrine and tolerate only those who entertain and make people feel good (2 Timothy 4:3–4). So we must carefully analyze and evaluate in the light of the Scriptures everything we hear—even what is taught and proclaimed by the most eloquent of speakers. We must not allow ourselves to be swayed by mere oratory—especially in the church! We need to be sure that the Bible teachers we listen to are "speaking the truth in Christ and not lying" (1 Timothy 2:7 NKJV).

Don't let "meaningless talk and deception" (Titus 1:10) confuse you. Eloquence is never a substitute for truth. *Richard DeHaan*

A Good Teacher

Read Titus 2:1–10

In everything . . . an example by doing what is good.

Titus 2:7

While a student at Bryan College, I came to know Bible teacher Irving Jensen. He was well-known for his course on Bible-study methods, and he has published dozens of books and magazine articles on the subject. He believed deeply in what he taught and was a very effective and influential teacher.

Jensen was so effective because he lived what he taught. His speech was sometimes hesitant, and he didn't use flashy classroom techniques, but he loved his students and taught us to love the Word of God by the way he lived and what he taught. He lived out the words of Titus 2:7–8, "In everything set them an example by doing what is good. In your teaching show integrity, seriousness and soundness of speech that cannot be condemned, so that those who oppose you may be ashamed because they have nothing bad to say about us."

We are to back up what we say about Christ with a lifestyle that is above reproach and cannot be condemned by our enemies. Our lives are to be so exemplary that people around us are attracted to the truth about Christ (v. 10).

Our words and our way of living should exemplify the message of Christ. By words and by deeds—that's how to be a good teacher.

David Egner

Do All the Good You Can

Read Titus 2:11–3:2

*[Jesus Christ] gave himself for us to
redeem us from all wickedness.*

Titus 2:14

At the church I attend, the Sunday morning service closes with a song based on John Wesley's words. We sing, "Do all the good you can, by all the means you can, in all the ways you can, in every place you can, at all the times you can, to everyone you can, as long as you ever can—do all the good you can." I've come to appreciate these words as a fitting challenge to live like Jesus, who "went around doing good" (Acts 10:38).

In Paul's letter to Titus, there are several references to doing good. We are told that a church leader is to be "one who loves what is good" (1:8). Christians are to be "eager to do what is good" (2:14) and "ready to do whatever is good" (3:1). Believers must "devote themselves to doing what is good" (3:8).

People everywhere are hungry for the reality of a personal touch from God, and we as Christians can do something about that. The wonderful gift of the love of Christ, which was given to us when we trusted in Him as our Savior, was never intended to be kept to ourselves. It should break out in acts of love, kindness, help, and healing wherever we are and in everything we do.

It's a great theme song for every Christian every day—"Do all the good you can."   *David McCasland*

Tiny Island

Read Titus 3:1–7

Slander no one, . . . be peaceable and considerate,
and always . . . be gentle toward everyone.
TITUS 3:2

Singapore is a tiny island. It's so small that one can hardly spot it on the world map. (Try it, if you don't already know where Singapore is.) Because it is densely populated, consideration of others is especially important. A man wrote to his fiancée who was coming to Singapore for the first time: "Space is limited. Therefore . . . you must always have that sense of space around you. You should always step aside to ensure you are not blocking anyone. The key is to be considerate."

The apostle Paul wrote to Titus, a young pastor: "Remind the people . . . to be obedient, to be ready to do whatever is good, to slander no one, to be peaceable and considerate, and always to be gentle toward everyone" (Titus 3:1–2). It has been said, "Our lives may be the only Bible some people read." The world knows that Christians are supposed to be different. If we are cantankerous, self-absorbed, and rude, what will others think about Christ and the gospel we share?

Being considerate is a good motto to live by and is possible as we depend on the Lord. And it is one way to model Christ and demonstrate to the world that Jesus saves and transforms lives.   *Poh Fang Chia*

PHILEMON

Notice the irony of the first sentence of Philemon: "Paul, a prisoner of Christ Jesus." He was a prisoner of Christ, a prisoner of the Roman state—yet he was seeking to set a slave free from the prison of slavery. Paul offers a hearty thank you to Philemon for his faith, and then he tells him he is praying for Philemon to understand his coming difficult request about Onesimus. He pleads with Philemon to let his faith control his reaction to Onesimus's return and to react to it in a godly way. Then Paul invites himself for a visit at Philemon's house after his release. True Christlike hospitality is key to everything that is happening in the book of Philemon.

OUTLINE

Paul's Thankfulness for Philemon Philemon 1:1–7
A Request for Forgiveness Philemon 1:8–16
A Promise from Paul Philemon 1:17–21
Greetings and Grace Philemon 1:22–25

Paul, the Aged

Read Philemon 1:1–9

Being such a one as Paul, the aged, . . .
I appeal to you for my son Onesimus.

PHILEMON 1:9–10 NKJV

Celebrating my sixtieth birthday really changed my perspective on life—I used to think people in their sixties were "old." Then I started counting the number of productive years I might have left and set the number at ten. I went along with this dead-end kind of thinking until I remembered a very productive coworker who was eighty-five. So I sought him out to ask what life after sixty was like. He told me of some of the wonderful ministry opportunities the Lord had given him over the last twenty-five years.

The apostle Paul, referring to himself as "aged" in Philemon 1:9, really resonates with my own sense of aging: "Being such a one as Paul, the aged, . . . I appeal to you for my son Onesimus" (vv. 9–10 NKJV). Paul was asking Philemon to take back his runaway servant Onesimus. Some scholars believe Paul was in his late forties or early fifties when he wrote this—certainly not a senior citizen by today's standards. But life expectancy in those days was much shorter. Yet despite awareness of his mature years, Paul went on to serve the Lord for several more years.

While we may experience physical or other kinds of limitations, what really matters is that we continue doing what we can for the Lord until He calls us Home.

Dennis Fisher

Removing the Barriers

Read Philemon 1:8–16

*He is very dear to me but even dearer to you, both
as a fellow man and as a brother in the Lord.*

Philemon 1:16

I saw Mary every Tuesday when I visited "the House"—a home that
helps former prisoners reintegrate into society. My life looked different
from hers: fresh out of jail, fighting addictions, separated from her son.
You might say she lived on the edge of society.

Like Mary, Onesimus knew what it meant to live on the edge of
society. As a slave, Onesimus had apparently wronged his Christian
master, Philemon, and was now in prison. While there, he met Paul and
came to faith in Christ (v. 10). Though now a changed man, Onesimus
was still a slave. Paul sent him back to Philemon with a letter urging
him to receive Onesimus "no longer as a slave, but better than a slave,
as a dear brother" (v. 16).

Philemon had a choice to make: He could treat Onesimus as his
slave or welcome him as a brother in Christ. I had a choice to make
too. Would I see Mary as an ex-convict and a recovering addict—or
as a woman whose life is being changed by the power of Christ? Mary
was my sister in the Lord, and we were privileged to walk together in
our journey of faith.

It's easy to allow the walls of socio-economic status, class, or cultural
differences to separate us. The gospel of Christ removes those barriers,
changing our lives and our relationships forever.   *Karen Wolfe*

HEBREWS

◆

Because the author did not identify a specific audience, it is not absolutely clear to whom this was being written. However, it is clear that the recipients were mostly, if not all, Jewish believers (and perhaps some nonbelievers) in Christian churches. There was some discouragement among these people because they were facing persecution, and they may have been wondering if they had chosen wisely in rejecting their ancient Jewish traditions for this new faith.

It appears that the book was written to some believers who were reconsidering their commitment to Jesus Christ, and the author is trying to assure them to stay in the faith.

OUTLINE

The Superiority of Jesus Hebrews 1:1–3:6

Warnings about Unbelief Hebrews 3:7–4:13

Jesus as High Priest Hebrews 4:14–7:28

The New Covenant of Jesus Hebrews 8:1–13

Jesus as Sanctuary and Sacrifice Hebrews 9:1–10:18

The Importance of Perseverance Hebrews 10:19–39

The Smiling Jesus

Read Hebrews 1:8–12

God, your God, has set you above your companions
by anointing you with the oil of joy.
HEBREWS 1:9

If you were to play the part of Jesus in a movie, how would you approach the role? That was the challenge faced by Bruce Marchiano, who played Jesus in the 1993 Visual Bible movie *Matthew*. Knowing that millions of viewers would draw conclusions about Jesus based on his work, the weight of getting Christ "right" felt overwhelming. He fell to his knees in prayer and begged Jesus for—well, for Jesus.

Bruce gained insight from the first chapter of Hebrews, where the writer tells us how God the Father set the Son apart by anointing Him "with the oil of joy" (1:9). This kind of joy is one of celebration—a gladness of connection to the Father expressed wholeheartedly. Such joy ruled in Jesus's heart throughout His life. As Hebrews 12:2 describes it, "For the joy set before him he endured the cross, scorning its shame, and sat down at the right hand of the throne of God."

Taking his cue from this Scriptural expression, Bruce offered a uniquely joy-filled portrayal of his Savior. As a result, he became known as "the smiling Jesus." We too can dare to fall to our knees and "beg Jesus for Jesus." May He so fill us with His character that people around us see the expression of His love in us!   *Elisa Morgan*

Able to Help

Read Hebrews 2:14–18

Because he himself suffered when he was tempted,
he is able to help those who are being tempted.

Hebrews 2:18

Joe's eight-week "break" from his job as a crisis care worker at a New York City church was not a vacation. In his words, it was "to live again among the homeless, to become one of them, to remember what hungry, tired, and forgotten feel like." Joe's first stint on the streets had come nine years earlier when he arrived from Pittsburgh without a job or a place to stay. For thirteen days he lived on the streets with little food or sleep. That's how God had prepared him for decades of ministry to needy people.

When Jesus came to earth, He also chose to share the experiences of those He came to save. "Since the children have flesh and blood, he too shared in their humanity so that by his death he might break the power of him who holds the power of death—that is, the devil" (Hebrews 2:14). From birth to death, nothing was missing from Christ's human experience—except sin (4:15). Because He conquered sin, He can help us when we're tempted to sin.

And Jesus doesn't need to reacquaint himself with our earthly cares. The One who saves us remains connected to us and is deeply interested in us. Whatever life brings, we can be assured that the One who rescued us from our greatest foe, the devil (2:14), stands ready to help us in our times of greatest need. *Arthur Jackson*

Buckling Up!

Read Hebrews 4:11–16

Let us then approach God's throne of grace with confidence.

HEBREWS 4:16

"The captain has turned on the seat belt sign, indicating that we are entering an area of turbulence. Please return to your seats immediately and securely fasten your seat belt." Flight attendants give that warning when necessary because in rough air, unbuckled passengers can be injured. Secured in their seats, they can safely ride out the turbulence.

Most of the time, life doesn't warn us of the unsettling experiences coming our way. But our loving Father knows and cares about our struggles, and He invites us to bring our cares, hurts, and fears to Him. The Scriptures tell us, "This High Priest of ours understands our weaknesses, for he faced all of the same testings we do, yet he did not sin. So let us come boldly to the throne of our gracious God. There we will receive his mercy, and we will find grace to help us when we need it most" (Hebrews 4:15–16 NLT).

In seasons of turbulence, going to our Father in prayer is the best thing we can do. The phrase "grace to help us when we need it"—means that in His presence we can be "buckled" in peace during threatening times, because we bring our concerns to the One who is greater than all! When life feels overwhelming, we can pray. He can help us through the turbulence.   *Bill Crowder*

Desiring Growth

Read Hebrews 5:11–14

Anyone who lives on milk . . . is not acquainted
with the teaching about righteousness.

HEBREWS 5:13

The axolotl (pronounced ACK suh LAH tuhl) is a biological enigma. Instead of maturing into adult form, this endangered Mexican salamander retains tadpole-like characteristics throughout its life. Writers and philosophers have used the axolotl as a symbol of someone who fears growth.

In Hebrews 5 we learn about Christians who were avoiding healthy growth, remaining content with spiritual "milk" intended for new believers. Perhaps because of fear of persecution, they weren't growing in the kind of faithfulness to Christ that would enable them to be strong enough to suffer with Him for the sake of others (vv. 7–10). Instead they were in danger of sliding backward from the Christlike attitudes they had already shown (6:9–11). They weren't ready for a solid diet of self-sacrifice (5:14). So the author wrote, "We have much to say about this, but it is hard to make it clear to you because you no longer try to understand" (v. 11).

Axolotls follow the natural pattern set for them by their Creator. But followers of Christ are designed to grow into spiritual maturity. As we do, we discover that growing up in Him involves more than our own peace and joy. Growth in His likeness honors God as we unselfishly encourage others. *Keila Ochoa*

Doing Our Role

Read Hebrews 6:9–12

*Each of you should use whatever gift you have received
to serve others, as faithful stewards of God's grace.*

1 PETER 4:10

When two of my grandchildren tried out for the musical *Alice in Wonderland Jr.*, their hearts were set on getting leading roles. Maggie wanted to be young Alice, and Katie thought Mathilda would be a good role. But they were chosen to be flowers. Not exactly a ticket to Broadway.

Yet my daughter said the girls were "excited for their friends who got the [leading roles]. Their joy seemed greater cheering for their friends and sharing in their excitement."

What a picture of how our interactions with each other in the body of Christ should look! Every local church has what might be considered key roles. But it also needs the flowers—the ones who do vital but not-so-high-profile work. If others get roles we desire, may we choose to encourage them even as we passionately fulfill the roles God has given us.

In fact, helping and encouraging others is a way to show love for Him. Hebrews 6:10 says, "[God] will not forget your work and the love you have shown him as you have helped his people." And no gift from His hand is unimportant: "Each of you should use whatever gift you have received to serve others, as faithful stewards of God's grace" (1 Peter 4:10).

Just imagine a church of encouragers diligently using their God-given gifts to His honor (Hebrews 6:10). Now, that makes for joy and excitement!   *Dave Branon*

Promise-Keepers

Read Hebrews 6:23–20

After waiting patiently, Abraham received what was promised.

HEBREWS 6:15

Gripped by the gravity of the promises he was making to LaShonne, Jonathan found himself stumbling as he repeated his wedding vows. He thought, *How can I make these promises and not believe they're possible to keep?* He made it through the ceremony, but the weight of his commitments remained. After the reception, Jonathan led his wife to the chapel where he prayed—for more than two hours—that God would help him keep his promise to love and care for LaShonne.

Jonathan's wedding-day fears were based on the recognition of his human frailties. But God, who promised to bless the nations through Abraham's offspring (Galatians 3:16), has no such limitations.

To challenge his Jewish Christian audience to perseverance and patience to continue in their faith in Jesus, the writer of Hebrews recalled God's promises to Abraham, the patriarch's patient waiting, and the fulfillment of what had been promised (Hebrews 6:13–15). Abraham and Sarah's status as senior citizens was no barrier to the fulfillment of God's promise to give Abraham "many descendants" (v. 14).

Are you challenged to trust God despite being weak, frail, and human? Are you struggling to keep your commitments, to fulfill your pledges and vows? In 2 Corinthians 12:9, God promises to help us: "My grace is sufficient for you, for my power is made perfect in weakness." For more than thirty-six years God has helped Jonathan and LaShonne to remain committed to their vows. Why not trust Him to help you?

Arthur Jackson

Stories in a Cabin

Read Hebrews 9:11–15

[Christ] went through the greater and more perfect tabernacle that is not made with human hands.

HEBREWS 9:11

The vintage cabin, expertly constructed from hand-hewn logs, was worthy of a magazine cover. But the structure itself was only half the treasure. Inside, family heirlooms clung to the walls, infusing the home with memories. On the table sat a handwoven egg basket, an ancient biscuit board, and an oil lamp. A weathered pork pie hat perched over the front door. "There's a story behind everything," the proud owner said.

When God gave Moses instructions for constructing the tabernacle, there was a "story" behind everything (Exodus 25–27). The tabernacle had only one entrance, just as we have only one way to God (see Acts 4:12). The thick inner curtain separated the people from the Most Holy Place where God's presence dwelt: Our sin separates us from God. Inside the Most Holy Place was the ark of the covenant, which symbolized God's presence. The high priest was a forerunner of the greater Priest to come—Jesus himself. The blood of the sacrifices foreshadowed Christ's perfect sacrifice: "He entered the Most Holy Place once for all by his own blood, thus obtaining eternal redemption" (Hebrews 9:12).

All these things told the story of Christ and the work He would accomplish on our behalf. He did it so that "those who are called may receive the promised eternal inheritance" (v. 15). Jesus invites us to be a part of His story. *Tim Gustafson*

What Can't Be Seen

Read Hebrews 11:1–6

*Faith is confidence in what we hope for and
assurance about what we do not see.*

HEBREWS 11:1

Historians say the Atomic Age began on July 16, 1945, when the first nuclear weapon was detonated in a remote desert of New Mexico. But Greek philosopher Democritus (c. 460–370 BC) was exploring the existence and power of the atom long before the invention of anything that could even see these tiny building blocks of the universe. Democritus comprehended more than he could see and atomic theory was the result.

The Scriptures tell us that the essence of faith is embracing what can't be seen. Hebrews 11:1 affirms, "Now faith is confidence in what we hope for and assurance about what we do not see." This assurance isn't the result of wishful or positive thinking. It's confidence in the God we can't see but whose existence is the truest reality in the universe. His reality is displayed in His creative works (Psalm 19:1) and made visible by revealing His invisible character and ways in His Son, Jesus, who came to show the Father's love to us (John 1:18).

This is the God in whom "we live and move and have our being," as the apostle Paul put it (Acts 17:28). As such, "we live by faith, not by sight" (2 Corinthians 5:7). Yet we don't walk alone. The unseen God walks with us every step of the way.   *Bill Crowder*

JAMES

◆

As is so often true with the churches who were getting letters from Paul and others, they were just learning to negotiate the waters of this new journey into Christianity. Therefore, there were a number of areas of mystery. For instance, what were they to do with trials that infiltrated their lives? Why were bad things happening to them if they were following the right way? James addresses this in his letter. Also, how were they to understand the relative importance of riches and poverty? Again, James tries to fill them in. And as usual with a helpful pastor, he supplies his readers with wisdom in a number of areas as they seek to live the Christlike life.

OUTLINE

It's in the Attitude

Read James 1:1–12

Consider it pure joy . . . whenever you face trials of many kinds.

JAMES 1:2

Regina drove home from work discouraged and tired. The day had started with tragic news in a text message from a friend, then spiraled downward in meetings with coworkers who refused to work with any of her ideas. As Regina was talking to the Lord, she thought it best to put the stress of the day aside. So she made a surprise visit with flowers to an elderly friend at a care center. Her spirits lifted as Maria shared how good the Lord was to her. She said, "I have my own bed and a chair, three meals a day, and help from the nurses here. And occasionally God sends a cardinal to my window just because He knows I love them and He loves me."

Attitude. Perspective. As the saying goes, "Life is ten percent what happens to us and ninety percent how we react to it." The people James wrote to were scattered because of persecution, and he asked them to consider their perspective about difficulties. He challenged them with these words: "Consider it pure joy . . . whenever you face trials of many kinds" (James 1:2).

We are each on our own journey of learning to trust God with hard circumstances. The kind of joy-filled perspective James talked about comes as we learn to see that God can use struggles to produce maturity in our faith.   *Anne Cetas*

Doers of the Word

Read James 1:19–27

Do not merely listen to the WORD, and so deceive yourselves. Do what it says.

JAMES 1:22

Just after we moved to a house in a new neighborhood, we invited my sister-in-law and her husband over for Sunday dinner. As we were greeting Sue and Ted at the door, an odd noise directed their eyes toward the kitchen. As I followed their gaze, I froze in horror. An errant hose of our old portable dishwasher was whipping about like the trunk of an angry elephant, spewing water everywhere!

Sue went into action mode. Dropping her purse, she was in the kitchen before me, shutting off the water and calling for towels and a mop. We spent the first fifteen minutes of their visit on our knees mopping the floor.

Sue is a doer—and the world is a better place because of the doers of the world. These are the people who are always ready to pitch in, to be involved, and even to lead if necessary.

Many of the doers of the world are also doers of the Word. These are the followers of Jesus who have taken the challenge of James to heart: "Do not merely listen to the word, and so deceive yourselves. Do what it says" (1:22).

Are you doing all that you know God wants you to do? As you read God's Word, put what you've learned into practice. First hear—then do. God's blessing comes as a result of our obedience (v. 25).

Cindy Hess Kasper

Hungry Now

Read James 2:14–18

*What good is it, my brothers and sisters, if someone
claims to have faith but has no deeds?*

JAMES 2:14

Thomas knew what he needed to do. Having been born to a poor family in India and adopted by Americans, upon a return trip to India he witnessed the dire needs of the children in his hometown. So he knew he had to help. He began making plans to return to the US, finish his education, save a lot of money, and come back in the future.

Then, after reading James 2:14–18 in which James asks, "What good is it . . . if someone claims to have faith but has no deeds?" Thomas heard a little girl in his native country cry out to her mother: "But Mommy, I'm hungry now!" He was reminded of the times he had been intensely hungry as a child—searching through trash cans for food. Thomas knew he couldn't wait years to help. He decided, "I'll start now!"

Today the orphanage he began houses fifty well-fed and cared-for children who are learning about Jesus and getting an education—all because one man didn't put off what he knew God was asking him to do.

James's message applies to us as well. Our faith in Jesus Christ provides us with great advantages—a relationship with Him, an abundant life, and a future hope. But what good is it doing anyone else if we don't reach out and help those in need? Can you hear the cry: "I'm hungry now?"   *Dave Branon*

Just a Spark

Read James 3:1–6

The tongue is a small part of the body, but it makes great boasts.
JAMES 3:5

"We're in the library, and we can see the flames right outside!" She was scared. We could hear it in her voice. We know her voice—the voice of our daughter. At the same time we knew her college campus was the safest place for her and her almost 3,000 fellow students. The 2018 Woolsey Fire spread more quickly than anyone anticipated—most of all fire personnel. The record heat and dry conditions in the California canyon, along with the legendary Santa Ana winds, were all the rather small sparks needed to ultimately burn 97,000 acres, destroy more than 1,600 structures, and kill three people. In the photos taken after the fire was contained, the usual lush coastline resembled the barren surface of the moon.

In the book of James, the author names some small but powerful things: "bits [in] the mouths of horses" and the rudders of ships (3:3–4). And while familiar, these examples are somewhat removed from us. But then he names something a little closer to home, something small that every human being possesses—a tongue. And while this chapter is first directed specifically to teachers (v. 1), the application quickly spreads to each of us. The tongue, small as it is, can lead to disastrous results.

Our small tongues are powerful, but our big God is more powerful. His help on a daily basis provides the strength to rein in and guide our words. *John Blase*

Cleaning Method

Read James 4:4–10

Wash your hands, you sinners, and purify your hearts.

JAMES 4:8

At the sink, two little children cheerfully sing the "Happy Birthday" song—two times each—while washing their hands. "It takes that long to wash away the germs," their mother tells them. So even before the COVID-19 pandemic, they had learned to take time to clean dirt from their hands.

Keeping things clean can be a tedious process, as we learned in the pandemic. Scrubbing away sin, however, means following focused steps back to God.

James urged believers in Jesus scattered throughout the Roman Empire to turn their focus back to God. Beset by quarrels and fights, their battles for one-upmanship, possessions, worldly pleasures, money, and recognition made them an enemy of God. He warned them, "Submit yourselves, then to God. Resist the devil, and he will flee from you. . . . Wash your hands, you sinners, and purify your hearts, you double-minded" (James 4:7–8). But how?

"Come near to God and he will come near to you" (v. 8). These are sanitizing words describing the necessity of turning to God to scour away the soil of sin from our lives. James then further explained the cleaning method: "Grieve, mourn and wail. Change your laughter to mourning and your joy to gloom. Humble yourselves before the Lord, and he will lift you up" (vv. 9–10).

Dealing with our sin is humbling. But, hallelujah, God is faithful to turn our "washing" into worship. *Patricia Raybon*

✦

Unexpected Change

Read James 4:13–17

You do not even know what will happen tomorrow.

JAMES 4:14

In January 1943, warm Chinook winds hit Spearfish, South Dakota, quickly raising the temperatures from -4° to 45°F (-20° to 7°C). That drastic weather change—a swing of 49 degrees—took place in just two minutes. The widest temperature change recorded in the USA over a twenty-four-hour period is an incredible 103 degrees! On January 15, 1972, Loma, Montana, saw the temperature jump from -54° to 49°F (-48° to 9°C).

Sudden change, however, is not simply a weather phenomenon. It's sometimes the very nature of life. James reminds us, "Now listen, you who say, 'Today or tomorrow we will go to this or that city, spend a year there, carry on business and make money.' Why, you do not even know what will happen tomorrow" (4:13–14). An unexpected loss. A surprise diagnosis. A financial reversal. Sudden changes.

Life is a journey with many unpredictable elements. This is precisely why James warns us to turn from "arrogant schemes" (v. 16) that do not take the Almighty into account. As he advised us, "You ought to say, 'If it is the Lord's will, we will live and do this or that'" (v. 15). The events of our lives may be uncertain, but one thing is sure: through all of life's unexpected moments, our God will never leave us. He's our one constant throughout life.   *Bill Crowder*

For the Long Run

Read James 5:7–11

Be patient, then, brothers and sisters, until the LORD's coming.

JAMES 5:7

A survey of more than one thousand adults discovered that most people take an average of seventeen minutes to lose their patience while waiting in line. Also, most people lose their patience in only nine minutes while on hold on the phone. Impatience is a common trait.

James wrote to a group of believers who were struggling with being patient for Jesus's return (James 5:7). They were living under exploitation and distressing times, and James encouraged them to set the timer of their temper, so to speak, for the long run. Challenging these believers to persevere under suffering, he tried to stimulate them to stand firm and to live sacrificially until the Lord returned to right every wrong. He wrote: "Be patient and stand firm, because the Lord's coming is near" (v. 8).

James called them to be like the farmer who waits patiently for the rain and the harvest (v. 7) and like the prophets and the patriarch Job who demonstrated perseverance in difficulties (vv. 10–11). The finish line was just ahead, and James encouraged the believers not to give up.

When we are being tried in a crucible of distress, God desires to help us continue living by faith and trusting in His compassion and mercy (v. 11). *Marvin Williams*

Kind Correction

Read James 5:19–20

Whoever turns a sinner from the error of
their way will save them from death.

JAMES 5:20

The early spring weather was refreshing and my traveling companion, my wife, couldn't have been better. But the beauty of those moments together could have quickly morphed into tragedy if it weren't for a red and white warning sign that informed me I was headed in the wrong direction. Because I hadn't turned wide enough, I momentarily saw a "Do Not Enter" sign staring me in the face. I quickly adjusted, but shudder to think of the harm I could have brought to my wife, myself, and others if I'd ignored the sign that reminded me I was going the wrong way.

The closing words of James emphasize the importance of correction. Who among us hasn't needed to be "brought back" by those who care for us from paths or actions, decisions or desires that could've been hurtful? Who knows what harm might have been done to ourselves or others had someone not courageously intervened at the right time.

James stresses the value of kind correction with these words, "Whoever turns a sinner from the error of their way will save them from death and cover over a multitude of sins" (5:20). Correction is an expression of God's mercy. May our love and concern for the well-being of others compel us to speak and act in ways that He can use to "bring that person back" (v. 19).   *Arthur Jackson*

1 PETER

◆

In order to properly encourage his readers as they faced hard times, Peter first reinforces the great rewards of salvation in Jesus Christ. Then he calls on his fellow believers to strive for a holy life both in the Christian community and before those outside the church. He also reminds them of Jesus's suffering as an encouragement, and Peter also proposes to them the idea that it was a privilege to suffer for Jesus's sake.

OUTLINE

Unseen Wonder

Read 1 Peter 1:3-9

*Though you have not seen him, you love him; and even
though you do not see him now, you believe in him.*

1 PETER 1:8

In the twilight of her years, Mrs. Goodrich's thoughts came in and out of focus along with memories of a challenging and grace-filled life. Sitting by a window overlooking the waters of Michigan's Grand Traverse Bay, she reached for her notepad. In words she soon wouldn't recognize as her own she wrote: "Here I am in my favorite chair, with my feet on the sill, and my heart in the air. The sun-struck waves on the water below, in constant motion—to where I don't know. But thank You—dear Father above—for Your innumerable gifts and Your undying love! It always amazes me—How can it be? That I'm so in love with One I can't see."

The apostle Peter acknowledged such wonder. He had seen Jesus with his own eyes, but those who would read his letter had not. "Though you have not seen him . . . you believe in him and are filled with an inexpressible and glorious joy" (1 Peter 1:8). We love Jesus not because we're commanded to, but because with the help of the Spirit (v. 11) we begin to see how much He loves us.

It's more than hearing that He cares for people like us. It's experiencing for ourselves the promise of Christ to make the wonder of His unseen presence and Spirit real to us at every stage of life.   *Mart DeHaan*

He Carried Our Burden

Read 1 Peter 1:18–25

*"He himself bore our sins" in his body on the cross, so
that we might die to sins and live for righteousness;
"by his wounds you have been healed."*

1 Peter 2:24

It's not unusual for utility bills to be surprisingly high. But Kieran Healy of North Carolina received a water bill that would make your heart stop. The notification said that he owed one-hundred-million dollars! Confident he hadn't used that much water the previous month, Healy jokingly asked if he could pay the bill in installments.

Owing a one-hundred-million-dollar debt would be an overwhelming burden, but that pales in comparison to the real—and immeasurable—burden sin causes us to carry. Attempting to carry the burden and consequences of our own sins ultimately leaves us feeling tired and riddled with guilt and shame. The truth is we are incapable of carrying this load.

And we were never meant to. As Peter reminded believers, only Jesus, the sinless Son of God, could carry the heavy burden of our sin and its weighty consequences (1 Peter 2:24). In His death on the cross, Jesus took all our wrongdoing on himself and offered us His forgiveness. Because He carried our burden, we don't have to suffer the punishment we deserve.

Instead of living in fear or guilt, the "empty way of life handed down to" us (1:18), we can enjoy a new life of love and freedom (vv. 22–23).

Marvin Williams

Caring Letters

Read 1 Peter 2:4–10

You are a chosen people, a royal priesthood, a
holy nation, God's special possession.

1 PETER 2:9

Decades ago, Dr. Jerry Motto discovered the power of a "caring letter." His research found that simply sending a letter expressing care to discharged patients who had previously attempted suicide reduced the rate of recurrence by half. Recently, health care providers have rediscovered this power when sending "caring" texts, postcards, and even social media memes as follow-up treatment for the severely depressed.

Twenty-one "books" in the Bible are actually letters—epistles—caringly written to first-century believers who struggled for a variety of reasons. Paul, James, and John wrote letters to explain the basics of faith and worship, and how to resolve conflict and build unity.

The apostle Peter, however, specifically wrote to believers who were being persecuted by the Roman emperor, Nero. Peter reminded them of their intrinsic value to God, describing them this way in 1 Peter 2:9, "You are a chosen people, a royal priesthood, a holy nation, God's special possession." This lifted their gaze to God's great purpose for them in their world: "that you may declare the praises of him who called you out of darkness into his wonderful light."

Our great God himself wrote a book filled with caring letters to us—inspired Scripture—that we might always have a record of the value He assigns us as His own. May we read His letters daily and share them with others who need the hope Jesus offers. *Elisa Morgan*

A Remarkable Life

Read 1 Peter 2:9–12

Be careful to live properly among your unbelieving neighbors.
1 PETER 2:12 NLT

I came to learn about Catherine Hamlin, a remarkable Australian surgeon, through reading her obituary. In Ethiopia, Catherine and her husband established the world's only hospital dedicated to curing women from the devastating physical and emotional trauma of obstetric fistulas, a common injury in the developing world that can occur during childbirth. Catherine is credited with overseeing the treatment of more than sixty thousand women.

Still operating at the hospital when she was ninety-two years old, and still beginning each day with a cup of tea and Bible study, Hamlin told curious questioners that she was an ordinary believer in Jesus who was simply doing the job God had given her to do.

I was grateful to learn about her remarkable life because she powerfully exemplified for me Scripture's encouragement to believers to live our lives in such a way that even people who actively reject God "may see your good deeds and glorify God" (1 Peter 2:12).

The power of God's Spirit that called us out of spiritual darkness into a relationship with Him (v. 9) can also transform our work or areas of service into testimonies of our faith. In whatever passion or skill God has gifted us, we can embrace added meaning and purpose in doing all of it in a manner that has the power to point people to Him.   *Lisa Samra*

"God Stuff"

Read 1 Peter 3:13–18

*Always be prepared to give an answer to everyone who
asks you to give the reason for the hope that you have.*

1 Peter 3:15

Most of Mike's coworkers knew little about Christianity, nor did they
seem to care. But they knew he cared. One day near the Easter season,
someone casually mentioned that they'd heard Easter had something to
do with Passover and wondered what the connection was. "Hey, Mike!"
he said. "You know about this God stuff. What's Passover?"

So Mike explained how God brought the Israelites out of slavery
in Egypt. He told them about the ten plagues, including the death of
the firstborn in every household. He explained how the death angel
"passed over" the houses whose doorframes were covered by the blood
of a sacrificed lamb. Then he shared how Jesus was later crucified at
the Passover season as the once-and-for-all sacrificial Lamb. Suddenly
Mike realized, *Hey, I'm witnessing!*

Peter the disciple gave advice to a church in a culture that didn't
know about God. He said, "Always be prepared to give an answer to
everyone who asks you to give the reason for the hope that you have"
(1 Peter 3:15).

Because Mike had been open about his faith, he got the chance
to share that faith naturally, and he could do so with "gentleness and
respect" (v. 15).

We can too. With the help of God's Holy Spirit, we can explain in
simple terms what matters most in life—that "stuff" about God.

Tim Gustafson

Starting Now

Read 1 Peter 4:7–11

Love each other deeply.

1 PETER 4:8

When my oldest sister's biopsy revealed cancer, I remarked to friends, "I need to spend as much time with Carolyn as possible—starting now." Some told me my feelings were an overreaction to the news. But she died within ten months. And even though I had spent hours with her, when we love someone there's never enough time for our hearts to love enough.

The apostle Peter called Jesus's followers in the early church to "love each other deeply" (1 Peter 4:8). They were suffering under persecution and needed the love of their brothers and sisters in their Christian community more than ever. Because God had poured His own love into their hearts, they would then want to love others in return. Their love would be expressed through praying, offering gracious hospitality, and gentle and truthful conversation—all in the strength God provided (vv. 9–11). Through His grace, God had gifted them to sacrificially serve each other for His good purposes. So that "in all things God may be praised through Jesus Christ" (v. 11). This is God's powerful plan that accomplishes His will through us.

We need others and they need us. Let's use whatever time or resources we have received from God to love—starting now. *Anne Cetas*

Being Real with God

Read 1 Peter 5:6–10

Cast all your anxiety on him because he cares for you.

1 Peter 5:7

I bow my head, close my eyes, lace my fingers together and begin to pray. "Dear Lord, I'm coming to you today as your child. I recognize your power and goodness . . . " Suddenly, my eyes snap open. I remember that my son hasn't finished his history project, which is due the next day. I recall that he has an after-school basketball game, and I imagine him awake until midnight finishing his schoolwork. This leads me to worry that his fatigue will put him at risk for the flu!

C. S. Lewis wrote about distractions during prayer in his book *The Screwtape Letters*. He noted that when our minds wander, we tend to use willpower to steer ourselves back to our original prayer. Lewis concluded, though, that it was better to accept "the distraction as [our] present problem and [lay] that before [God] and make it the main theme of [our] prayers."

A persistent worry or even a sinful thought that disrupts a prayer may become the centerpiece of our discussion with God. God wants us to be real as we talk with Him and open up about our deepest concerns, fears, and struggles. He is not surprised by anything we mention. His interest in us is like the attention we would receive from a close friend. That's why we're encouraged to give all of our worries and cares to God—because He cares for us (1 Peter 5:7).   *Jennifer Benson Schuldt*

2 PETER

Peter wanted to remind believers that they already had what they needed through God's "divine power" and that they could escape the world's corruption. He then gave them the eight traits that could help them be strong in Jesus. They were then equipped to hear the bad news—that there were others who were out to deceive them for their own gain. The strength and godly power he introduced the book with were vital as the people became aware of charlatans and false teachers in the church.

OUTLINE

Unimaginable Promises

Read 2 Peter 1:2-8

He has given us his very great and precious promises.
2 PETER 1:4

In our moments of greatest failure, it can be easy to believe it's too late for us—that we've lost our chance at a life of purpose and worth. That's how Elias, a former inmate at a maximum-security prison in New York, described feeling as a prisoner. "I had broken . . . promises, the promise of my own future, the promise of what I could be."

It was Bard College's "Prison Initiative" college degree program that began to transform Elias's life. While in the program, he participated on a debate team, which one year debated a team from Harvard—and won. For Elias, being "part of the team . . . [was] a way of proving that these promises weren't completely lost."

A similar transformation happens in our hearts when we begin to understand that the good news of God's love in Jesus is good news for us too. It's not too late, we begin to realize with wonder. God still has a future for me.

And it's a future that can neither be earned nor forfeited, dependent only on God's extravagant grace and power (2 Peter 1:2–3). A future where we're set free from the despair in the world and in our hearts into one filled with His "glory and goodness" (v. 3). A future secure in Christ's unimaginable promises (v. 4); and a future transformed into the "freedom and glory of the children of God" (Romans 8:21).

Monica La Rose

Shakespeare's Translator

Read 2 Peter 1:16–2:3

No prophecy of Scripture came about by the
prophet's own interpretation of things.

2 PETER 1:20

Some have speculated that William Shakespeare helped translate the King James Bible. They say that he inserted a cryptogram (a message written in code) while he translated Psalm 46. In this psalm, the forty-sixth word from the beginning is "shake" and the forty-sixth word from the end is "spear." Furthermore, in 1610, while the King James Bible was being translated, Shakespeare would have been forty-six years old. Despite these coincidences, no serious evidence supports this theory.

Some people also claim to have found hidden meanings when interpreting the Bible. Certain cults will cite a verse out of context, only to lead someone into heretical doctrine. Some quote John 14:16 (NKJV), for example, and say that the "Helper" refers to their "new revelation." When compared with other Scripture, however, the Helper whom Jesus sent to us is obviously the Holy Spirit (John 16:7–14; Acts 2:1–4).

The apostle Peter wrote, "No prophecy of Scripture is of any private interpretation" (2 Peter 1:20 NKJV). To interpret a biblical passage accurately, we must always consider the context and compare it with other Scripture. This respects the clear meaning of the Bible without trying to find hidden meaning in it. *Dennis Fisher*

DECEMBER 4

Dressed to Deceive

Read 2 Peter 2:1–3, 12–19

Watch out for false prophets. They come to you in sheep's clothing, but inwardly they are ferocious wolves.

MATTHEW 7:15

Hiking in the mountains of Utah, Coty Creighton spotted a goat that didn't look like the rest of the herd. A closer look revealed that the unusual animal was actually a man dressed as a goat. When authorities contacted the man, he described his costume as a painter's suit covered in fleece, and he said he was testing his disguise for a hunting trip.

The hunter's deception reminds me of Jesus's words: "Watch out for false prophets. They come to you in sheep's clothing, but inwardly they are ferocious wolves" (Matthew 7:15). False teachers do not bear the fruit of God's Spirit (Galatians 5:22–23). Rather, they "follow the corrupt desire of the flesh and despise authority" (2 Peter 2:10). They are bold, egotistical, and given to greed (vv. 10, 14). Ruled by their own desires, they exploit people by using "fabricated stories" (v. 3). The Bible says these wayward spiritual leaders are headed for destruction and will take many unsuspecting and undiscerning people with them (vv. 1–2).

Jesus, the Good Shepherd, rather than pursuing personal gain, laid down His life for His sheep. God does not want anyone to be misled by false teaching. He wants us to be aware of those who deceive, and follow Him instead—the true Shepherd of our souls. *Jennifer Benson Schuldt*

All Aboard

Read 2 Peter 3:1–13

The LORD is . . . patient with you, not wanting anyone to perish.

2 PETER 3:9

One day when I dropped my husband off at our local train station, I watched as the conductor scanned the area for stragglers. A woman with wet hair bounded from the parking lot and up into the train. Then, a man in a dark suit strode to the platform and climbed aboard. The conductor waited patiently while several more latecomers sprinted to the tracks and boarded at the last moment.

Just as the conductor was patient with people boarding the train, God patiently waits for people to come to know Him. However, someday Jesus will return and "the heavens will disappear with a roar; the elements will be destroyed by fire" (2 Peter 3:10). When this happens, or when our physical bodies die, it will be too late to establish a relationship with God.

"The Lord is . . . patient with you," Peter says, "not wanting anyone to perish, but everyone to come to repentance" (v. 9). If you have delayed deciding to follow Christ, there is good news—you can still commit yourself to Him. "If you declare with your mouth, 'Jesus is Lord,' and believe in your heart that God raised him from the dead, you will be saved" (Romans 10:9). He is calling. Will you run in His direction?

Jennifer Benson Schuldt

He's Got This

Read 2 Peter 3:14–18

But grow in the grace and knowledge of
our LORD and Savior Jesus Christ.

2 PETER 3:18

Pastor Watson Jones remembers learning to ride a bike. His father was walking alongside when little Watson saw some girls sitting on a porch. "Daddy, I got this!" he said. He didn't. He realized too late that he hadn't learned to balance without his father's steadying grip. He wasn't as grown up as he thought.

Our heavenly Father longs for us to grow up and "become mature, attaining to the whole measure of the fullness of Christ" (Ephesians 4:13). But spiritual maturity is different from natural maturity. Parents raise their children to become independent, to no longer need them. Our divine Father raises us to daily depend on Him more.

Peter begins his letter by promising "grace and peace . . . through the knowledge of God and of Jesus our Lord," and he ends by urging us to "grow in" that same "grace and knowledge of our Lord and Savior Jesus Christ" (2 Peter 1:2; 3:18). Mature Christians never outgrow their need for Jesus.

Watson warns, "Some of us are busy slapping Jesus's hands off the handlebars of our life." As if we didn't need His strong hands to hold us, to pick us up, and to hug us when we wobble and flop. We can't grow beyond our dependence on Christ. We only grow by sinking our roots deeper in the grace and knowledge of Him.   *Mike Wittmer*

1 JOHN

◆

John was not one to waste a good introduction. Both this letter and his complete gospel (which was written even later than this) begin similarly by emphasizing Jesus's existence with God from eternity past. He then tackled the subject of sin—which some in the church were claiming to be free from. John emphasized love and its essential nature for Christians. And he reiterated how important it is to recognize Jesus for who He really is.

OUTLINE

John's Purpose in Writing 1 John 1:1–4

Walking in the Light; Dealing with Sin 1 John 1:5–2:14

What to Avoid 1 John 2:15–27

The Life of the Child of God 1 John 2:28–5:5

Salvation Assurance 1 John 5:6–15

Believers and Sin 1 John 5:16–21

Stories of Jesus

Read 1 John 1:1–4, 24–25

Jesus did many other things as well.

JOHN 21:25

As a girl I loved to visit my small local library. One day, looking at the bookshelves holding the young adult section, I reasoned I could probably read every book. In my enthusiasm I forgot one important fact—new books were regularly added to the shelves. Although I gave it a valiant effort, there were simply too many books.

New books continue to fill more and more bookshelves. The apostle John likely would be amazed with the availability of books today since his five New Testament books, the gospel of John; 1, 2, and 3 John; and Revelation, were handwritten on parchment scrolls.

John wrote those books because he felt compelled by the Holy Spirit to give Christians an eyewitness account of Jesus's life and ministry (1 John 1:1–4). But John's writings contained only a small fraction of all that Jesus did and taught during His ministry. In fact, John said that if everything Jesus did were written down, "the whole world could not contain the books that would be written" (John 21:25 NLT).

John's claim remains true today. Despite all the books that have been written about Jesus, the libraries of the world still cannot contain every story of His love and grace. We can also celebrate that we have our own personal stories to share, and we rejoice that we will be proclaiming them forever! (Psalm 89:1).   *Lisa Samra*

How to Stay on Track

Read 1 John 2:18–27

The Spirit teaches you everything you need to know,
and what he teaches is true—it is not a lie.

1 JOHN 2:27 NLT

As the world's fastest blind runner, David Brown of the US Paralympic Team credits his wins to God, his mother's early advice ("no sitting around"), and his running guide—veteran sprinter Jerome Avery. Tethered to Brown by a string tied to their fingers, Avery guides Brown's winning races with words and touches.

"It's all about listening to his cues," says Brown, who says he could "swing out wide" on 200–meter races where the track curves. "Day in and day out, we're going over race strategies," Brown says, "communicating with each other—not only verbal cues, but physical cues."

In our own life's race, we're blessed with a Divine Guide. Our Helper, the Holy Spirit, leads our steps when we follow Him. "I am writing these things to you about those who are trying to lead you astray," wrote John (1 John 2:26). "But you have received the Holy Spirit, and he lives within you, so you don't need anyone to teach you what is true. For the Spirit teaches you everything you need to know" (v. 27 NLT).

John stressed this wisdom to the believers of his day who faced "antichrists" who denied the Father and that Jesus is the Messiah (v. 22). We face such deniers today as well. But the Holy Spirit, our Guide, leads us in following Jesus. We can trust His guidance to touch us with truth, keeping us on track.   *Patricia Raybon*

Our True Selves

Read 1 John 3:1–3

We know that when Christ appears, we shall be like him.

1 JOHN 3:2

Inside my parents' old photo album is a picture of a young boy. He has a round face, freckles, and straight, light-blond hair. He loves cartoons, hates avocados, and owns just one record, by Abba. Also inside that album are pictures of a teenager. His face is long, not round; his hair is wavy, not straight. He has no freckles, likes avocados, watches movies rather than cartoons, and would never admit to owning an Abba record! The boy and the teenager are little alike. According to science they have different skin, teeth, blood, and bones. And yet they are both me. This paradox has baffled philosophers. Since we change throughout our lives, who is the real us?

The Scriptures provide the answer. From the moment God began knitting us together in the womb (Psalm 139:13–14), we've been growing into our unique design. While we can't yet imagine what we'll finally become, we know that if we're children of God we'll ultimately be like Jesus (1 John 3:2)—our body with His nature, our personality but His character, all our gifts glistening, all our sins gone.

Until the day Jesus returns, we're being drawn toward this future self. By His work, step by step, we can reflect His image ever more clearly (2 Corinthians 3:18). We aren't yet who we're meant to be, but as we become like Him, we become our true selves. *Sheridan Voysey*

The Ultimate Sacrifice

Read 1 John 3:16–23

This is how we know what love is: Jesus Christ
laid down his life for us. And we ought to lay
down our lives for our brothers and sisters.

1 JOHN 3:16

When Deng Jinjie saw people struggling in the water of the Sunshui River in the Hunan province of China, he didn't just walk by. In an act of heroism, he jumped into the water and helped save four members of a family. Unfortunately, the family left the area while he was still in the water. Exhausted from his rescue efforts, Jinjie was overwhelmed and swept away by the river current and drowned.

When we were drowning in our sin, Jesus Christ gave His life to come to our aid. We were the ones He came to rescue. He came down from heaven above and pulled us to safety. He did this by taking the punishment for all of our wrongdoing as He died on the cross (1 Peter 2:24) and three days later was resurrected. The Bible says, "This is how we know what love is: Jesus Christ laid down His life for us" (1 John 3:16). Jesus's sacrificial love for us now inspires us to show genuine love "with actions and in truth" (v.18) to others with whom we have relationships.

If we overlook Jesus's ultimate sacrifice on our behalf, we'll fail to see and experience His love. Today, consider the connection between His sacrifice and His love for you. He has come for your rescue.

Jennifer Benson Schuldt

Fearless Love

Read 1 John 4:7–12

We love because he first loved us.
1 JOHN 4:19

For years I wore a shield of fear to protect my heart. It became an excuse to avoid trying new things, following my dreams, and obeying God. But fear of loss, heartache, and rejection hindered me from developing loving relationships with God and others. Fear made me an insecure, anxious, and jealous wife, and an overprotective, worrying mother. As I continue learning how much God loves me, however, He's changing the way I relate to Him and to others. Because I know God will care for me, I feel more secure and willing to place the needs of others before mine.

God is love (1 John 4:7–8). Christ's death on the cross—the ultimate demonstration of love—displays the depth of His passion for us (vv. 9–10). Because God loves us and lives in us, we can love others based on who He is and what He's done (vv. 11–12).

When we receive Jesus as our Savior, He gives us His Holy Spirit (vv. 13–15). As the Spirit helps us know and rely on God's love, He makes us more like Jesus (vv. 16–17). Growing in trust and faith can gradually eliminate fear, simply because we know without a doubt that God loves us deeply and completely (vv. 18–19).

As we experience God's personal and unconditional love for us, we grow and can risk relating to Him and others with fearless love.

Xochitl Dixon

Aunt Betty's Way

Read 1 John 5:1–6

This is how we know that we love the children of God:
by loving God and carrying out his commands.

1 JOHN 5:2

When I was young, whenever my doting Aunt Betty visited, it felt like Christmas. She'd bring Star Wars toys and slip me cash on her way out the door. Whenever I stayed with her, she filled the freezer with ice cream and never cooked vegetables. She had few rules and let me stay up late. My aunt was marvelous, reflecting God's generosity. However, to grow up healthy, I needed more than only Aunt Betty's way. I also needed my parents to place expectations on me and my behavior, and hold me to them.

God asks more of me than Aunt Betty. While He floods us with relentless love, a love that never wavers even when we resist or run away, He does expect something of us. When God instructed Israel how to live, He provided Ten Commandments, not ten suggestions (Exodus 20:1–17). Aware of our self-deception, God offers clear expectations: we're to "[love] God and [carry] out his commands" (1 John 5:2).

Thankfully, "[God's] commands are not burdensome" (v. 3). By the Holy Spirit's power, we can live them out as we experience God's love and joy. His love for us is unceasing. But the Scriptures offer a question to help us know if we love God in return: Are we obeying His commands as the Spirit guides us?

We can say we love God, but what we do in His strength tells the real story. *Winn Collier*

2 JOHN

◆

The essence of John's teaching in this short letter can be summed up with two words: love and truth. He writes of the truth, "which lives in" believers, and he finds great joy in discovering that his spiritual children are "walking in the truth." Next, he implores his reader to "walk in love." Yet he does not want believers to extend hospitality to those who do not teach the truth. So love has its limits.

OUTLINE

The Flip Side of Love

Read 2 John 1:1–11

Grace, mercy and peace from God the Father and from Jesus Christ, the Father's Son, will be with us in truth and love.

2 JOHN 1:3

The Roman inns during the time of Christ had a reputation so bad that rabbis wouldn't even permit cattle to be left at them. Faced with such bad conditions, traveling Christians usually sought out other believers for hospitality.

Among those early travelers were false teachers who denied that Jesus was the Messiah. This is why the letter of 2 John tells its readers there is a time to refuse to extend hospitality. John had said in a previous letter that these false teachers were "antichrist—denying the Father and the Son"(1 John 2:22). In 2 John he elaborated on this, telling his readers that whoever believes Jesus is the Messiah "has both the Father and the Son" (v. 9).

Then he warned, "If anyone comes to you and does not bring this teaching, do not take them into your house or welcome them" (v. 10). To extend hospitality to someone preaching a false gospel would actually help keep people separated from God.

John's second letter shows us a "flip side" of God's love. We serve a God who welcomes everyone with open arms. But genuine love won't enable those who deceitfully harm themselves and others. God wraps His arms around those who come to Him in repentance, but He never embraces a lie.   *Tim Gustafson*

Ring the Bell

Read 2 John 1:1–6

I urge you . . . to reaffirm your love to him.

2 CORINTHIANS 2:8

The story is told of a king who had a silver bell placed in a high tower of his palace early in his reign. He announced that he would ring the bell whenever he was happy. That way, his subjects would know of his joy.

The people listened for the sound of that silver bell, but it remained silent. Days turned into weeks, and weeks into months, and months into years. But no sound of the bell rang out to indicate that the king was happy.

The king grew old and gray, and eventually he lay on his deathbed in the palace. As some of his weeping subjects gathered around him, he discovered that he had really been loved by his people all through the years. At last the king was happy. Just before he died, he reached up and pulled the rope that rang the silver bell.

Think of it—a lifetime of unhappiness because he didn't know that he was warmly loved and accepted by his loyal subjects.

Like that monarch, many lonely souls live out their days without the joy of knowing they are loved and appreciated by others. Do you know people who need an encouraging word? If so, tell them how much they mean to you. It may be just what's needed to bring joy into their lives.   *Richard DeHaan*

Godspeed!

Read 2 John 1:1–11

If anyone comes to you and does not bring this teaching,
do not take them into your house or welcome them.

2 John 1:10

In 1962, John Glenn made history as the first American to orbit the Earth. As his rocket lifted off from Cape Canaveral, fellow astronaut Scott Carpenter said, "Godspeed, John Glenn." "Godspeed" comes from the expression, "May God prosper you."

Though we don't often hear this word today, the apostle John used it in his second epistle: "If there come any unto you, and bring not this doctrine, receive him not into your house, neither bid him God speed" (v. 10 KJV).

John has been referred to as "the apostle of love," so why would he warn believers against pronouncing a blessing on others? Traveling evangelists were dependent on the hospitality of Christians to provide them with room and board. John was telling the believers that biblical truth is important. If itinerant missionaries were not preaching doctrine consistent with apostolic teaching, believers were not to bless their work by providing lodging or financial assistance.

This is also true for believers today. We are to treat everyone with kindness because God is kind to us. But when asked to financially support an endeavor, it's important to always ask Him for wisdom. The Spirit who guides us into truth (John 16:13) will show us when it is appropriate to bid Godspeed to those we encounter. *Dennis Fisher*

3 JOHN

◆

Simply put, this was a thank you note to Gaius accompanied by a word of warning about a man in the church who was causing trouble with his attitude. John said thanks to Gaius for being so hospitable to people he didn't even know when they paid him a visit. Then there is Diotrephes, who did everything wrong: he wouldn't listen to John, he didn't want visiting teachers participating at his church, and he rejected good hospitality. He was everything a Christian leader should not be.

OUTLINE

To My Dear Friend

Read 3 John 1

The elder, to my dear friend Gaius, whom I love in the truth.

3 JOHN 1:1

What the apostle John did for his friend Gaius in the first century is a dying art in the twenty-first century. John wrote him a letter.

One writer for *The New York Times*, Catherine Field, said, "Letter-writing is among our most ancient of arts. Think of letters and the mind falls on Paul of Tarsus," for example. And we can add the apostle John.

In his letter to Gaius, John included hopes for good health of body and soul, an encouraging word about Gaius's faithfulness, and a note about his love for the church. John also spoke of a problem in the church, which he promised to address individually later. And he wrote of the value of doing good things for God's glory. All in all, it was an encouraging and challenging letter to his friend.

Digital communication may mean letter-writing on paper is fading away, but this shouldn't stop us from encouraging others. Paul wrote letters of encouragement on parchment; we can encourage others in a variety of ways. The key is not the way we encourage others, but that we take a moment to let others know we care for them in Jesus's name!

Think of the encouragement Gaius experienced when he opened John's letter. Could we similarly shine God's love on our friends with a thoughtful note or an uplifting text?   *Dave Branon*

DECEMBER 17

No Greater Joy

Read 3 John 1

*I have no greater joy than to hear that my
children are walking in the truth.*

3 John 1:4

Bob and Evon Potter were a fun-loving couple with three young sons when their life took a wonderful new direction. In 1956 they attended a Billy Graham Crusade in Oklahoma City and gave their lives to Christ. Before long, they wanted to reach out to others to share their faith and the truth about Christ, so they opened their home every Saturday night to high school and college students who wanted to study the Bible. A friend invited me, and I became a regular at the Potters' house.

This was a serious Bible study that included lesson preparation and memorizing Scripture. Surrounded by an atmosphere of friendship, joy, and laughter, we challenged each other, and the Lord changed our lives during those days.

I stayed in touch with the Potters over the years and received many cards and letters from Bob, who always signed them with these words: "I have no greater joy than to hear that my children are walking in the truth" (3 John 1:4). Like John writing to his "dear friend Gaius" (v. 1), Bob encouraged everyone who crossed his path to keep walking with the Lord.

A few years ago I attended Bob's memorial service. It was a joyful occasion filled with people still walking the road of faith—all because of a young couple who opened their home and their hearts to help others find the Lord.   *David McCasland*

Imitate the Good

Read 3 John 1

Dear friend, do not imitate what is evil but what is good. Anyone who does what is good is from God. Anyone who does what is evil has not seen God.

3 JOHN 1:11

Most people would agree that life is a painful mixture of good and bad. It's true in marriage, friendship, family, work, and church. Yet we are surprised and disappointed when self-centeredness takes the stage within a fellowship of those who seek to worship and serve Christ together.

When the apostle John wrote to his friend Gaius, he commended the truthful living and generous hospitality of those in his church (3 John vv. 3–8). In the same fellowship, however, Diotrephes, "who wants to be head of everything" (v. 9 PHILLIPS), had created an atmosphere of hostility.

John promised to deal personally with Diotrephes on his next visit to the church. In the meantime, he urged the congregation: "Dear friend, do not imitate what is evil but what is good. Anyone who does what is good is from God. Anyone who does what is evil has not seen God" (v. 11). John's words echo the instruction of Paul to the Christians in Rome: "Do not be overcome by evil, but overcome evil with good" (Romans 12:21).

In a heated conflict, we may be tempted to "fight fire with fire." Yet John urges us to turn away from what is bad and follow what is good. This is the pathway that honors our Savior.   *David McCasland*

JUDE

---◆---

Error is creeping into the church of Jesus Christ, so Jude moves from writing about salvation to addressing this growing problem of false teaching. Using Old Testament stories as his jumping off point, Jude speaks of people who are rejecting authority, speaking abusively, and look out for themselves only. He says they "boast among themselves and flatter others for their own advantage" (v. 16). He then offers an antidote: be built up in the faith, pray in the Spirit, remain in God's love, show mercy to doubters, and witness to them.

OUTLINE

Greetings from Jude Jude 1:1–4

Instruction about False Teachers Jude 1:5–23

Benediction Jude 1:24–25

To Pray or Prey

Read Jude 1:1–19

Certain individuals whose condemnation was written about long ago have secretly slipped in among you. . . . [They] deny Jesus Christ, our only Sovereign and LORD.

JUDE 1:4

The headline read: "Cathedral Once Revered as a Sanctuary Now a Den of Thieves and Killers." The article told about a church that has been plagued by violence. A night watchman was murdered. Then his replacement was beaten. And within one week, seven parishioners who went to church to pray were mugged.

A local official sadly observed, "The place to pray has now become a place to prey—that's P-R-E-Y."

When Jesus lived on earth, He said to the money changers in the temple, "'It is written,' he said to them, '"My house will be a house of prayer"'; but you have made it '"a den of robbers."'" (Luke 19:46). And Jude spoke of another kind of thievery. He referred to certain men in the church who had "secretly slipped in" and were motivated by greed (Jude 1:4).

Still today, dishonest and scheming men lurk within the church. They use their positions to prey on the unsuspecting with their false teaching. Jude exhorted believers to be strong in their faith so they could repel these "ungodly people" (v. 4).

We thank God for every born-again servant of the Lord who preaches the gospel and teaches the Word, and whose methods are consistent with His message. We must beware of "thieves and robbers," however, who are more interested in preying on people than in praying for people.

Mart DeHaan

Instinctively Wrong

Read Jude 1:18–20

*You, dear friends, by building yourselves up in your
most holy faith and praying in the Holy Spirit.*

JUDE 1:20

Saul Gellerman, in his book *How People Work*, says, "Solving tough organizational problems may require counter-intuitive strategies." In business, *counter-intuitive* is a fancy way of referring to ideas that go against common sense.

Consultants who advocate such thinking are simply reinforcing the advice of Jesus. Over and over, He urged His followers to do what God said was right, not what desire, instinct, and intuition told them to do.

Desire says, "I want it." Jesus said, "It is more blessed to give than to receive" (Acts 20:35).

Instinct says, "Me first." Jesus said, "The last will be first, and the first will be last" (Matthew 20:16).

Intuition says, "I'll feel better if I get revenge." Jesus said, "Do good to those who hate you" (Luke 6:27).

Wanting something doesn't make it good. Achieving something doesn't make it valuable. And having strong feelings about something doesn't make it right. As Jude wrote, those who follow their own desires and instincts lead others into conflict and division (1:18–19).

The alternative is to be spiritual, which means doing what does not come naturally. In fact, it requires supernatural strength that only God can give.　　　　　　　　　　　　　　　　*Julie Ackerman Link*

Keep the Romance

Read Jude 1:17–23

Keep yourselves in God's love.

JUDE 1:21

The great American statesman and lawyer William Jennings Bryan (1860–1925) was having his portrait painted. The artist asked, "Why do you wear your hair over your ears?"

Bryan responded, "There is a romance connected with that. When I began courting Mrs. Bryan, she objected to the way my ears stood out. So, to please her, I let my hair grow to cover them."

"That was many years ago," the artist said. "Why don't you have your hair cut now?"

"Because," Bryan winked, "the romance is still going on."

Is the romance still going on in our relationship with Jesus? When we first came in faith to Christ, we experienced the joy of knowing our sins were forgiven and we were adopted into His family. Our hearts were full and overflowing with love for the Lord. We longed to please Him.

As time passed, however, the zeal of our first love may have begun to cool. That's why we need to take to heart the words of Jude in his brief letter. He wrote, "Keep yourselves in God's love" (1:21). Jesus used similar terms when He said, "Remain in my love" (John 15:9–10). We nurture that love when we focus on pleasing Him instead of ourselves.

Keep the romance going.   *David Egner*

How to Stand Firm

Read Jude 1:24–25

To him who is able to keep you from stumbling.
JUDE 1:24

It was a cold, icy winter's day, and my mind was focused on getting from my warm vehicle to a warm building. The next thing I knew I was on the ground, my knees turned inward and my lower legs turned outward. Nothing was broken, but I was in pain. The pain would get worse as time went by, and it would be weeks before I was whole again.

Who among us hasn't taken a spill of some sort? Wouldn't it be nice to have something or someone to keep us on our feet all the time? While there are no guarantees of surefootedness in the physical sense, there is One who stands ready to assist us in our quest to honor Christ in this life and prepare us to stand joyfully before Him in the next.

Every day, we face temptations (and even false teachings) that seek to divert us, confuse us, and entangle us. Yet, it's not ultimately through our own efforts that we remain on our feet as we walk in this world. How assuring to know that when we hold our peace when tempted to speak angrily, to opt for honesty over deceit, to choose love over hate, or to select truth over error—we experience God's power to keep us standing (Jude 1:24). And when we appear approved before God when Christ returns, the praise that we offer now for His sustaining grace will echo throughout eternity (v. 25). *Arthur Jackson*

PART 9

◆

Prophecy

Revelation

In Genesis 3:15, the first prophecy contained in Scripture was recorded. It was a prediction that someday the damage done by the serpent in the garden of Eden would be remedied. That prophecy was fulfilled in Jesus through His death, burial, and resurrection. And now, in Revelation, we see the final prophecies of the Bible—including the final destruction of the one who led Adam to fall back in Genesis. The prophetic message of Revelation, while it contains many confusing and sometimes unusual images, is simply this. At the end of time, Jesus will triumph, and He will usher in an unspeakably amazing future for all who have trusted in Him. It is a magnificent picture of God's majesty and power and love.

REVELATION

The seven churches of Asia had received various messages from the writers of the epistles, but this message was different. This would be a word-for-word message from Jesus himself—with each letter specifically crafted to meet the key need of each church. That was the content of the chapters two and three of Revelation. Next, things got fantastic for John. He was transported to a place where he was "before the throne room of God." Before him were opened amazing visions of seals and scrolls, and he heard trumpets and singing. He experienced God's ultimate victory over evil, and he was finally, at the end, introduced to the new heaven and the new earth. In events that hardly have words worthy of their description, John opened up a new world of hope and grandeur—all reflecting the glory and majesty of God.

OUTLINE

Debt Eraser

Read Revelation 1:4–7

[Jesus Christ] loves us and has freed us from our sins by his blood.
REVELATION 1:5

Stunned is just one word that describes the response of the crowd at the 2019 graduation ceremony at Morehouse College in Atlanta, Georgia. The commencement speaker announced that he and his family would be donating millions of dollars to erase the student debt of the entire graduating class. One student—with $100,000 in loans—was among the overwhelmed graduates who expressed their joys with tears and shouts.

Most of us have experienced indebtedness in some form—having to pay for homes, vehicles, education, medical expenses, or other things. But we've also known the amazing relief of a bill being stamped "PAID"!

After declaring Jesus as "the faithful witness, the firstborn from the dead, and the ruler of the kings of the earth," John worshipfully acknowledged His debt-erasing work: "To him who loves us and has freed us from our sins by his blood" (Revelation 1:5). This statement is simple, but its meaning is profound. Better than the surprise announcement the Morehouse graduating class heard is the good news that the death of Jesus (the shedding of His blood on the cross) frees us from the penalty that our sinful attitudes, desires, and deeds deserve. Because that debt has been satisfied, those who believe in Jesus are forgiven and become a part of God's kingdom family (v. 6). This good news is the best news of all!   *Arthur Jackson*

Our New Name

Read Revelation 2:1–7

*I will also give that person a white stone
with a new name written on it.*

REVELATION 2:17

She called herself a worrier, but when her child was hurt in an accident, she learned how to escape that restricting label. As her child was recovering, she met each week with friends to talk and pray, asking God for help and healing. Through the months as she turned her fears and concerns into prayer, she realized that she was changing from being a worrier to a prayer warrior. She sensed that the Lord was giving her a new name. Her identity in Christ was deepening through the struggle of unwanted heartache.

In Jesus's letter to the church at Pergamum, the Lord promises to give to the faithful a white stone with a new name on it (Revelation 2:17). Biblical commentators have debated over the meaning, but most agree that this white stone points to our freedom in Christ. In biblical times, juries in a court of law used a white stone for a not-guilty verdict and a black stone for guilty. A white stone also gained the bearer entrance into such events as banquets; likewise, those who receive God's white stone are welcomed to the heavenly feast. Jesus's death brings us freedom and new life—and a new name.

What new name do you think God might give to you?

Amy Boucher Pye

DECEMBER 25

Light of the World

Read Revelation 3:14–22

*Here I am! I stand at the door and knock. If anyone
hears my voice and opens the door, I will come in.*

REVELATION 3:20

One of my favorite pieces of art hangs in the Keble College chapel in Oxford, England. The painting, *The Light of the World* by English artist William Holman Hunt, shows Jesus holding a lantern in His hand and knocking on a door to a home.

One of the intriguing aspects of the painting is that the door does not have a handle. When questioned about the lack of ways to open the door, Hunt explained that he wanted to represent the imagery of Revelation 3:20, "Here I am! I stand at the door and knock. If anyone hears my voice and opens the door, I will come in."

The apostle John's words and the painting illustrate the kindness of Jesus. He gently knocks on the door of our souls with His offer of peace. Jesus stands and patiently waits for us to respond. He does not open the door himself and force His way into our lives. He does not impose His will on ours. Instead, He offers to all people the gift of salvation and light to guide us.

To anyone who opens the door, He promises to enter. There are no other requirements or prerequisites.

If you hear the voice of Jesus and His gentle knock on the door of your soul, be encouraged that He patiently waits for you and will enter if you welcome Him in.   *Lisa Samra*

The Not-So-Wonderful Wizard

Read Revelation 4:4–11

*There before me was a throne in heaven
with someone sitting on it.*

REVELATION 4:2

In *The Wonderful Wizard of Oz*, Dorothy, the Scarecrow, the Tin Man, and the Cowardly Lion return to Oz with the broomstick that empowered the Wicked Witch of the West. The Wizard had promised, in return for the broomstick, that he would give the four their deepest desires: a ride home for Dorothy, a brain for the Scarecrow, a heart for the Tin Man, and courage for the Cowardly Lion. But the Wizard stalls and tells them to come back the next day.

While they plead with the Wizard, Dorothy's dog Toto pulls back the curtain, behind which the Wizard spoke, to reveal that the Wizard isn't a wizard at all, He's just a fearful, fidgety man from Nebraska.

It's said that the author, L. Frank Baum, had a serious problem with God, so he wanted to send the message that only we have the power to solve our problems.

In contrast, the apostle John pulls back the veil to reveal the truly Wonderful One behind the "curtain." Words fail John (note the repeated use of the preposition *like* in the passage), but the point is well made: God is seated on His throne, surrounded by a sea of glass (Revelation 4:2, 6). Despite the troubles that plague us here on earth (chapters 2–3), God isn't pacing the floor and biting His nails. He's actively at work for our good, so we can experience His peace.   *David Roper*

DECEMBER 27

Worth It, or Worthy?

Read Revelation 5:6–12

Worthy is the Lamb, who was slain.

REVELATION 5:12

Helen Roseveare, an English missionary physician in the African Congo, was taken prisoner by rebels during the Simba Rebellion in 1964. Beaten and abused by her captors, she suffered terribly. In the days that followed, she found herself asking, "Is it worth it?"

As she began to ponder the cost of following Jesus, she sensed God speaking to her about it. Years later she explained to an interviewer, "When the awful moments came during the rebellion and the price seemed too high to pay, the Lord seemed to say to me, 'Change the question. It's not, "Is it worth it?" It's "Am I worthy?"'" She concluded that in spite of the pain she had endured, "Always the answer is 'Yes, He is worthy.'"

Through God's grace at work within her during her harrowing ordeal, Helen Roseveare decided that the Savior who had suffered even death for her was worthy to be followed no matter what she faced. Her words, "He is worthy" echo the cries of those surrounding Jesus's throne in the book of Revelation: "In a loud voice they were saying: 'Worthy is the Lamb, who was slain, to receive power and wealth and wisdom and strength and honor and glory and praise!'" (5:12).

Our Savior suffered and bled and died for us, giving himself entirely, so that we may freely receive eternal life and hope. His all deserves our all. He is worthy!   *James Banks*

Just a Touch

Read Revelation 9:1–8

Then he placed his right hand on me and said, "Do not be afraid. I am the First and the Last."

REVELATION 1:17

It was just a touch, but it made all the difference to Colin. As his small team was preparing to do charitable work in a region known for hostility to believers in Jesus, his stress level began to rise. When he shared his worries with a teammate, his friend stopped, placed his hand on his shoulder, and shared a few encouraging words with him. Colin now looks back on that brief touch as a turning point, a powerful reminder of the simple truth that God was with him.

John, the close friend and disciple of Jesus, had been banished to the desolate island of Patmos for preaching the gospel, when he heard "a loud voice like a trumpet" (Revelation 1:10). That startling event was followed by a vision of the Lord himself, and John "fell at his feet as though dead." But in that frightening moment, he received comfort and courage. John wrote, "He placed his right hand on me and said, 'Do not be afraid. I am the First and the Last'" (v. 17).

God takes us out of our comfort zone to show us new things, to stretch us, to help us grow. But He also brings the courage and comfort to go through every situation. He won't leave us alone in our trials. He has everything under control. He has us in His hands. *Tim Gustafson*

A Joyful Celebration

Revelation 19:1–9

The wedding of the Lamb has come.

REVELATION 19:7

My friend Sharon passed away one year prior to the death of my friend Dave's teenage daughter Melissa. They both had been tragically killed in car accidents. One night both Sharon and Melissa were in my dream. They giggled and talked as they hung streamers in a large banquet hall and ignored me when I stepped into the room. A long table with white tablecloths had been set with golden plates and goblets. I asked if I could help decorate, but they didn't seem to hear me and kept working.

But then Sharon said, "This party is Melissa's wedding reception."

"Who's the groom?" I asked.

Neither responded but smiled and looked at each other knowingly. Finally, it dawned on me—it's Jesus!

"Jesus is the groom," I whispered as I woke up.

My dream brings to mind the joyful celebration believers in Jesus will share together when He returns. It's portrayed in Revelation as a lavish feast called "the wedding supper of the Lamb" (19:9). John the Baptist, who prepared people for the first coming of Christ, had called Him "the Lamb of God, who takes away the sin of the world" (John 1:29). He also referred to Jesus as "the bridegroom" and to himself as the "friend" (like the best man) who waited for Him (3:29).

On that banquet day and for all eternity we will enjoy unbroken fellowship with Jesus, our groom, and with Sharon and Melissa and all of God's people.

Anne Cetas

The Beautiful Bride

Read Revelation 19:4–9

*The wedding of the Lamb has come, and
his bride has made herself ready.*

REVELATION 19:7

I have officiated at a lot of weddings. Often planned according to the dreams of the bride, each of the weddings has been unique. But one thing is the same: adorned in their wedding dresses with hair beautifully done and faces aglow, brides steal the show.

I find it intriguing that God describes us as His bride. Speaking of the church, He says, "The marriage of the Lamb has come, and his Bride has made herself ready" (Revelation 19:7 ESV).

This is a great thought for those of us who have become discouraged about the condition of the church. I grew up as a pastor's kid, pastored three churches, and have preached in churches all over the world. I've counseled both pastors and parishioners about deep and troubling problems in the church. And though the church often seems unlovable, my love for the church has not changed.

But my reason for loving the church has changed. I now love it most of all for whose it is. The church belongs to Christ; it is the bride of Christ. Since the church is precious to Him, it is precious to me as well. His love for His bride, as flawed as we may be, is nothing less than extraordinary!   *Joe Stowell*

A Good Ending

Read Revelation 22:1–5

*The throne of God and of the Lamb will be in the city,
and his servants will serve him. They will see his face.*

REVELATION 22:3–4

As the lights dimmed and we prepared to watch the movie *Apollo 13*, my friend said under his breath, "Shame they all died." I watched the movie about the 1970 spaceflight with apprehension, waiting for tragedy to strike, and only near the closing credits did I realize I'd been duped. I hadn't known or remembered the end of the true story—that although the astronauts faced many hardships, they made it home alive.

In Christ, we can know the end of the story—that we too will make it home alive. By that I mean we will live forever with our heavenly Father, as we see in the book of Revelation. The Lord will create a "new heaven and a new earth" as He makes all things new (21:1, 5). In the new city, the Lord God will welcome His people to live with Him, without fear and without the night. We have hope in knowing the end of the story.

What difference does this make? It can transform times of extreme difficulty, such as when people face the loss of a loved one or even their own death. Though we recoil at the thought of dying, we can embrace the joy of the promise of eternity. We long for the city where no longer will there be any curse, where we'll live forever by God's light (22:5).

Amy Boucher Pye

THE WRITERS

◆

James Banks Pastor, Peace Church, Durham, North Carolina. Author: *Prayers for Prodigals, Praying the Prayers of the Bible,* and *Praying Together.*

John Blase Author: *Touching Wonder: Recapturing the Awe of Christmas* and *All Is Grace: A Ragamuffin Memoir.*

Henry Bosch (1914–1995) Original managing editor of *Our Daily Bread* (1956–1981).

Amy Boucher Pye Writer, speaker, retreat leader. Lives in North London, England. Author: *Finding Myself in Britain* and *The Living Cross.*

Dave Branon Former senior editor, Our Daily Bread Publishing. Author: *Beyond the Valley* and *The Lands of the Bible Today.*

Anne Cetas Former managing editor, *Our Daily Bread* (retired). Author: *Finding Jesus in Everyday Moments.*

Poh Fang Chia Editor, Our Daily Bread Ministries, Singapore.

Winn Collier Author: *Restless Faith, A Burning in My Bones,* and *Let God.*

Bill Crowder Former vice president of ministry content, Our Daily Bread Ministries. Author: *Wisdom for Our Worries, God of Surprise,* and *Gospel on the Mountains.*

Lawrence Darmani Novelist and publisher in Accra, Ghana. Author: *Grief Child.*

Dennis DeHaan (1932–2014) Former editor, *Our Daily Bread.*

Mart DeHaan Former president, Our Daily Bread Ministries. Author: *A Matter of Faith: Understanding True Religion.*

Richard DeHaan (1923–2002) Former president, Our Daily Bread Ministries. Founder of the ministry's television program *Day of Discovery*, which was on the air from 1968 until 2016.

Xochitl Dixon Blogs at xedixon.com. Author: *Waiting for God* and *Different Like Me.*

David Egner Former editor, Our Daily Bread Ministries. Author: *Praying with Confidence.*

Dennis Fisher Former senior research editor, Our Daily Bread Ministries. Former chairperson, C. S. Lewis Studies Consultation for the Evangelical Theological Society.

Tim Gustafson Editor, Discovery Series of Our Daily Bread Ministries; former managing editor, *Our Daily Bread.* Author: *Brother to Brother.*

C. P. Hia Special assistant to the president, Our Daily Bread Ministries. Based in Singapore.

Kirsten Holmberg Speaker and author, residing in Idaho. Author: *Advent with the Word: Approaching Christmas through the Inspired Language of God.*

Adam Holz Director, Focus on the Family's website Plugged In. Author: *Beating Busyness.*

Arthur Jackson Midwest region urban director, PastorServe. Former pastor.

Cindy Hess Kasper Former senior content editor, Our Daily Bread Ministries; has written for *Our Daily Bread* since 2006.

Alyson Kieda Former editor, Our Daily Bread Ministries.

Randy Kilgore Writer and workplace chaplain; founder of Desired Haven Ministries, Massachusetts. Author: *Made to Matter: Devotions for Working Christians*.

Leslie Koh Editor, Our Daily Bread Ministries, Singapore. Former journalist for *The Strait Times* in Singapore.

Monica La Rose Editor, Our Daily Bread Ministries. Has a master's in theology from Calvin Seminary, Grand Rapids.

Albert Lee Former assistant to the president, Our Daily Bread Ministries. Based in Singapore.

Julie Ackerman Link (1950–2015) Began writing for *Our Daily Bread* in 2000. Author: *Above All, Love* and *Hope for All Seasons*.

David McCasland Longtime writer for *Our Daily Bread* beginning in the late 1990s. Author: *Oswald Chambers: Abandoned to God* and *Eric Liddell: Pure Gold*.

Elisa Morgan Cohost of *Discover the Word* and *God Hears Her*. President emerita of Mothers of Preschoolers (MOPS) International. Author: *Praying Like Jesus*, *You Are Not Alone*, and *Christmas Changes Everything*.

Keila Ochoa Works with Media Associates International to help train writers worldwide. Author of a number of books in the Spanish language.

Remi Oyedele Works in the business world as a senior director of continuous improvement. Blogs at wordzpread.com.

Glenn Packiam Lead pastor, New Life Downtown, Colorado Springs. Author: *Blessed Broken Given: How Your Story Becomes Sacred in the Hands of Jesus*, *Discover the Mystery of Faith*, and *Secondhand Jesus*.

Patricia Raybon Writer, journalist, supporter of Bible-translation projects. Author: *I Told the Mountain to Move* and *My First White Friend*.

David Roper Former pastor. Author: *Out of the Ordinary, Psalm 23*, and *The Strength of a Man*.

Lisa Samra Writer, facilitator of mentoring relationships with women, developer of groups focusing on spiritual formation.

Jennifer Benson Schuldt A technical writer living in the Chicago area. Has written for *Our Daily Bread* since 2015.

Julie Schwab Adjunct professor, Cornerstone University, Purdue Global, and Southern New Hampshire.

Joe Stowell Former president: Moody Bible Institute (Chicago) and Cornerstone University (Grand Rapids). Author of over twenty books.

Marion Stroud (1940–2015) Wrote for *Our Daily Bread* beginning in 2014. Author: *Dear God, It's Me and It's Urgent* and *It's Just You and Me, Lord*.

Herb Vander Lugt (1920–2006) Author and former senior research editor for Our Daily Bread Ministries.

Sheridan Voysey Writer, speaker, broadcaster in Oxford, England. Author: *Resurrection Year* and *Resilient*.

Linda Washington Has written both fiction and nonfiction for all ages. Author: *God and Me*; coauthor: *The Soul of C. S. Lewis*.

Marvin Williams Pastor, Trinity Church, Lansing, Michigan. Author: *Loving God, Loving Others*.

Mike Wittmer Professor of Bible, Grand Rapids Theological Seminary; pastor, Cedar Springs Baptist Church. Author: *Heaven Is a Place on Earth, The Last Enemy*, and *Despite Doubt*.

Karen Wolfe Graduate of New Orleans Baptist Theological Seminary, writer, lives in Georgia.

Joanie Yoder (1934–2004) Writer for 10 years, *Our Daily Bread*. Author: *God Alone*.

Spread the Word
by Doing One Thing.

- Give a copy of this book as a gift.
- Share the QR code link via your social media.
- Write a review of this book on your blog, favorite bookseller's website, or at ODB.org/store.
- Recommend this book to your church, small group, or book club.

Connect with us. 🅵 📷 🐦

Our Daily Bread Publishing
PO Box 3566, Grand Rapids, MI 49501, USA
Email: books@odb.org

Love God. Love Others.

with 🌾 Our Daily Bread.

Your gift changes lives.

Connect with us. 🄵 📷 𝕏

Our Daily Bread Publishing
PO Box 3566, Grand Rapids, MI 49501, USA
Email: books@odb.org